# NAHGANNE

## TALES OF THE NORTHERN SASQUATCH

RED GROSSINGER

Foreword: Raymond Yakeleya

Calgary, Alberta, Canada

DURVILE.COM

UpRoute Imprint of Durvile Publications Ltd.
Calgary, Alberta, Canada
www.durvile.com



Library and Archives Cataloguing in Publications Data

NAHGANNE
TALES OF THE NORTHERN SASQUATCH

Grossinger, Red; Author
Yakeleya, Raymond; Foreword
Théroux, Rich; Illustrations

1. Sasquatch | 2. First Nations | 3. Indigenous | 4. Yukon | 5. Paranormal

*Scan QR Code for expanded Nahganne information*

The UpRoute "Spirit of Nature" Series
Series Editors, Raymond Yakeleya and Lorene Shyba

Issued in print and electronic formats
ISBN: 978-1-988824-59-8 (pbk); 978-1-990735-19-6 (e-pub)
978-1-990735-20-2 (audiobook)

Front cover illustration and Sasquatch drawings throughout, Rich Théroux
Book design, Lorene Shyba

Durvile Publications recognizes the land upon which our studios are located.
We extend gratitude to the Indigenous Peoples of Southern Alberta, which include the Siksika, Piikani, and Kainai of the Blackfoot Confederacy; the Dene Tsuut'ina; and the Chiniki, Bearspaw, and Wesley Stoney Nakoda First Nations; and the Region 3 Métis Nation of Alberta.

Durvile Publications would like to acknowledge the financial support of the Government of Canada through Canadian Heritage Canada Book Fund and the Government of Alberta, Alberta Media Fund.

Printed and bound in Canada. First Printing. 2022.

# *Dedication*

I dedicate this book to those who had the internal fortitude to tell me about their encounters and experiences with Sasquatch and who may help in getting more people to come forward.

# Contents

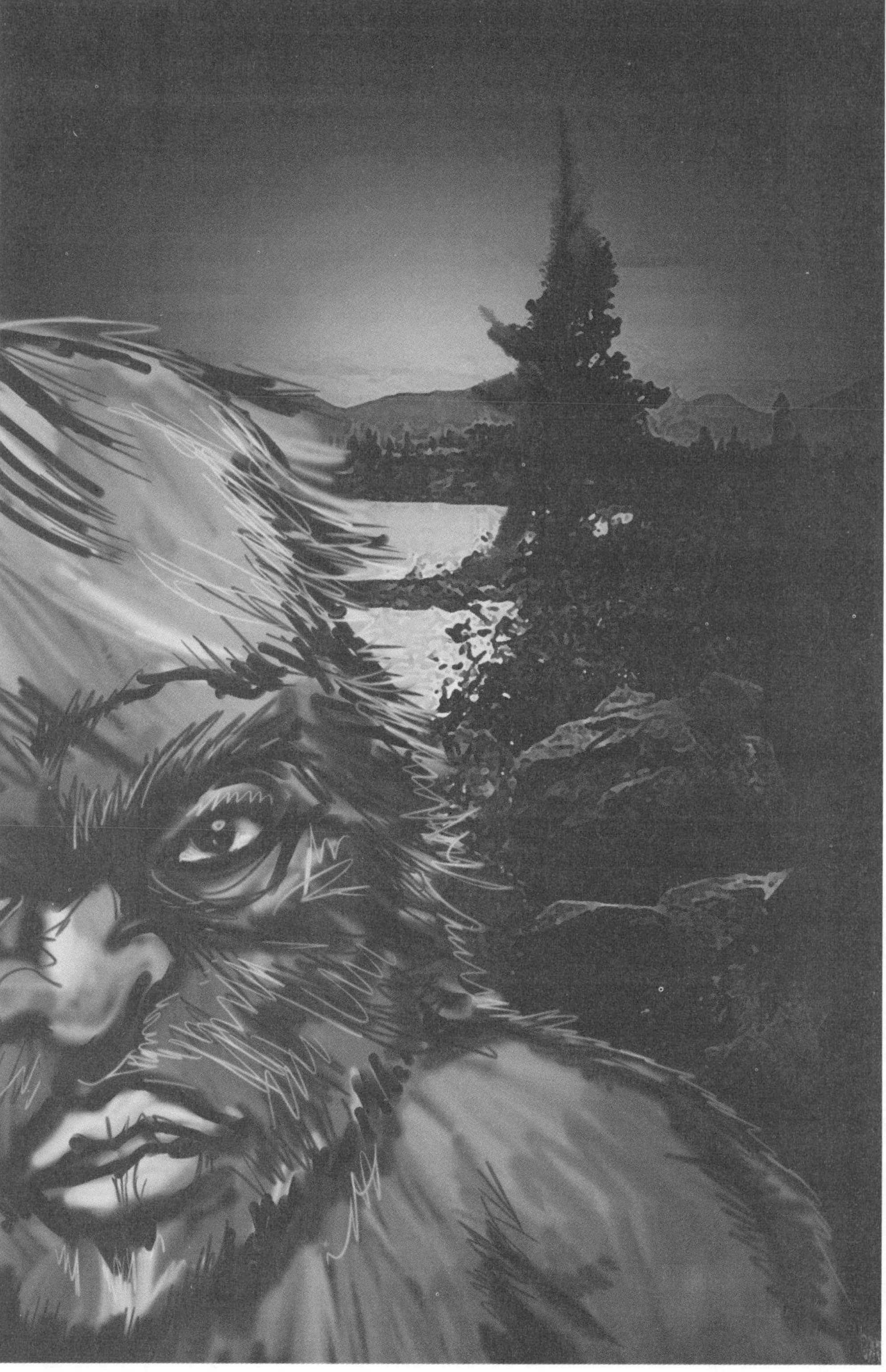

# Foreword

## Raymond Yakeleya

THE DENE FIRST NATIONS PEOPLE of the North know the Nahganne to be real creatures with mysterious powers. We know that they are intelligent, have strong feelings of family, and even their own language. Our People's relationship with Nahganne may go back as far as the last Ice Age, 25,000 years ago. It would seem that it was about this time that Nahganne came across the land bridge from Siberia to North America—at about the same time our People were also migrating and beginning to populate this continent. It may well be that there has been interaction between our two species since this time.

Despite this longtime association with Nahganne, there are still many things about this interesting creature that we do not know. I hope that this book will support Red Grossinger's research into the Sasquatch and bring the focus forward so that people can talk openly and without shame about their experiences.

By sharing our stories, I think we can learn more about this mysterious creature and find the answer to some of our unsettled questions. In what areas are Nahganne most concentrated? What do they eat? What is their purpose? A primary aim of this book is to learn and try to understand these creatures, and then treat them with respect and care.

I remember when my grandmother Elizabeth Yakeleya would talk with me, she would always stress never to hurt Nahganne. What I learned from my granny was kindness—kindness to everything. Hurting Nahganne is not something our Elders would promote, and I have never heard of any

Dene person shooting it or harming them in any way. Our People are more likely to help them by allowing Nahganne to steal meat from our hunting and fishing camps. I don't think I have ever heard the Dene say anything bad if Nahganne stole fish or meat—they know they must eat too. There's a lot of knowledge to learn from the creatures, and we are just beginning to scratch the surface.

When I was a boy about to go on a hunting trip with my Uncle Gordon, my granny looked at me seriously and said, "Raymond, be careful, Nahganne is out there." Parents always worry about their kids when they are in the bush. Out in the bush you always have to gather water, wood, and spruce boughs for the flooring of tents or tipis. In some times of the year, you go out to collect berries too. Parents do not like to see young people go off by themselves.

My family has had many experiences with Nahganne. My dad's sister, my aunt, was taken by them. It was autumn, and the family were fishing for herring and other types of fish at Mahoney Lake. While there, my aunt was grabbed by a Nahganne, and she started screaming right away, "Ama, Ama," which means mother. As soon as she started yelling, a big wind came up—I have heard from my Auntie Charlotte that Nahganne have power over elements, like the wind. The family heard my young aunt screaming right away, and Grandpa Bernard took off after my aunt to get her back. He ran after her until the Nahganne dropped her, then Grandpa Bernard tucked her under his arm and carried her to safety.

One of the things the Sahtù People say is if a girl is taken and she comes back, she will not live long. They say that because they believe the experience of being taken by the Nahganne, the Sasquatch, frightens the heart. A week after they got my aunt back, she passed away.

Auntie Charlotte also told me that Nahganne have power over the elements, and they also seem to have power over dogs and dog teams. They can compel dogs to quiet down. It also seems to me that the Nahganne are more concentrated in certain parts of the land.

The second instance of a Nahganne in my hometown, Tulita in the Northwest Territories, happened in the 1940s to the daughter of a woman named Marina Francis. Marina Francis was often around when I grew up. She was an elderly, single, widowed woman who lived beside one of my aunts on the riverbank overlooking the Mackenzie River. I remember that the other boys and I would help her out by chopping and splitting wood for her. Marina Francis's daughter was her only child, and her husband trained their daughter in the same way he would have trained a son. Therefore, she knew how to use guns, set traps, skin animals, catch fish, and set nets. Marina Francis's daughter know all the basic things that Dene boys learn in order to survive off the land.

It seems like the Nahganne go around Dene camps and they're always on the search for food. One of the things our People had were dog teams. When our People hear dogs barking, especially at night, they are always on alert and suspect a number of things: it could be wolves or bears, or it could be Nahganne. The dogs are the first defence that we have out in the bush. But despite all this, Marina Francis's daughter was taken. The daughter was by herself when she was stolen, and like many cases of Nahganne incidences, it was autumn.

Marina Francis's daughter later told my grandmother where the Nahganne took her and that it was at the rocky top of an old mountain. She told my grandma Elizabeth she remembers something over her head and that she couldn't see where she was going. She was missing for two or three days before she managed to get away from the Nahganne when it went off to look for food. She escaped, but the

Nahganne noticed she was gone and followed her, screaming. She hid from Nahganne inside a hole in the ground and stayed very quiet, very still, until morning. Nahganne never found her, and she made her way back to her family. But sure enough, just like my aunt, she sadly did not live long after the encounter. She spoke about this incident to Tulita People before she passed and we hope to get more about this and other stories about Nahganne from the Elders so we can find out more of her encounter.

I have another aunt, Muriel, who was originally from Déline, a neighbouring community of Tulita and the only really big community on Great Bear Lake. Aunt Muriel told me about Dene men who used to work at the Port Radium Mine in the 1940s, and maybe even the 1930s, getting the ore out—the material that was turned into atomic bombs in World War II for the Hiroshima and Nagasaki bombs. She said that at those mining camps during the night, Nahganne would come around to the family tents, communicating to each other by whistling and knocking stones together. They would have a stone in each hand, and one would hit once, another would hit twice, and then three times. They knew where each other were, and the people in the tents could hear them.

A few of my other family members have had experiences with Nahganne. My Uncle Walter was an experienced trapper. He was once tracking a trail of big footprints in the snow that had a very big stride. The Nahganne is described as over seven feet tall, broad-shouldered, covered in fur, and fast-moving. The stride of the footprints in the snow was too big and long to have been human, so believing it to be the trail of a Nahganne, Uncle Walter followed it for quite a long time.

Suddenly, the footprints ended. Uncle Walter looked around, but there was nothing. He wondered to himself,

"Where did it go?" he said to me. "It was as if it turned into a bird and flew off."

This is not the first time I've heard of a story like this. I've heard other tribes and Indigenous People say similar things—that Nahganne can change its shape—shapeshift maybe or go into another dimension. So, we're always observing and seeing the same thing. It doesn't mean we know what it means, but we know that it happens.

My brother Dwayne, as a young boy, also ran into a Nahganne. Dwayne and his best friend Peter Andrew were on a boat on the Keele River in the early 1970s when they looked across to the land and spotted Nahganne. Dwayne explained to me that he looked into its eyes from about twenty feet away, and I remember him saying, "Raymond, his eyes were red." When I asked him years later, as a man in his forties, "How do you feel about it now when you think about it?" he said something unusual. He said, "When I think about it, it still haunts me to this day." I also spoke with Peter Andrew about this incident and he confirmed Dwayne's story, as they both saw the Nahganne at the same time. Peter said to me, "We were just young boys at the time and it really shook us up."

Nahganne have powers that we don't quite understand. They will communicate with you by whistling at you. They have good olfactory senses. You know, the power of smell is strong. Nahganne will sometimes go to a woman when she's menstruating—you know he's got her scent.

I truly appreciate what Red is doing by bringing the topic of Sasquatch forward so people can talk openly and without shame. A lot of Elders are reticent to talk about Nahganne—this is not something our People talk about openly. It is almost taboo. Many of our Elders are passing on, the people who have true knowledge, and I think now's the time to ask these questions. How do you protect your kids if we don't talk about it? How do we pass this traditional knowledge on?

You could say our Dene People, especially Elders, are specialists in certain things. Some know about stars, some know about animals, and some know about plants. And so, when you bring up a subject like Nahganne, some will talk with you, and some will not. I always say to them, "Look at us younger people. We want you Elders to pass along knowledge to the new generation." And you say okay, you think that's a really good idea. But you've got to give us the traditional knowledge so that we can pass it along. If you keep it to yourself, when are we going to pass it along?

We need to pass along the truth, that being the most important element of what our people know. And so, many of them say, "Yes, you're right," and they'll sit down and talk because it's about respecting our young people and respecting ourselves as a people in our knowledge. I think that is also the intention of this book—to understand and pass on knowledge about Nahganne, Sasquatch of the North. It also provides us with ways we can protect ourselves should we encounter one in the bush. We need to know this!

*— Raymond Yakeleya, 2022*

*Originally from Tulita in the Northwest Territories, Raymond Yakeleya is a writer/filmmaker and an editor of Durvile & UpRoute Books' Spirit of Nature series.*

# Preface

## *About the Reports*

> Fair things pass by, unheeded as a threshold brook . . . —*John Keats, 1818*

> The important thing is not to stop questioning. Curiosity has its own reason for existence. One cannot help but be in awe when he contemplates the mysteries of eternity, of life, of the marvelous. —*Albert Einstein 1955*

My first experience with Sasquatch is traced back to when I was camping along Yukon's Takhini River back in July of 1997.

Being an avid outdoor person, I spend most of my summers camping, hiking, canoeing, and fishing at various locations around the Yukon, and one of my favourite places to set up camp is the Takhini River Campground.

On this one occasion, I was fly fishing at one of my "secret fishing spots" along the Takhini River, when I experienced odd rustling sounds and fleeting movements from the nearby bushes. On a few occasions, I would briefly observe some sort of two-legged creature, yet I could not determine what it was other than being the source of these strange activities.

A week or so later, I approached a close friend from the Teslin Tlingit First Nation (TTC) with this puzzling incident; she responded that I had experienced an activity related to what she called a "bushman," better known as Sasquatch.

From that day on, I read as many books as I could about these large human-like bipedal giants and I joined a number of Sasquatch Organizations.

My newfound interests led me to compile a number of Sasquatch-related activities that have occurred in the Yukon, investigating these sightings and incidents, and keeping records.

As years progressed, people from around the Yukon heard of my interest in Sasquatch. They started sharing their own personal experiences with me, after which I felt obliged to present these encounters and occurrences to other people who were interested in the subject.

And this is it, folks, a chronological presentation of encounters and occurrences reports that I have received, and some that I have experienced while investigating these reports relating to the activities of these bipedal forest giants that took place around the Yukon.

My Reports are presented as follows:

1. The type of encounter or occurrence experienced, by region;
2. The location of these activities using the Geographic Coordinate System (GCS) with latitude and longitude—I subsequently pinpoint the location where these activities took place using topographical map, with the name of the map, its identification number, and the location, by using a Grid Reference System;
3. A detailed description of the activities that occurred at each specific location;
4. A bit about local history;

5. Some information concerning the local geography by describing the land around these activities and the food available; and
6. A description of the investigation that I conducted, with the resulting analyses and my own impressions.

In addition, there is a bit of human background information, tidbits of details about the people of the Yukon, with a few nuggets of local history. Many of these reports reflect the nature of our Yukon First Nations and their deep attachment to the land; and finally, there are stories about the Yukoners and others, who have made, and still make, the Yukon what it is today.

Enjoy the read, folks!

*— Red Grossinger,*
*Whitehorse, 2022*

# Introduction

## Giant Bipedal Hirsute Hominoids

> You see, but you do not observe.
>
> — *Sherlock Holmes, 1891*
>
> What may be real for one person is but a hallucination for another.
>
> — *Red Grossinger, 2020*

THIS BOOK is about the giant bipedal, forest-dwelling, hirsute hominoid entities. For as long as humans have been around Northern Canada, the activities of these giants have been observed in many places around this great land, but only a few persons have taken the time to share their stories of coming in contact with these forest giants. In the North, they have been given many regional names, such as Nahganne and Kietch Sa'be, but they are most commonly known as Sasquatch.

Although I have some 150 reports about Sasquatch on file at this time, only 70 reports are in this book, the majority originating from Yukon Indigenous Peoples, including Dene, Dena, Gwich'in, Tlingit, Tutchone, Tagish, Champagne and Aishihik, Tahltan, Métis, Kwanlin Dün, and Tr'ondëk Hwëch'in. The reports not included lacked substance, specific details, or clarity; or were false, not really plausible, or not fully investigated.

When investigating a report, I try to study all the details in order to get a full idea of what actually took place—this includes where, how, and when did it take place, who witnessed the event, and is the witness dependable and reliable. Only the facts are included in my final reports. Sasquatch gender is not specifically identified in most of the following case study reports or stories so I have used they/their and sometimes it/its instead of conjecturing female or male gender.

Being of mixed Huron/Algonquin and European ancestry myself, I understand the reluctance of many Indigenous People to come forward with their Sasquatch experiences, yet in my views, they are the most experienced persons on the subject matter, along with "bush wise" white folk.

THE TERM SASQUATCH was coined by John W. Burns in 1929. Burns was then a schoolteacher and government agent at the Chehalis First Nation Reserve, just west of Harrison Hot Springs, in the Province of British Columbia, Canada.

At the time, he was writing about activities of interest for a local newspaper, and most of his stories were about these forest giants. So, in order to make his work more interesting, he borrowed the Halkomelem dialect word "Sasq'ets," from the Sts'Ailes First Nation, and made up the term "Sasquatch" to describe these gigantic, hair-covered, human-like bipedal creatures that members of the local First Nations had come in contact with on many occasions when venturing out hunting or fishing.

In the 1930s and 1940s, Burns described a number of accounts concerning various Sasquatch sightings along the Fraser River Valley; one of these articles was actually published in *Macleans* Magazine. The encounters with these forest giants he wrote about were reported to him by members of the Chihalis and Sts'Ailes First Nations.

Many people interested in the existence of these uncatalogued and unclassified hominoids have advanced the notion that the North American gigantic wild hominoid species, identified as Sasquatch, are actually the descendants of the Asian *Gigantopithecus Blacki*.

The term *Gigantopithecus Blacki* was originally coined by the German paleontologist Ralph von Koenisgswald (1902–1982) when referring to the hairy Asian Gigantic Apes, which were known to exist in Asia when, in 1936, gigantic molars were found in Hong Kong.

The German Anatomist Franz Weidenreich (1873–1948) made a controversial assertion by writing that "*Gigantopithecus*

*Blacki"* was "more human-like than ape-like," in his book entitled *Apes, Giants and Man* published in 1946.

In 1956, a massive jawbone, dated to be about one million years old (1 Mya) was discovered in a cave at Liuchen, China, and was identified by Chinese scientists as being the remains of a *Gigantopethicus Blackie.* Later, in 1965, twelve gigantic teeth were discovered at Wuming, also in China. These were dated to be 350,000 years of age. Since then, upward of one thousand gigantic teeth have been found throughout Asia, all of them identified by Chinese scientists to be from *Gigantopethicus Blackie.* From these findings, it was deduced by the same Chinese scientists, that *Gigantopethicus Blackie* would weigh some 545 kilograms (1,200 lbs.) and be about 3.05 meters tall (10 ft).

In North America, only a few scientists have taken the time to seriously study the subject of Sasquatch; one of these scientists was Dr. Grover Krantz (1931–2002), who, in 1992, used the term "*Gigantopithecus Canadensis*" to describe the North American Gigantic Apes in his research and the many resulting books he wrote on the subject.

Recent writings by Dr. John Bindernagel (1941–2018) in *North America's Great Ape: The Sasquatch,* published in 1998 and *The Discovery of Sasquatch: Reconciling Culture, History and Science in the Discovery Process,* published in 2010, are serious presentations of evidence proving the actual existence of this hominoid. Besides providing valuable evidence, Dr. Bindernagel's objective studies may have helped sway the bias against this controversial subject within the scientific community.

It is the opinion of Dr. Krantz, along with a few other scientists and writers in this field of research, that the Sasquatch's ancestors were from Eurasia, which would mean they simply followed the *Homo sapiens* during their migrations from Asia to North America by way of the Isthmus of Beringia. During two periods of time, colder temperatures resulted in the build-up of more ice around the northern seas. This resulted in opening an isthmus, a mostly dry piece of land, connecting the continent of Asia to the continent of America, first from about 38 to 34 Kya and then again between 30 to 15 Kya. This route often called the Beringia Land Bridge, became the doorway to North America.

Dr. Jeff Meldrum, a respected Professor of Anatomy and Anthropology at the Idaho State University and Editor-in-Chief of the scientific journal *The Scientific* Inquiry, wrote an enlightening scientific book entitled *Sasquatch: Legend Meets Science*, published in 2006. In this book, Meldrum provides "undisputable, evidence-based scientific analyses concerning the Sasquatch, with unparalleled open-mindedness, thoroughness, and objectivity," according to Dr. Esteban Sarmiento, of the American Museum of Natural History, in New York.

Dr. W. Henner Fahrenbach, retired Zoologist and a reputed scientist at the Oregon Primate Research Center's Electron Microscopy Laboratory, published an article in the scientific journal *Cryptozoology* in 1998 entitled "Sasquatch Size, Scaling and Statistic." This article included a number of graphs using material from Sasquatch researchers and writers John Green, J.R. Napier, J.A. Hewkin, and P. Byrne to depict aspects of the Sasquatch based on accumulated reports of large human-like footprints. When asked about most scientists' reluctance to do more research on the subject of Sasquatch, Fahrenbach replied: "It is easy to be put off, if you don't know anything about it... however, this is generally uncharacteristic for a scientist to respond that way."

French-born cryptozoologist Dr. Marie-Jeanne Koffman spent over twenty years researching the *Almasty* (Sasquatch) in the Caucasus Region from the South Russian steppes to the plateaus of Anatolia in Armenia and Iran. In December 1994, she wrote a scientific paper, with an addition to it in January 1995, entitled "Relic Humanoids in Antiquity." In it, she describes Sasquatch in detail and relates it to past hominoid encounters through world history.

A specific content of her paper is the interpretation of a Phoenician plate dated from 700 BCE, upon which a hairy man-like bulky biped is depicted. She further describes a cup dated from around the 5th century BCE that depicts the capture of an "unidentifiable anthropomorphic troglodytic ape" which resemble a "giant hairy human being." In addition, she further explains the existence of the "Wild Man Enkidu", as part of the *Epic of Gilgamesh,* dating this Wild Man from about 2,650 BCE. Further in her paper, she makes mention of many beasts looking like "giant hairy humans" that can be found in the content of various bibles and other religious books.

The well-known Belgian-born scientist, explorer, researcher, and writer in the field of zoology, Dr. Bernard Heuvelmans (1916-2001), better known as "The Father of Cryptozoology," spent his entire life researching unknown, unclassified and uncatalogued creatures from around the world. In many of his books, he mentions the relationship between *Homo neanderthalensis, Homo sapiens,* and *Gigantopithecus,* the unclassified gigantic apes discovered in Asia.

As reported by the US writer Michael McLeod, in his book entitled *Anatomy of a Beast: Obsession and Myth on the Trail of Bigfoot,* published in 2011: "In recent years, fossils of *Gigantopithecus Blacki* and of *Homo erectus* have been found together in both China and Vietnam, thus showing evidence they coexisted."

The first mention of bushmen (Sasquatch) in North America is traced to the Hudson Bay Company explorer and fur trader, E. Umfreville (1755–1799), who in 1790 wrote about the local Indigenous people talking about "large human-like creatures," referred to as "*Weedegoag,*" while he was working along the North Saskatchewan River, in what is now Alberta, Canada.

In 1811, the fur trader David Thompson (1770–1857), working for the North West Company, came across a number of "large human-like footprints" measuring some 35.56 cm (14 in) in length, around the area of present-day Jasper, in Alberta as well. In 1818, a trapper named Ross Cox (1793–1853), who was trapping along the Columbia River, in what is today the state of Montana, mentioned about the "wild and huge human-like beings," that he had observed during the period of 1812 to 1817.

A Protestant Missionary by the name of Elkanah Walker (1805–1877), wrote reports about "giant bipedal primates" living in the area of the present-day state of Washington and province of British Columbia, in 1840. The Irish adventurer and frontier artist Paul Kane (1810–1871) was a short distance away from Mount St. Helens in the state of Washington, when, on 26 March 1847, he wrote in his diary "...that mountain has never been visited by either whites or Indians; the latter assert that it is inhabited by a race of beings of a different species, who are cannibals, and whom they hold in great dread ..."

In 1892, Theodore Roosevelt (1858–1919), the 26th President of the United States, wrote a book entitled *The Wilderness Hunter*, in which he described his adventures in the Pacific Northwest and wrote about an "apelike creature of gigantic stature covered in hair... and which left behind large, deep human-like footprints."

In 1893, E.R. Young (1879–1905), a Methodist missionary, mentioned that "Weendagoos were often observed" in what is now Alberta.

In the Yukon, the first report of Sasquatch dates back to 1899. At the time, a number of prospectors were working in the area of the Indian River, just south of present-day Dawson City, and they reported observing some "giant hair-covered beings, looking like men."

This happened during the famous Klondike Gold Rush, when some forty-thousand men and women rushed in, expecting to find gold wherever they looked. People did not pay much attention to reports of these sightings by fellow prospectors at that period of time, as they were too busy searching for that elusive Klondike gold and making money through various enterprises. They wanted nothing but money, gold, or souls.

After reading, researching, and studying the works of many scientists who have taken the time to seriously study this phenomenon and have written their findings about these giant bipedal ambulating entities we call Sasquatch, I am convinced they are real and do exist. Today, these Sasquatch creatures are well and alive in the Yukon. In my writings I refer to Sasquatch as "giant bipedal, forest-dwelling, hirsute hominoid entities." These entities are still unclassified and uncatalogued.

Members of the Yukon Indigenous community have known about Sasquatch for a long time and have simply taken them for granted. However, the Sasquatch have remained mostly unknown for most non-Indigenous people, as only a few scientists have had the internal fortitude, the guts, and the courage to seriously tackle their existence.

In this book, *Nahganne: Tales of the Northern Sasquatch,* I describe many unexpected, vivid sightings of these creatures, the discoveries of large human-like footprints, loud unidentifiable vocals, along with other unexplainable events and strange, odd occurrences. These sightings have been experienced by a large number of Yukoners from various backgrounds and ethnicities, around this great land of Beringia, believed to be associated with the Sasquatch.

There is a myriad of names for these entities in the Yukon. Besides Nahganne and Sasquatch: I have heard of Big Man, Black Cannibal, Black Indian, Bocq, Bushman, Forest Giant, Hairy Giant, Hairy One, Hairy Man, Keecho, Kushka, Kushtaka, Loup-Garou (Often wrongly referred to as roogaroo), Stickman, Wild Indian, Wild Man, Wild People, Windago, Wood Being, and Wood Man. Oh...I almost forgot the silly, ridiculous term, Bigfoot.

It should be noted that Sasquatch is the preferred term used by serious researchers, enthusiasts, and writers, such as Krantz, Bindernagel, Fahrenbach, Meldrum, Murphy, Alley, Green, Steenburg, Napier, Hewkins, and Byrne. We have used the term Nahganne to title the book in deference to the term used by many First Nations Peoples of the North.

Sasquatch have been seen along roads and highways, by rivers and lakes, up on hills and mountainsides, deep in valleys and in dense forests. They have been seen around campgrounds and on hiking trails, sometimes looking through windows and walking in communities. They have been reported stealing fish at fish camps, stealing freshly killed animals from hunters, and generally searching for food.

Large human-like footprints have been discovered at many locations, along with handprints and knuckle prints. People have reported an odd, unidentified, strong pungent smell, perhaps used by Sasquatch as an attempt to scare and discourage people from getting too inquisitive. Various types of vocals have been heard in the woods from loud shrieks, to whoops, to roaring screams, to ear-piercing cries, to whisperings of sort and moderate whimpers. The sounds of wood knocks and rocks being banged together have been heard as well as if some of these creatures were communicating with each other, announcing the arrival of visitors into their territories perhaps, or even trying to communicate with these visitors—who knows?

Many of the Indigenous populations in North America have adopted what has become to be known as "The Seven Sacred Teachings." These teachings are the spiritual foundation based in a firm belief in the "Great Spirit," with the understanding that all living beings on Earth have a spirit which is the essence of life.

This is further advanced by the various ceremonial practices of each First Nation as each "teaching" is represented by an animal, such as, Truth is the Turtle; Wisdom is the Beaver; Humility is the Wolf; Love is the Eagle; Respect is the Bison; Courage is the Bear; and Honesty, which is represented by the Sasquatch under the name of Kietch Sa'be.

Honesty is defined as "Worthy of being depended upon; marked by truth, facts, real and genuine; not willing to cheat or defraud; not deceptive or fraudulent; without pretensions or false accusations."

Some First Nations members have suggested that Nahganne or Kietch Sa'be teaches respect of the land and all its inhabitants. This creature is said to be the protector of the land and will appear when the Earth is being misused.

Back in 2006, I was investigating a number of large human-like footprints discovered close to the community of Pelly

Crossing, in central Yukon, when a resident Elder of the Selkirk First Nation (SFN) told me that "Keecho will help us in time of need."

Readers will notice the similarity between Kietch Sa'be and Keecho. While Kietch Sa'be is pronounced Kee Shae, and Keecho is pronounced Kee Shoo. So, I probably heard what the SFN Elder said to me a bit differently, due to his accent and by all indication he was talking about the same entity.

In 2019, I was talking about Sasquatch with a Roman Catholic nun who was visiting Whitehorse and she later mentioned to me that she believes "...Sasquatch are animal spirit entities, without souls." Another woman I talked with who held a Master of Theology surmised the Sasquatch phenomena as follows: "As angels are the souls of people, Sasquatch are the spirits of animals"

SASQUATCH HAVE BEEN observed by many people of various backgrounds and ethnicities by bush-wise white folks and by Indigenous Peoples who have lived here all their lives. These Indigenous Peoples are the keepers of this great land we call the Yukon after all . . . therefore, accepting their accounts about the actual existence of Sasquatch, should not be that difficult.

# PART I

# SASQUATCH REPORTS *from the* NORTH

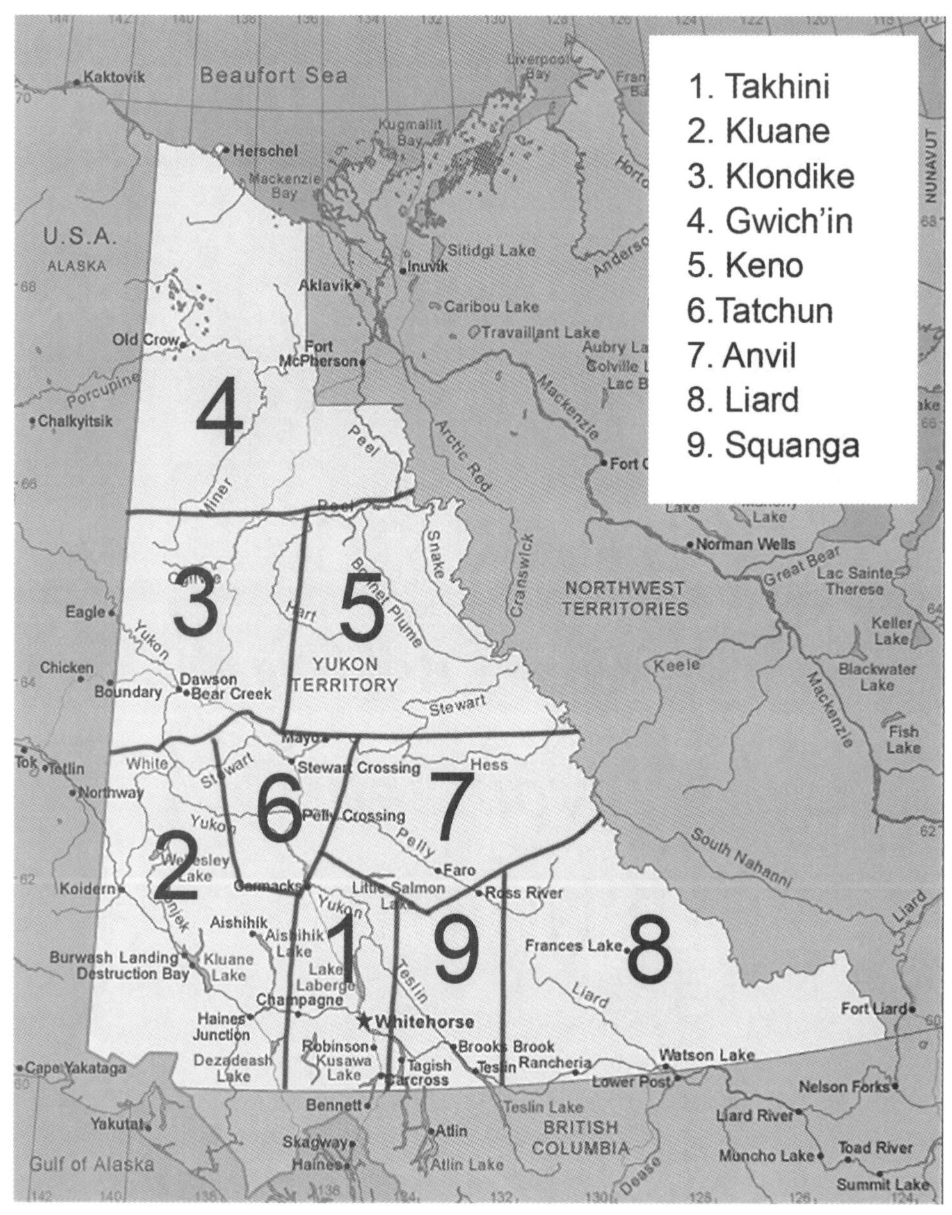


*Regions of Yukon*
*Corresponding to Reports and Stories in*
*Nahganne: Tales of the Northern Sasquatch*

# Introduction to the Reports

## Strange Things Done...

> There are strange things done, in the midnight sun... — *Robert W. Service (1867–1957), the bard of the Yukon. He wrote this back in 1910, from his small Dawson City cabin, bringing the lives and activities of Dawsonites, sourdoughs, Yukoners, and all those gold-crazy prospectors to life in the form of poems, ballads, and stories.*
>
> *I add:* There are stranger things done yet during our dark Northern nights, and even during plain bright daylight, by our Wild Men of the Yukon, the Northern Sasquatch." — *Red Grossinger, 2022*

IN PART I "Sasquatch Reports from the North," encounters and occurrences are presented in chronological order, each corresponding to a specific region of the Yukon, as shown on the Yukon Regions Map on the opposite page. Most reports originated from members of First Nations Peoples, some by other Indigenous Peoples from across Canada, a few from bush-wise white folk, and some are describing my own experiences. I have collected reports of Sasquatch activities from every region of the Yukon and many parts of northern British Columbia, Northwest Territories, and Alaska. Only a few selected Reports are included in this book due to space limitations but updates and further Reports can be found by scanning the QR code in the margin.

*Scan QR Code for expanded information*

Whenever possible, I have talked with the witnesses of these Reports to get their full stories. Some of the witnesses were not available to speak with me directly for various reasons—some are long dead, for instance, but their stories lived on through oral telling. Sometimes I asked my community contacts and colleagues to conduct interviews for me to get the full story when witnesses were reluctant to speak with me directly. As for the matter of privacy, most people who share Sasquatch stories with me insist that their names not be used, so I make it my overall policy to keep their trust by preserving their anonymity.

There were reports that came my way that appeared totally unfounded to me, and upon further investigation, I found them to be bogus. These have obviously not been included. However, as I am a forward-looking, optimistic person with an open, inquisitive mind, I sometimes accepted that what was reported could well be possible. This is especially true when the information came from a First Nations person, as their legends and oral teachings acknowledge Nahganne/Sasquatch as entities to be respected.

Most of these Reports I selected for this book were reported to me directly, or are occurrences that I have experienced myself while investigating other Reports. I was able to access most of the geographic locations where these incidents reportedly occurred to make further investigation and determine the validity of what witnesses said. Each report was treated independently and was traced to its source as much as possible.

A number of Reports came from sources that were not easily traceable. However, in all cases, I was able to determine the locations of these encounters and occurrences using the intimate knowledge of the North that I have acquired by living here since 1980 and by travelling around this great landscape.

There are many other encounters and occurrences that have been observed by people who have not had the intestinal fortitude to report them. They were likely afraid of being ridiculed. This is a totally normal human reaction and well understood. In other cases, encounters and occurrences may have been dismissed by witnesses. They may well have thought to themselves that what they had observed were hallucinations—that they were seeing things, or that it was some sort of dream.

I venture the opinion that only about 10 – 15 per cent of people who have experienced something unusual that might be related to a Sasquatch think of reporting their experiences. If they went to the police with such a report, what would the police do? Basically, nothing, as they have other things to take care of. If they report to a Conservation Officer, the report goes in an "unknown file," never to be seen again. If it is reported to the newspapers, it may get printed with an impressionable, attention-gathering type of headline, and then, mostly forgotten.

In short, there are very few obvious places where encounters or occurrence can be reported and taken seriously. I am known to take reports seriously and so people often turn to me through an ad I run in the *The Whitehorse Star*. This ad has enabled many people to contact me.

Of significance in this book, as foreword writer Raymond Yakeleya will attest, are Reports pointing at the possibility of Sasquatch being supernatural. In Report #27 for example, there is mention of telepathic communication between a female Sasquatch and a witness. This encounter took place in 2000, Report #27, close to Meziadin Junction, on BC Highway #37, in northern British Columbia.

There are three sighting reports where the witnesses explained to me how Sasquatch entities disappeared right in front of them. I had the good fortune of being able to discuss the details of such puzzling disappearances with the witnesses. One such encounter occurred by Duncan Creek in the Keno Region in July of 2008, Report #37, when the witness came face to face with two Sasquatch, one of which was visibly pregnant, on a trail leading to Duncan Creek. During this encounter, both Sasquatch disappeared in front of the witness.

There was another encounter which took place in August of 2011, Report #50, by Moose Creek in the Keno Region as well, where two people observed a Sasquatch suddenly becoming invisible and, seemingly, to shape-shift into a raven.

A more interesting encounter yet occurred in Crestview, a subdivision of Whitehorse, in the Takhini Region, in July of 2011. This is Report #47 where the witness observed a Sasquatch at a distance of 2 m (6 ft), walking right beside him for a distance of ninety metres, before the entity became gradually translucent, then transparent, and finally became totally invisible.

The manner in which such disappearances took place still leaves me puzzled and is simply without explanation. How does a visible entity simply become invisible in front of a witness? Why? Where does it go? What has happened? Is it some mind-set play, some not-yet understood abilities? Some cloaking abilities? Are they walking through portals?

Other questions still remain, such as, do Sasquatch make use of fire? As it was mentioned by a Northwest Territories Dene man, some people in the NWT reported to him to have observed fire smoke exiting from a cave complex, yet such caves were not used by any human being. Who then were using the fires?

A First Nations man of the Kluane First Nation in western Yukon has mentioned that he observed what is commonly called "Little People" a number of times, close to the small community of Destruction Bay. What and who are they?

Enthusiasts in this field of endeavour have advanced many theories as to how such creatures could become invisible, from paranormal to multi-dimensional abilities and so on. Yet, nothing that would enlighten what I would call a "regular guy like me," a non-scientifically trained but open-minded person.

I WILL CONCLUDE with two comments: The first is addressed to people who may have seen or experienced something that may indicate the passage of these giant bipedal, forest-dwelling, hirsute hominoid entities somewhere in the North. If you have or even think that you may have had an encounter with Sasquatch, please contact me at sasquatchyukon@hotmail.com and let's talk about it. The second is addressed to the scientific community. As advanced by scientists Juan Campanario and Brian Marten in their paper "Challenging dominant physics paradigms" (published in *Journal of Scientific Exploration vol. 18, no. 3, Fall 2004, pp. 421-438):*

> Challenging scientific orthodoxy is difficult, because most scientists are educated and work within current paradigms and fundamental theories based on scientific methodologies

> that have strong resistance to anything unconventional. And furthermore, there are no career incentives to examine unconventional ideas challenging established beliefs.

Biologist, theorist, naturalist, and writer E.O. Wilson asserts, in his 'scale of credibility,' that to gain acceptance from the scientist world, an encounter or an occurrence has to go from "interesting" to "suggestive" to "persuasive" and finally to "compelling" then, given time, to "obvious," before being accepted.

Is that not currently the case with Sasquatch? In my opinion, those of us seriously involved in the existence of Sasquatch, either as amateur researchers or as "Sasquatch enthusiasts," as I prefer calling myself, have accepted these occurrences as being "obvious."

We understand the resistance in researching such an unconventional subject. We know there have been scientists whose careers have been destroyed by advancing unconventional subjects such as Sasquatch; Dr. Grover Krantz, whom I wrote about in the Introduction, is one example.

Peers are a difficult bunch to please, as they have very orthodox-set minds, resulting from years of being shut-out of other realities, either by unawareness or plain unwillingness to accept the currently available evidence.

However, regardless of these obstacles, the time has come to finally classify and catalogue these hominoid entities, the North American Great-Ape called Nahganne by some, Sasquatch by others. In the following "Reports from the North," I have done my level best to do exactly that.

## *The 1970s*

### Report #1
### ANVIL REGION
### Sighting by Faro in 1970
### Location: Coord. 62o 13'41 N 133o 20'26 W
### (Map: Faro 105 K/3: GR 855 005)

This following Report #1 was provided to me by a Ross River First Nations woman when I was interviewing her about other Sasquatch activities she had observed—namely the 2010 encounter described in report #41. It so happened that she had mentioned this 2010 encounter to her father at which time he told her about this Faro sighting. She, in turn, passed the story to me. The council woman's father was working at the Faro mine at the time and his workmate explained to him how he had watched the Sasquatch in question. He had observed a tall bipedal creature walking around the town in the winter of 1970, appearing to be checking garbage cans and walking with a significant limp.

**Encounter:** The ambulating creature in question, described as a Sasquatch by the witness, a male in his mid-30s at the time, was going from garbage can to garbage can, apparently searching for food. Of course, garbage cans are a great source of food, and once a Sasquatch realizes such, they will return to find more food, just as bears would do on a regular basis.

**Local History:** For many years in the 1950s and 1960s, the area north of the Pelly River (Tu Desdes Tue) and west of the Community of Ross River had been the subject of intense prospecting by a man by the name of Al Kulan. In the mid-1960s, he discovered the largest vein of lead and zinc ever found, and shortly thereafter, the Cyprus Anvil Mining Corporation constructed what was to become the largest lead and zinc mine in the world, with silver and gold being side products. To house the many employees, up to 2,100 in January 1982, a town site was constructed in the spring of 1969, which formed the community of Faro, located on the Robert Campbell Highway, Yukon Highway #4, some 161 km (100 mi) east of the community of Carmacks.

But as luck would have it, a good portion of the newly built town was razed to the ground as a result of a nearby wild forest fire in the summer of 1969. However, since such an important mining operation had to move on, the burned portion was immediately rebuilt. The mine remained in operation with trucks of the White Pass and Yukon Route transporting the ore concentrates in large buckets from Faro to Whitehorse 24 hours a day. These same buckets would then be loaded on the trains of WP & YR and transported to the town of Skagway, some 171 km (106 mi) away in Alaska, where the content would be loaded on-board ships to further destinations. In 1982, the mine experienced an ugly and fierce strike, while this was going on the price of metals fell drastically, and the combination of both forced the mine to shut down.

In 1985, as the price of metals regained value, another company called Curragh Resources took over the mine and started shipping the ore concentrates directly to Skagway by trucks. The railway, owned by White Pass and Yukon Route, had stopped operating between Whitehorse and Skagway in 1982, at the time when the original Faro Mine shut down.

After Curragh Resources suffered a major disaster in Nova Scotia in 1993, they had been forced to shut down the Faro Mine operation due to financial difficulties. In 1995, the Anvil Range Mining Corp acquired the mine site and operated it until 1998.

Today, in 2022, the Canadian government is still conducting a cleanup operation with the objective of returning the ground in the area of the mine pit to a condition that would protect the surrounding land and water. The property was left in very bad condition after the forced closure and the bankruptcy of Curragh Resources and Anvil Range Mining. Most creeks in the area were devoid of fish and the surrounding land was poisoned by lead and other mining byproducts. The Faro Mine has not reopened since, resulting in the population dwindling to a handful of people. Subsequently, however, it has become a retirement community and has a population of 449 residents, as of September 2020.

The railway is still operating but only as a tourist train offering scenic rides through the White Pass between Skagway, Alaska and Carcross, Yukon during the summer months. As for Al Kulan, who had originally discovered the largest-ever deposit of lead, zinc, silver, and gold in the world, he had semi-retired, spending his winters in Vernon, British Columbia and returning to the Yukon in the summers to do what he liked best—to prospect for minerals. In the summer of 1977, he was back in the community of Ross River when he was unfortunately murdered in the local saloon.

**Investigation:** There is not much more in this sighting report to investigate or analyze; however, it was mentioned in the report that the bipedal ambulating entity in question was limping badly from what appeared to be their right leg. That would limit their hunting abilities, and they would therefore have to take a chance in going into the communities for an easy source of food.

The woman's father mentioned another 1970 Sasquatch sighting from the community of Ross River, some 69 km (43 mi) further east. As she described it, her father spoke of a bipedal ambulating entity, described as a Sasquatch, with a noticeable limp, checking out garbage cans for food. This comprises the next report, Report #2, from the community of Ross River, some 69 km (43 mi) east of Faro, dated 1970 as well, which mentions a bipedal ambulating entity, described as a Sasquatch, with noticeable limping, checking out garbage cans for food.

Could these two sightings be from the same wild man? Very possibly.

## Report #2
## ANVIL REGION
## Sighting by the Ross River Airport in 1970
## Location: Coord. 61o 58'22 N 132o 26'26 W
## (Map: Ross River 105 F/16: GR 342 735)

While conducting the interview with Ross River Dena Council woman, Report #1, she mentioned another sighting to me.

**Encounter:** Her father, who resided in Ross River at the time, told her about how he observed an injured, limping, big, bipedal, entity walking at the edge of town and who crossed an open field adjacent to the airport. Her father said he then observed that the Sasquatch, as he described the entity, wandered around the community checking the garbage containers.

The small village of Ross River is the home of the Ross River Dena Council (RRDC), with some 412 residents as of September 2020, most of whom are of First Nation ancestry. The community is located some 230 km (143 mi) east of the community of Carmacks and 69 km (43 mi) east of the community of Faro on the Robert Campbell Highway, Yukon Highway #4.

The report mentions that this creature was observed a short time after the similarly injured bipedal entity, described in Report #1, was observed in the town of Faro.

**Local History:** This location at the confluence of the Ross River *(Takaden'I Tue)* and the Pelly River (Tu Desdes Tue) had been a fall gathering place for Indigenous Peoples for as long as they can remember. They would fish the rivers and trade with each other before departing to their individual wintering spots not too far away.

In 1901, a white man by the name of Tom Smith started a trading post on the north side of the Pelly River for the purpose of purchasing fur from the First Nations gathered here. He called the trading post Smith's Landing. During that winter, some fifteen Indigenous families decided to stay for the winter rather than moving on to their usual winter location. During the following two years, more and more family members travelled from the Kaska regions of both the Yukon and the Northwest Territories along the Mackenzie River to sell their furs. However, as competition would have it, in 1903 another man built a second trading post on the south side of the Pelly River to take advantage of the larger fur business.

By 1914, over a thousand people from Indigenous Nations would gather here in late summer and fall. A large number would remain for the winter, resulting in Smith's Landing becoming a small community of its own. The name of the community was changed to Ross River in 1914 when the firm Taylor and Drury purchased the trading post.

By this time other trading posts had been built at such locations as Pelly Banks, Sheldon Lake *(Shutset'i)*, Frances Lake, and along the MacMillan River. In 1916 a severe influenza epidemic hit the community, and many lost their lives. In the following years, the price of fur went down, and by the time the Canol Road was constructed in 1942-1943, most other trading posts had closed down, leaving Ross River the only one in operation. With the arrival of the US Army construction crew to construct the Canol Pipeline along with the Canol Road, South and North, the community became quite active for a time with hundreds of US soldiers camped around the community.

**Geography:** The community of Ross River is in a large flood plain valley at the confluence of the Ross River, flowing from the north, and the Pelly River, flowing from the east. One would notice the high clay bluffs immediately past the floodplain making room for a series of mountains further north where these fossilized footprints were discovered.

**Investigation:** The important aspect of these two reports is that the reported Sasquatch showed significant limping while walking, and the timing of both encounters, the same day at two locations, just a few hours apart. Similarly, in August of 2014 two reports mentioned an encounter and an occurrence a short distance away from each other, Reports #55 & 56.

The entity described as a Sasquatch, was reported to have a height of between about 182.5 cm (72 in or 6 ft) and 213 cm (84 in or 7 ft). According to my "Quick Calculation Method", presented later in this book, a creature of 182.5 cm (72 in or 6 ft) would leave footprints just a bit less than 30.5 cm (12 in), which would indicate a young creature. Such Sasquatch would weigh about 229 kg (504 lbs) in the medium category and about 286 kg (630.5 lbs) if of the heavier set and have a step of 117 cm (46 in or 3 ft 10 in). The average daily calorie requirement would be about 5,230 calories per day to remain healthy. A creature standing at a height of 200 cm (78.5 in or 6.5 ft) medium-size would weigh about 248 kg (546 lbs) and up to 310 kg (683.5 lbs).

For the larger, heavy-type with a footprint of about 33 cm (13 in), such Sasquatch would have a step of about 127 cm (50 in or 4 ft 2 in). Such a creature would require some 5,660 calories per day to remain in good health.

On the other hand, a Sasquatch that is 213 cm tall (84 in or 7 ft) would weigh about 267 kg (588 lbs) if of medium build and up to 334 kg (736 lbs) for the larger more muscular Sasquatch.

A creature of that height would leave a footprint measuring about 35.5 cm (14 in) and would have a step of about 137 cm (54 in or 4 ft 6 in). Such a creature would need about 6,010 calories per day to remain healthy. Judging height has always been a problem for most witnesses, especially at a distance of more than 100 m (330 ft).

These are a few Sasquatch-related activities reported close by: a sighting by Dragon Lake in 1975, Report #); a sighting by the Lapie River pull out in 2004 Report #33; the Faro sighting in 1970 Report #1; and vocals along Swim Lake Road in 2010 Report #45.

**Note:** During the summer of 1985, a number of fossilized footprints were found encrusted in rocks about 30 km. (21 miles) north of the community of Ross River and a short distance from the North Canol Road, on the northwest side. Those footprints were identified to be from the *Parasaurolophus walkeri* which was a crested hadrosaur that lived during the Late Cretaceous Period some 76.5 to 73 Mya (million years ago). According to information about such animals, this hadrosaur would have been some 10 meters (33 ft) long, would usually be biped as well as a quadruped at times, and had a vegetarian diet. These animals originated from Asia and would have come across to North America at some period of time when the two continents were somehow connected during the period of 76 to 73 Mya. No skeletons of the *Parasaurolophus walkeri* were ever found in the Yukon to date; however, quite a few skeletons were located amongst the Badlands of Alberta, in Utah, and in New Mexico. The Anvil Region was covered by ice from about 4.7 Mya until about 10 Kya (thousand years ago).

## Report #3
## TAKHINI REGION
## Sighting at Pump House Lake with Rock Throwing Occurrence in 1974
## Sighting Location: Coord. 60o 43'33 N 135o 09'49 W (Map: Whitehorse 105 D/11: GR 911 322)

**Rock Throwing Location:** Coord. 60o 43'26 N 135o 09'54 W
On the following page is a diagram of Pump House Lake Area, made by your author Red Grossinger. In the summer of 2015, I was contacted by a man who wanted to share an encounter with what he described as a Sasquatch.

**Encounter:** During a late summer evening in June of 1974, the witness, a young lad of 17 years of age at the time, along with his 15-year-old younger brother, decided to catch a few trout and drove to a small man-made water reservoir located a few kilometres west of Whitehorse, known locally as the Pump House Lake and/or Pump House Pond. There they were subjected to rocks being thrown at them and, a few minutes later, observed a tall ambulating entity, which the witness called a Sasquatch, cross the road in front of them.

**Local History:** This small lake is part of a waterway system built by the Yukon Electrical Company Limited starting in 1949, taking water from various lakes to small power generating stations along the way. One of the stations is located some 150 m (500ft) down from Pump House Lake, using water from a diversion of Porter Creek, which first empties from Fish Lake through Fish Creek, then through Louise and Jackson Lakes to a small power generating station on Porter Creek, which was again diverted in 1955 to another small generating station connecting this water diversion to McIntyre Creek. A small dam was built at the same time, resulting in a water reservoir, which was then known as "McIntyre Creek Pound." Now it is better known as Pump House Lake, which is located some 30 km (18 mi) west of downtown Whitehorse.

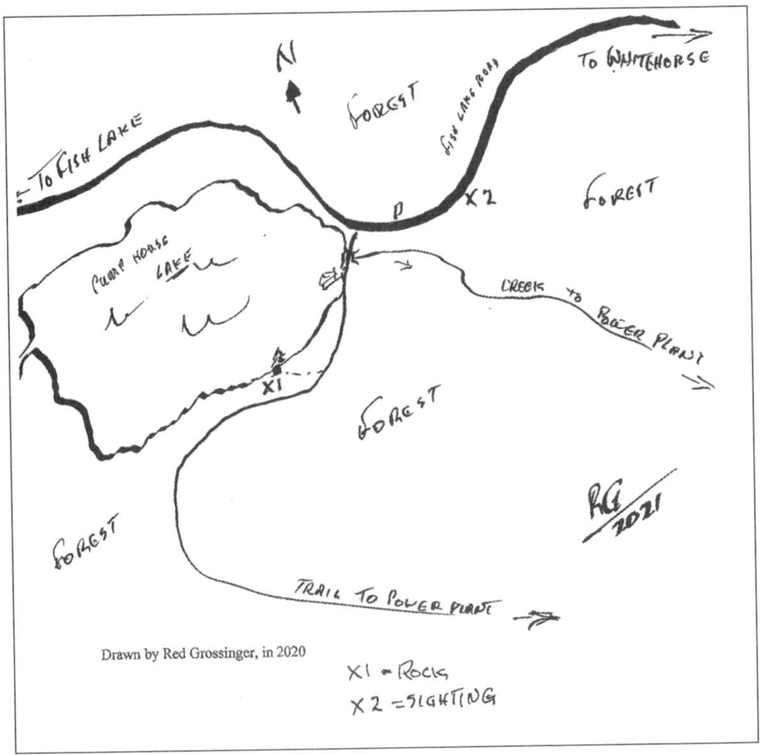


*Takhini Region: Rock Throwing Occurrence and Sighting at Pump House Lake, June 1974.*

**Investigation:** The man in question, who is a Métis from the Prairies, no longer resides in Whitehorse, although his sister and mother still do. Actually, his sister, who I have known for a number of years, is the one that informed him of my research work with Sasquatch. It so happened that in September of 2015 he was visiting his ailing mother in Whitehorse, so we made arrangements to meet at 1400 hours (2 pm) on Wednesday, September 2, 2015, at the intersection of Fish Lake Road and the Alaska Highway. After a short introduction, we drove to Pump House Lake, and we walked directly to the location where he had been subjected to rocks being thrown at his younger brother and him.

**Encounter continues:** The witness and his brother had arrived at the lake at about 1930 hours (7:30 pm), parked their car at the gate by the pump house and walked some 300 m (1,000 ft) to their usual fishing spot on the eastern side of the lake where their small, home-made wooden raft was tied to a close by tree. They jumped onto it and started fishing. They had fished for a while, catching a few trout, and at around 2100 hours (9 pm) decided it was time to get back home.

They paddled their small raft back to its mooring, secured it and started to climb the steep shore to the trail, a distance of about 10 m (33 ft), straight up. (I walked it and measured it.) As they were starting to climb the bank in the direction of the trail, they heard the sound of a large rock falling into the lake, 3 m (10 ft) behind them. This rock would have been thrown above their heads. Just a few seconds later, another large rock came splashing down at the same location. Thinking it was someone playing a joke on them, the witness yelled out: "There are people fishing down at the lake, stop fooling around." The witness stated that he was getting angry so he ran up the bank to see who was throwing the rocks. But there was no one there. What he did notice, though, was a very strong and pungent smell in the air, which he described as being akin to the smell of a "wet grizzly bear." This really got him worried as he explained to me, so he called out to his brother to hurry up. They walked briskly back to the car, constantly looking around to see whatever may be close to them. On a few occasions, they heard some shuffling sounds in the bush on their right-hand side and observed swift movements, but saw nothing definitive. They arrived at the car a few minutes later, placed their fishing gear into it and started on their journey back to town.

As it was now getting a bit darker, the driver turned the headlights on. They had proceeded just a few metres when something bolted out of the bush from their right-hand side, east side, and ran across the road about 2 m (6 ft) ahead of them. The ambulating entity they then observed was really tall, as the witness mentioned, at least 243 cm (8 ft) tall and possibly even up to 274 cm (9 ft) and was covered in darkish brown and black hair. As it crossed the road, it turned its head in the direction of the car for a second and the witness stated that its eyes were reflecting in the car's headlight. The bipedal, ambulating entity crossed the six-metre (19 ft 6 in) wide road, which I measured, in three long steps that took no more than three seconds and disappeared in the dense forest on the west side of the road. Upon returning home, the witness and his brother mentioned what they had experienced to their parents. However, the reaction of their parents was simply that the young guys "should stop fooling around and making up stories." They never since discussed their sighting with anyone else.

**Continuing the investigation:** The witness and I then walked back to our vehicles where he pointed out the location where the ambulating entity had crossed the road. As part of the investigation, after the witness had departed, I conducted various measurements of the distance between the lake and the length of the ground to the trail, the distance to this trail, and then measurements of the road where the sighting occurred. The distance from the water's edge and the trail at the fishing spot is 10 m (33 ft), the length at a direct angle, was about 8 m (26 ft). The width of the road where the sighting occurred was measured to be six m (19 ft 6 in) wide. The bipedal ambulating entity crossed the road in three long steps while running, as the witness explained to me, which would mean that each step was some two metres long, 200 cm (6ft 4 in).

Now what human being can do that, I ask? Through my calculation a step of 200 cm (78 in) would indicate a step maker of being about 312 cm (10ft 3 in or 123 in) tall, weighing between 442 and 483 kg (974 and 1,066 lbs) and having a footprint of some 51.435 cm (20.25 in). This would indicate that a Sasquatch of that size would require about 10,000 calories per day to remain healthy. These calculations would fit in quite closely with the rough height mentioned to me by the witness during the interview, being between 243 cm (8 ft) and 274 cm (9 ft).

**A question comes to mind:** Could it be possible that this creature was actually in the process of capturing fish in the area when these young lads came to fish? And that they were not happy at all to share the area? Of interest: there have been two more sighting reports that have occurred close by, within a kilometre radius actually. They are mentioned further on as Report #6 and Report #43. I should mention that I have fished that same pond, along with my sons, on quite a few occasions since 1980 catching rainbow trout, Arctic char and Arctic graylings and I have walked along the many trails around the area, which provides me with a very good knowledge of the region.

## Report #4
## ANVIL REGION
## Sighting by Dragon Lake in 1975
## Location: Coord. 62o 33'27 N 131o 20'25 W
## (Map: Sheldon Lake 105 J; GR 080 039)

A HUNTER contacted me in the summer of 2014 to report that he had come across a large, human-like creature, described as being a Sasquatch, when he was hunting along the North Canol Road in August of 1975.

**Encounter:** According to the witness, the Sasquatch was first observed standing on a small elevation between the shores of Dragon Lake *(Tuetset'i)* and the North Canol Road, at the point where the road is the closest to the lake, just after a left-hand turn and beside a boat access trail to the lake, some 100 km (62 mi) north of the Community of Ross River. The witness is a Mik'maq First Nation man, originally from the Province of New Brunswick, who was working and residing in Whitehorse at the time. Being an avid hunter, as he explained, he was out hunting on the North Canol Road looking for a moose at the start of the hunting season, which in the Yukon opens on the First of August each year.

I should mention that in October 1982, I was out hunting along the same area of the road as well and shot a moose a bit further down the road, about 20 km (12.5 mi) to right across from Sheldon Lake. I have returned to the area on a number of occasions, the last time being in 2010; therefore, I know the area well.

This area is very popular for moose hunting, although, as I write this, the Ross River Dena Council (RRDC) is claiming total ownership of the area along with hunting restrictions, as the area is part of their traditional territory historically; however, the Ross River Dena Council has not signed into the Yukon Final Land Claim Agreement as of yet.

**Geography**: The North Canol Road follows the Ross River Valley *(Takaden'I Tue)* for most of the way to just north of Sheldon

Lake *(Shuta Dene Ko)*. At one point, it veers right in a northeast direction leading to the Northwest Territories. This a fairly wide valley, with a mostly low-lying swampy area covered by the type of plants found in wet terrain, along with black spruce and willow trees. The valley is flanked on both sides by fairly tall mountains, being the lower elevations of the Selwyn Mountain Range. Besides animals such as bear, caribou, deer, hare, moose, and lynx being found in the area large numbers, there is a also wide array of vegetation.

There was a previous sighting, in 1949, from the North Canol Road by the South MacMillan River some 30 km (20 mi) further north. I have not investigated this sighting, nor have I investigated the two other sighting reports from the area of the community of Ross River: one just beside the airport, in town in 1970, Report #2, and one on the Robert Campbell Highway, Yukon Highway #4, in 2004, Report #33.

**Investigation:** When I spoke to him, the witness stated that he was driving at a low speed looking for moose or signs thereof when he approached the area where the Sasquatch was observed for a few seconds. He stated that he could not figure out what he was looking at and then it dawned on him that it was the creature known as a Sasquatch.

He mentioned that the creature was at least 213 cm (84 in or 7 ft) tall and possibly taller; it was totally covered in dark hair, being some 45 to 50 m away (150 ft) or so. He could not make out any specific details that he remembers and further stated that he did not even think of looking for facial details and could only state that it was huge, extraordinarily big.

As soon as the Sasquatch noticed the truck, he stepped off from the high piece of ground and started walking in the direction of the lake and out of sight. The sighting was no longer than thirty seconds, according to the witness. The witness then pulled into the small trail leading to the boat ramp to see if he could get a second look at the creature, but without success. He remained in his location for a few minutes, then continued on his hunting quest.

The only reason he contacted me is that he noticed the "Sasquatch Research" sign on my truck when I stopped at the vegetable stand where he worked. A couple of days later, when I returned to this vegetable stand again, he contacted me to tell his story.

He judged the Sasquatch as being some 213 cm (7 ft) tall. Which by my calculations, would have a footprint of about 35.85 cm (14 in), a step of about 137 cm (54 in or 4.5 ft) and probably a weight of about 267 kg (588 lbs) if of the medium size and some 334 kg (734 lbs) if of a larger size. Such a creature would need about 6,148 calories per day to remain healthy.

I would venture to mention this Sasquatch would have been a young one, due to the height mentioned, as the average Yukon Sasquatch stands at about 254 cm (8ft 4 in).

**NOTE:** There is an interesting story of a Sasquatch kidnapping a young girl close by this very location. It is mentioned in the "Interesting Sasquatch Stories from the Yukon" portion of this book.

## Report #5
## SQUANGA REGION
## Sighting by Jakes Corner in 1975
## Location: Coord. 60o 20’22 N 133o 59’03 W (Map: Squanga Lake 105 C/5: GR 570 893)

A First Nations man from the Teslin Tlingit Council (TTC) was on his way back to Teslin from Whitehorse in the early evening of Saturday, October 4, 1975, where he had been visiting family and friends, when he observed a Sasquatch standing beside the highway.

**Encounter:** Just about half a kilometre past Jakes Corner, the man noticed what he thought was a hitchhiker standing on the right-hand side of the road. So, he pulled his car over and stopped by the individual at the side of the road, with the intention of picking up the hitchhiker. He then realized that his would-be hitchhiker was a grey-faced, hairy creature, reflecting a blueish tint that he identified as a Sasquatch in his report. At the time he had mentioned his sighting to a few members of TTC, one of whom is a good friend of mine. Later on, when she became aware of my interest in Sasquatch, she told me the full story. The exact location was described to be about 0.5 km (0.3 mi) east of Jakes Corner, on the Alaska Highway, Yukon Highway #1. Jakes Corner is located at the Junction of the Alaska Highway and the Tagish Road, Yukon Highway # 8, some 85 km (53 mi) east of Whitehorse.

**Local History:** Jakes Corner was the site of a highway construction camp during the construction of the Alaska Highway. From here, the Alaska Highway went to Whitehorse and a secondary road was built to join the Alaska Highway to the First Nation community of Tagish and then to the railhead at the community of Carcross. In the 1950s, another road was built to connect the Alaska Highway, close to Jakes Corner, to the community of Atlin on the shores of Atlin Lake in British Columbia.

**Geography:** Almost across from Jakes Corner, on the south side of the road, one faces the high peak of Mount White, which rises to an elevation of 1,529 m (5,016 ft). The west face of Mount White is extremely steep; the land between the mountain and the highway is low, swampy land crossed by Little Atlin Creek, while another set of mountains is located on the north side of the highway. This is where the creature recognized as a Sasquatch was sighted. The forest is very dense around these parts, mostly black spruce with the odd willows on the lower lands and poplars on the higher grounds. There are a high number of moose in this area as well as the Carcross/Tagish woodland caribou herd. Mount White is also home to a large herd of sheep and a few observation sites are accessible from the Atlin Road.

The usual array of smaller animals are found in the area and plenty of fish, mostly Arctic grayling, northern pike, and ling cod are in the close by Little Atlin Lake.

**Investigation:** The height of the creature was reported to be only about 117 cm tall (65 in or 5 ft 5 in) or so. This would probably indicate a juvenile Sasquatch, which would have a footprint of only about 28 cm (11.5 in). Such a creature would only weigh about 210 kg (475 lbs), but if he were exceptionally heavy, he could have been about 262 kg (590 lbs) and have a step of some 112 cm (44 in or 3 ft 8 in). The daily food requirement of such a creature would be about 4,802 calories per day to remain healthy. The Sasquatch's face was described as being greyish, which is quite common in other reports.

The reported bluish tint is also interesting, as there was a similar colour description of a Sasquatch sighted beside the Carcross Road at the Cowley Stretch in mid-January 2006, Report #34. The bluish tint of the hair was very similar as explained to me by the Cowley Stretch's witness. It is my opinion that the cause of this bluish tint would mostly be the reflection of the vehicle headlights on the Sasquatch's hair when it is cold out and after a bit of snow has fallen.

There was no mention of snow in this report, but as a long time Yukon resident, I know for a fact that it is cold in the Yukon during the evenings in early October, with the temperature dipping well below the freezing point most of the time, which would cause frost to stick to a warm body covered with hair. Therefore, this bluish tint might have been reflected from the vehicle headlights.

To test this point, I would encourage readers to make an experiment with someone wearing a warm fur coat at night during a cold period, with the headlight from a car shining on that person just to see what the reflection would be.

## Report #6
## TAKHINI REGION
## Sighting by Icy Water Fish Farm on Fish Lake Road in 1976
## Location: Coord. 60o 43'21 N 135o 10'39 W (Map: Whitehorse 105 D/11: GR 904 320)

While investigating a sighting report by Pump House Lake, I was talking with a fisherman friend of mine who mentioned that he had discussed the subject of Sasquatch with a First Nations couple who were fishing at the same location the year before, which would have been in 2014.

**Encounter:** My fisherman friend, a Tlingit First Nation man, told me that the couple in question were from the Kwanlin Dün First Nation (KDFN), and were on their way to Fish Lake in mid-July of 1976, driving the original Fish Lake Road, when they noticed a large, dark figure sort of bend over in the swamp, just a couple of metres to their right-hand side. As they approached closer, the figure stood up looking at them and slowly walked away to the nearby bush. The KDFN couple identified the entity as a Sasquatch. The KDFN couple never mentioned this sighting to anyone until talking with my Tlingit friend in 2014.

**History:** The location where the sighting took place is part of a fairly large swamp connected to Fish Creek. Some 200 m (620 ft) away from this location was a large copper mine, which was in operation by Whitehorse Copper Co. at the time, and just a few metres from the intersection of the Fish Lake Road and the Copper Haul Road, which was used to haul copper from the mine pits to the mill about 12 km (8 mi) away. Whitehorse Copper Co. had some twenty mine pits at various locations in the area and operated until 1981, when the price of copper plummeted. To this day, people come across many mine pits located along the Copper Haul Road.

**Investigation:** On Wednesday, September 2, 2015, I was investigating a sighting of a rock-throwing incident that had taken place by Pump House Lake in 1974, when I met my Tlingit friend who was intrigued by the investigation I was conducting and shared his meeting with the KDFN couple who had observed this Sasquatch in the Fish Creek swamp in 1976. I know the area quite well, having fished along the creek on many occasions and having explored the many trails found in the area. There have been two other Sasquatch sightings within a 2-kilometre radius ,Reports #3 and #43.

## Report # 7
## TAKHINI REGION
## Sighting by Long Lake Road in 1978
## Location: Coord. 60o 43'44 N 135o 03'08 W
## (Map: Whitehorse 105 D/11: GR 971 328)

As I was going through old reports I had on file, I came upon one from a young First Nations boy who, at the time, was 15 years of age and originally from the Kwanlin Dün First Nation (KDFN). The boy mentioned that he observed what he referred to as a Sasquatch close to the Yukon River downstream from the Robert Campbell Bridge within the Whitehorse city limits.

**Encounter:** The young fellow in question was on his way to his favourite fishing spot at around 0800 hours (8 am), in August of 1978. Walking from downtown Whitehorse, he first crossed the Robert Campbell Bridge onto the east side of the Yukon River, then turned left, walking in a northerly direction on a gravel road leading away from the bridge in the direction of Long Lake (One of 203 lakes named Long Lake in Canada) on a road commonly called the Long Lake Road by the locals, but which actual name is Wickstrom Road. This road follows the Yukon River on the east side of the river. From Long Lake on, the road becomes the Livingstone Trail, eventually reaching the former gold fields of Livingstone Creek on the east shores of the Big Salmon River.

At one point, after climbing a small hill and going down the other side, he turned left onto a smaller trail which would eventually take him to the river's edge, some six kilometres from the bridge. As he approached a large clearing, just past a small utility shed, he noticed a tall and thin dark black figure, top-heavy with a slightly hunched back and long arms at a distance of about 30 m (100 ft) away or so and just about in the middle of the clearing.

The figure was sort of jumping and dancing around a tall aspen tree with its arms flailing about in an excited manner, looking as if it were amusing itself. At one point, the figure, which the witness later identified as a Sasquatch, moved closer to the tree, then put its hand out, reaching for and grasping a large branch at about shoulder height. The creature then made what appeared to be an attempt to climb the tree.

The witness then states that, as the creature tried to lift itself up, the branch it was holding on broke with a loud noise, and the creature fell to the ground. While all this was taking place, the young man was hiding behind the shed so as not to be seen by the creature but was still able to observe the action. When the creature fell to the ground, our young fisherman took advantage of the distraction and started off running back to town.

A few days later, our young fisherman mentioned the incident to his friends and family; however, they mostly regarded the event as wild imagination on the part of the young fellow and total nonsense.

The day after he mentioned the event, the young man went back to the sighting location with a friend to look for the broken tree branch and maybe some footprints. By all indication, he found the tree in question, but he could not locate the broken branch and did not notice any tracks in the immediate vicinity of the tree or in the clearing. The report states the clearing to be located about 6 km (4 mi) downstream from Whitehorse, on the eastern shore of the river at a distance of about 500 m (1,650 ft) from the shores of the Yukon River, as written by the young fella.

**Investigation:** During my investigation of the sighting, I walked along the Yukon River from the Robert Campbell Bridge to locate the exact sighting location. I would dispute the location as described by the witness, as the 6 km (4 mi) he stated in the Report would have required him to climb one of the steep hills located before and another one past Long Lake. He would then have had to walk down a sharp treacherous incline to get to the riverbank, which distance at that specific point would have been much further than stated.

There is no mention of Long Lake itself in the report, except for the name of the road; therefore, the location in question had to be before Long Lake. That lake is 4 km (2.5 mi) down the road from the Robert Campbell Bridge, which crosses the Yukon River in downtown Whitehorse leading to the sub-division of

Riverdale. The Robert Campbell Bridge is presently one of three ways to get to the east shore of the river. One of the other routes is to cross at the power dam, which is usually closed to any public traffic anyway, and the other way is to cross the Millennium Trail pedestrian bridge, which did not exist at the time of the reported sighting.

Distances for a young person who does not drive a car can be very confusing, especially if you have to walk to get where you want to go.

Therefore, I would place the actual sighting location close to what was then locally known as the old fox farm, about 1.6 km (1 mi) down the road from the bridge. All other descriptions of the location would fit with this site. The buildings around the site burned down in 2000, and new housing has sprung up in the area. This location is presented because I was a resident of Whitehorse in 1980, two years after the reported sighting took place, and that is the only location that would fit. Being an avid fisherman myself, I used to fish up and down the Yukon River in those days and probably fished the same spot. In case anyone wonders, I left the Yukon in June of 1983 and returned for good in August of 1986.

Our witness was a young fellow in his mid-teens at the time who had been residing in Fort St. John, BC with his KDFN mother, and had been spending the summer visiting his father in Whitehorse while on his way to his favourite fishing spot, where he had fished on many occasions before. The young fellow in question only reported this encounter in November of 1995, and I became aware of it in 2010.

**Local History:** Prior to the full-time settlement of what is now the city of Whitehorse by the first white folks during the Klondike Gold Rush of 1896, this part of the Yukon was inhabited by the Indigenous People of the Kwanlin Dün First Nation (KDFN) and the Ta'an Kwäch'än Council (TKC). Members of these First Nations would fish at the Whitehorse rapids, located by what is known today as Miles Canyon and Schawka Lake. They would fish for various types of salmon and other fish, mostly in the rapids downstream from the canyon and also hunt for caribou, elks, and moose around the nearby mountain slopes.

The Kwanlin Dün First Nation People would winter in the immediate area, while the Ta'an Kwäch'än People would winter on the east shore of nearby Lake Laberge, about 30 km (21 mi) downstream from Whitehorse. Soon after the discovery of gold in 1896, thousands of mad gold seekers travelled the Chilkoot Trail to Bennett Lake during the following two years, built boats of all sorts and as soon as the ice broke would have been on their way, Klondike bound. Many perished attempting to navigate Miles Canyon and the Whitehorse Rapids, but most just carried on to the Klondike, driven by the overwhelming madness of getting to the gold fields ahead of the others and claiming all that gold. This madness became known as gold fever, and many people perished by it or actions resulting from this madness. Starting in 1897 and during 1898, small paddle boats were constructed at Bennett City at the end of the Chilkoot Trail, at the far end of Bennett Lake. These paddle wheelers would take the gold seekers and their kit as far as Canyon City, where they and their goods would be unloaded from these small paddle boats and transported by horse-pulled tramways. The first such tramway was located on the east side of the Yukon River, then, as business competition would have it, another one started operating on the west side of the river. Both tramways ended downstream from the rapids at a location that is now the city of Whitehorse, and the goods would be re-loaded in larger paddle wheelers for the journey to Dawson City and the Klondike Gold Fields.

The resulting camp, downstream from the rapids, originally became known as Closeleigh for a short period of time in 1898, and the following year the name was changed to Whitehorse. These rapids became known as the Whitehorse Rapids, as its turbulent waters looked much like the head and mane of wild white horses and is the source of the name "Whitehorse."

In 1899, a railway line reached the then-small settlement of Whitehorse, which soon became the centre for rail transportation between Skagway, Alaska and Whitehorse, Yukon, and the centre of river transportation and navigation as well, between

Whitehorse and Dawson City in the Klondike Region, where the famous gold rush was happening. The arrival of the railway to Whitehorse meant the end of the paddle wheelers on the upper portion of the Yukon River and the southern lakes, from Bennett City in BC to Whitehorse in the Yukon.

Many of the Indigenous Peoples became wood cutters at the time of the gold rush, and for some time after, provided fuel wood for the paddle boats. Some also worked as river guides and river pilots—their intimate knowledge of the river and the land being in high demand.

As well, a large number of Indigenous People were busy hunting for fresh meat for all these newcomers, and it was noted that as a result, games were driven further and further away from their regular locations, closer to the Yukon River. The Yukon First Nations Peoples were employed in these capacities until an all-seasons road was built between Whitehorse and Dawson City in 1954, thus killing the paddle wheelers and all its related employment. As these logs were cut for some sixty years, the northern boreal forest was decimated for quite a distance on both sides of the Yukon River, between Whitehorse and Dawson City. We can still see the scars of old tree stumps and remains of old wood camps when walking around the forest today, just about everywhere you venture along the river. Most trees one sees today are second- and third-generation growth.

**Geography:** The area where the sighting took place is part of the northern boreal forest with small sandy rolling hills mostly covered with aspen, birch, black and white spruce, lodgepole pine, poplar, and willow. As well, there are many small pot-hole lakes, remnant of the last ice age, and a few rocky outcrops that can be located in the immediate area. Eventually, these rolling hills would join the rocky slopes of the mountain known locally as Grey Mountain, a.k.a. Canyon or Cap Mountain, which raises to an elevation of 1,836 m (6,023 ft) some 6 km (4 mi) in an east-southeast direction from the sighting location. Past Grey Mountain to the east and north is pure wilderness for hours of flying time with many high mountains and deep valleys, part of what is known as the Yukon Plateau and where very few people have ever set foot. There are plenty of animals roaming the boreal forest around the Whitehorse area today, as this is now a no-hunting zone. One often comes across bears, caribou, cougars, coyotes, deer, elk, and moose. Smaller animals would include beavers, frogs, grouse, hares, lynx, otters, rodents, and porcupines. Along lakes and waterways, ducks, geese, swans, and many other types of large and small birds reside as well as large numbers of fish in the waters. Additionally, there are also about a thousand varieties of plants around the area, most of them edible, each specific to its growing zone and much too numerous to specify. Suffice to say that there is plenty of food for Sasquatch to survive all year round.

**Other Occurrences:** To my knowledge, there were several more sightings in the immediate area of Whitehorse prior to this one. As well, I experienced an unidentified, strange, foul smell close by. I observed a series of large foot impressions and a number of tree-related events close to where these sightings took place.

**Further Investigative Comments:** This report was made in 1995 about an encounter that occurred in 1978. The witness stated that he remembers the sighting quite well, but it took him almost seventeen years to make a report. No specific reasons were given as to why it took him so long to come out and report it. However, one has to consider the human aspect of this Sasquatch phenomenon.

This is a sad but true fact that people have a feeling of being ridiculed and are frightened that they will be made fun of when reporting such an occurrence to the authorities.

I know the area in question very well; my residence is presently located 3.5 km (2.3 mi) away from where this sighting reportedly occurred, and I used to fish the very same part of the Yukon River when I first resided here from 1980 to 1983. The only details of value being presented by the witness about the ambulating entity sighted by the young lad are that it was tall, thin, with dark black hair and long arms, and the figure observed was "top-heavy," which I take as meaning that the observed entity was muscular around the upper body. The figure was slightly hunchbacked, which I take as possibly describing an older creature, yet still black—but then again, it was described as "prancing around," sort of dancing and jumping.

If you were to notice a human being doing the exact same thing, he/she would have a slightly hunched back as well. The approximate height of the Sasquatch is not mentioned anywhere in the report. At one point, the witness states that the reported Sasquatch reached for a branch at shoulder height, but he does not mention which hand was used or the height of the branch. The reported creature's noticeable excitement towards the tree may well have been the result of having cornered some game animal in the tree in question, such as a porcupine or squirrel, for example, expecting it to be its next meal.

Just for the record, according to my calculations, based on research work and with data compiled from many scientists and Sasquatch researchers, the average Sasquatch would be 238 cm tall (94 in or 7 ft 10 in) and weigh about 295 kg (651 lbs). Such a creature would have a footprint of about 39 cm (15.5 in) and a step of 152 cm (60 in or 5 ft), measured from the tips of the toes of one footprint to the tips of the toes of the following footprint. To maintain healthy activities a Sasquatch of such a height and weight would need about 6,688 calories of food per day.

Other reported Sasquatch sightings in the general area all indicated that the entity being observed averaged a height of about 213 cm (84 in or 7 ft), such would indicate a footprint of 35.5 cm (14 in) with a step of 138 cm (54 in or 4 ft 6 in) and would weigh around 267 kg (588 lbs).

There are a few other reports mentioned for the area, a foul-smell occurrence in 2010, Report #44, and a foot track in 2011, Report #11.

# *The 1980s*

**Report # 8**
**TATCHUN REGION**
**Foul Smell at Tatchun Lake Campground in 1984**
**Location: Coord. 62o 17'52 N 136o 08'25 W**
**(Map: Carmacks 115 I: GR 042 007)**

A MAN CONTACTED ME to report that he had experienced a strange, unexplained, short-term, extremely foul and pungent smell in early September 1984, at the location of the present-day Tatchun Lake Campground, about 8 km (5 mi) up the Frenchman Lake Road from its intersection with the North Klondike Highway, Yukon Highway #2.

The man in question was employed by Yukon Government Parks and Recreation Department at the time of the occurrence. He was then in his mid-40s, a white man who had lived in the Yukon for about twenty years by that time, an avid fisherman and sometime hunter. At the time, he was involved in the planning and construction of Yukon Territorial Campgrounds throughout the Yukon; therefore, he is very familiar with the Yukon wilderness.

I have known this fellow for over thirty-five years and he is certainly what I would consider bush-wise, totally reliable, and trustworthy. In 1990 he arranged for me to get a contract with the Yukon Parks and Recreation Department to transport, by boat, a number of campground tables, fire pits, and toilets to the sites of new campgrounds being developed along the Thirty Mile stretch of the Yukon River, which starts at the outflow of Lake Laberge to the confluence of the Teslin River with the Yukon River, at the former riverside community of Hootalinqua.

At the time of the occurrence, he was conducting a preliminary survey of an area on the northwest side of Tatchun Lake, with the intention of locating a suitable place to construct a new campground. The Frenchman Lake Road had recently been built for the specific purpose of opening access to the lake from that side.

**Local History:** A small trail has existed for some time in this immediate area, reportedly way back in time when the Little Salmon/Carmacks First Nation (LSCFN) used that route to access Frenchman Lake; however, this trail was not suitable for regular traffic, never mind RVs, motor homes, campers, and travel trailers. However, it has recently been upgraded and is now usable by all types of vehicles.

There is an interesting display in the community of Carmacks called the Tagé Cho Hudän Interpretive Centre, where the First Nation ancestors of the present-day Little Salmon/Carmacks First Nation or Tsawnjik Dün First Nation, as it is now called. This display depicts a woolly mammoth being trapped using ropes made of willows and animal hides and eventually being killed for food and clothing.

This depiction not only shows hunting and trapping methods used at the time but refers to the immediate area as being ice-free, thus part of the larger Beringia land mass. Interestingly, more recent research concerning Beringia shows the immediate area around what is now the community of Carmacks as being ice-free for millions of years, yet the first *Homo sapiens* migration to eastern Beringia, in what is now Alaska and the Yukon, occurred during a period of time dated to have occurred at between 30 Kya to 15 Kya. I calculated the fastest advance of *Homo sapiens* would have been about 100 km (62 mi) per generation at the most. Which would be roughly about thirty years per generation in those days. In order to reach this area, the time-lapse would have been somewhere around seventeen generations or a bit over five hundred years from the time the first *Homo sapiens* set foot onto the soil of what is now North America to reach the area of the community of Carmacks, a distance of about 1,700 km (1,055 mi) or so.

So that would indicate the possibility of the Indigenous Aboriginal Beringians being the very first ancestors of our present-day Indigenous Peoples. They would have arrived in this area between 29,500 years ago and 14,500 years ago at the earliest. Research has indicated that the woolly mammoth disappeared from the present Carmacks area some 10 Kya, while a small herd remained alive until about 1,700 years ago around Wrangel Island in Alaska.

In the latest news, in late June 2022, the full body of a baby woolly mammoth was discovered in the Klondike Goldfields, by miners working Eureka Creek. The woolly mammoth had been frozen in ice age permafrost for some 35,000 years, and has been named "Nun cho ga" by Elders of the Tr'ondëk Hwëch First Nation.

**Occurrence:** The man in question had driven to the northwest shores of Tatchun Lake using a small bush trail, hardly usable for 4 x 4 pickup trucks, where he was surveying the area for a suitable location to develop a new campground, which was to be located somewhere close by and alongside the lake. The way the new road was to be constructed would provide limited access to the lake due to the type of terrain.

He and his crew had originally selected three possible locations on the various maps available and his job was to make a final selection based on a number of specific criteria. He had separated from the other two members of his group at another location, and they were in their own truck. Having previously turned down the first location they had visited, they went to another location while he went to this specific location on his own. The plan was for them to complete the survey, then return to Whitehorse right after, and he would return on his own once he had completed his survey.

He had arrived at this location around 1330 hours (1:30 pm) and was by the lake when he decided to return to his truck at about 1400 hours (2 pm).

The area was covered with tall lodgepole pines, and there were a large number of dead trees, which, when the area was cleared, would be used for firewood. Upon climbing up from the lake, he was crossing some dead trees when his left foot slipped, and he got his left leg impaled by a sharp broken tree branch.

Lying there wondering what to do next, the entire forest around him suddenly became deadly quiet: all the birds stopped flying, no squirrels around, no birds chirping, nothing but total dead silence. This is when an extremely pungent smell that he really cannot describe came upon him. He mentioned the smell to be extremely strong, pungent, and making his eyes burn and run with tears, but he could not describe the actual content of that smell. The smell lasted about a minute, and he stayed there, mostly lying on the tree branches for the next ten minutes, trying to figure out first what had happened, and then secondly what to do next. He knows for sure that it was not a bear or any such animal, he knows what bears smell like, and the smell was not even close to that of a bear. He simply does not know any animals that would project such a stink, while making all other creatures of the wild to go silent for such a period of time. Finally, after about ten minutes, he managed to get untangled from the broken branches, got up, and made his way back to the truck the best he could. After performing first-aid to his leg, he drove directly back to Whitehorse and went to the Whitehorse General Hospital for treatment.

**Investigation:** When I first interviewed him in 2009, he explained his experience the best he could, trying to describe the smell he had been subjected to. I went on to mention my own experience with a similar smell occurrence and explained what I had experienced and how it had happened, describing what I had smelled and how I had felt. He agreed that the smell was somewhat similar.

I have camped at the Tatchun Lake Campground on many occasions through the years, and although I have noticed some strange tree formations, there is nothing that, in my view, would indicate any other activity signs related to Sasquatch. The area in question is very dense with tall, bent-over lodgepole pines and willow trees with large white spruce trees closer to the lake. Any creature can stand still just a couple of metres (a couple of yards) from a person and not be seen. This campground is well-used by those who like fishing as there are large northern pike and lake trout being taken from Tatchun Lake—and I, for one, sure have taken my share through the years. I have been returning to the site on many occasions and will keep returning whenever I can to conduct more research around the area and enjoy the fishing, even though these days only barbless single hooks are permitted. The Tatchun Lake access road is located about 40 km (25 mi) north of the community of Carmacks on the North Klondike Highway, Highway #2. While the Tatchun Lake campground is located about 8 km (5 mi) up the Frenchman Lake Road. Frenchman Lake, where I experienced a similar occurrence in 2003, is located another 30 km (21 mi) further down the Frenchman Lake Road, in a north-northeast direction, which eventually reaches the Robert Campbell Highway, Yukon Highway #4. There is a sighting by the mouth of the lake, which took place in 1995, Report #21, and a foul-smell occurrence at Frenchman Lake in 2003 Report #30.

## Report # 9
## SQUANGA REGION
## Animal Reaction at the Teslin Microwave Tower in 1984
## Location: Coord. 60o 12'38 N 132o 48'57 W
## (Map: Teslin 105 C/2: GR 211 767)

A GOOD FRIEND OF MINE, a First Nations man in his mid-40s at the time, told me that in late September of 1984, he and his wife, who is from the the Teslin Tlingit Council, had witnessed some strange behaviour from their dog.

**Occurrence:** They had driven to the local microwave tower in late September to look at the autumn foliage. As they arrived, they let their dog out of the car to run around, as they had always done before. But this time, the dog acted very strangely; after wandering about for a couple of minutes, the dog quickly returned to the car shaking and generally behaving in a scared and unfamiliar manner.

**Local History:** This unusual occurrence took place by the tower located some 12 km (7 mi) west of the community of Teslin and 3 km (2 mi) north, off the Alaska Highway, Yukon Highway #1. This microwave tower is part of a series of towers erected by our local phone company Northwestel, a subsidiary of Bell Canada, which provides communications services to communities in Canada's North from the Yukon across the Northwest Territories and as far as Nunavut and some portions of northern BC.

The man who reported this to me was originally from the Iroquois First Nation around Chatham, Ontario. He has been living in the Yukon for over thirty-five years, and he actually married a woman from the Teslin Tlingit First Nation. In addition to looking at the autumn foliage around Teslin Lake, they were also checking for possible tracks left by animals that may have been around the hill. This microwave tower in question is located on a fairly small mountain at an elevation of only 1,320 m (4,330 ft).

Most of the trees are balsam poplars and willows with the

odd stands of white spruce and lodgepole pine around a fairly rocky terrain. There are numerous animal activities around this area, ranging from the larger types to much of the small animals, and there is no other road access further north from where this tower is located or around the immediate area.

I have known this couple for over twenty years, and we have become good friends. They are both of Indigenous descent, although from different First Nations in different parts of Canada. They had been residing in Whitehorse until the summer of 2019 and moved back to Teslin when they have been offered a new house by the TTC.

I actually employed the man as a security guard when I was the manager of a private security firm working out of Whitehorse a few years ago. (Sadly, he passed away in 2020.)

**Investigation:** As soon as their dog was let out of the vehicle, it ran into the bush at full speed, just as it always did before, with not a care in the world, just running free.

However, this time it had returned in about two minutes, running twice as fast, it seemed, and wanted to get back in the vehicle, totally scared of something, acting in a manner that the couple had never observed before.

As it got back in the vehicle, the dog was trying to hide under the back seat, shaking—it was very unusual and something the dog had never done before, according to the owners. As mentioned later by the owners, this dog had chased bears before and all sorts of animals without any fear or any past reaction, so they could not understand what would have scared their dog in such a way.

After observing this strange behaviour and unfamiliar reaction, the couple were somewhat on alert, and a short while later they sensed something odd, something they had never sensed before, a feeling they were not wanted, a strange unexplainable anxiety of sorts, and decided that indeed something was not quite right. This is when they decided to leave the area, so they got into their vehicle, returning home to the community of Teslin a short distance away.

They had not mentioned this incident to anyone before and only shared this odd occurrence with me after they found out about my interest in the Sasquatch phenomenon and various activities or occurrences possibly related to these gentle giants of the forests. The same couple experienced a vocal occurrence by Brooks Brook in 1995, Report #17.

The area around Teslin has experienced many Sasquatch-related activities, which are identified in this book under the Squanga Region.

I should mention there are quite a few other reports similar to this one, relating to odd, unfamiliar pet dog reactions.

## Report #10
## LIARD REGION
## Sighting at the Kotaneelee Natural Gas Field in 1989
## Location: 60o 07'31 N 124o 07'37 W (Map: La Biche River 95 C, SE Corner, 1/250,000 & Yukon Bedrock Geology Map)

A MAN OF IRISH DESCENT contacted me to report that he, along with a co-worker from the Liard First Nation, had experienced a Sasquatch sighting.

**Encounter:** This man and his co-worker were taking a walk after dinner at a gas exploration site dining hall when they observed a tall and rather skinny ambulating bipedal creature, which he identified as being a Sasquatch, with grey-whitish looking hair, performing a sort of dance in a clearing illuminated by the light of a full moon during the early evening. These gentlemen were working at a natural gas exploration camp located east of Mount Martin, with an elevation of 1,359 m (4,460 ft), in the Liard Plateau at the southeast corner of the Yukon. Just a few kilometres west of the Northwest Territories borders and a few kilometres north of the British Columbia border, in the area known today as the Kotaneelee Natural Gas Fields.

The sighting occurred in early October of 1989, at around 2100 hours (9 pm). The man in question was about 45 years of age at the time and was a member of crew working for a natural gas exploration company, which was exploring in the area at the time. The witness was originally from the province of Newfoundland and Labrador and had been working in natural gas exploration for over fifteen years when this sighting took place. He had worked in many places around the world, including Argentina and some other South American locations, before joining this company in the Yukon.

I had known the man in question for about five years before he related this sighting to me in 2005, after he heard about the Sasquatch sighting by a group of First Nations people in the community of Teslin and was informed that I was also researching the Sasquatch phenomenon. As he was part of the exploration crew, he was working two weeks in the field and then two weeks off at home, "two on, two off," as it is referred to in this type of business. He contacted me during his time off at home and explained how the sighting occurred.

He was taking a stroll with another crew member in the early evening; the weather was nice for the time of the year, and there was no wind that he noticed.

When they came to a small clearing about 300 m (1,000 ft) from the camp's bunkhouse, they noticed a creature which was identified as a Sasquatch by the witness/reporter, sort of dancing in the full moonlight in the middle of the clearing, waving its arms around and jumping about in a comical sort of way.

The creature must have heard the two people approaching, as within a few seconds of these two gentlemen arriving in the vicinity, it disappeared into the close-by forest.

**Local History:** Oil and natural gas explorations started in the late 1970s in this area, resulting in quite a few finds in what became known as the Liard Basin Exploration Zone. When natural gas was found between the Kotaneelee Mountain Range in the Northwest Territories, just north of the BC border and southwest of Mount Martin in the Yukon, the area was named the Kotaneelee Natural Gas Fields. These gas fields were closed for good in 2018. The only access to the location was by air for a long time; however, before the gas extraction operation began, a road was finally built to connect the gas fields to the Alaska Highway, Yukon Highway #1, through Northern BC.

**Geography:** The area is located in a valley with mostly low swampy grounds and muskeg, surrounded by mountains. This area is known for a number of hot springs close by, flowing freely. Aspens and black spruce are the most common trees along with balsam poplars, black cottonwoods, lodgepole pines, and willows. Wildflowers abound as well. This mostly low ground provides good forage for animals such as elk and moose, along with the smaller animals and their predators. A generally warmer regional climate with plenty of large wild plants not

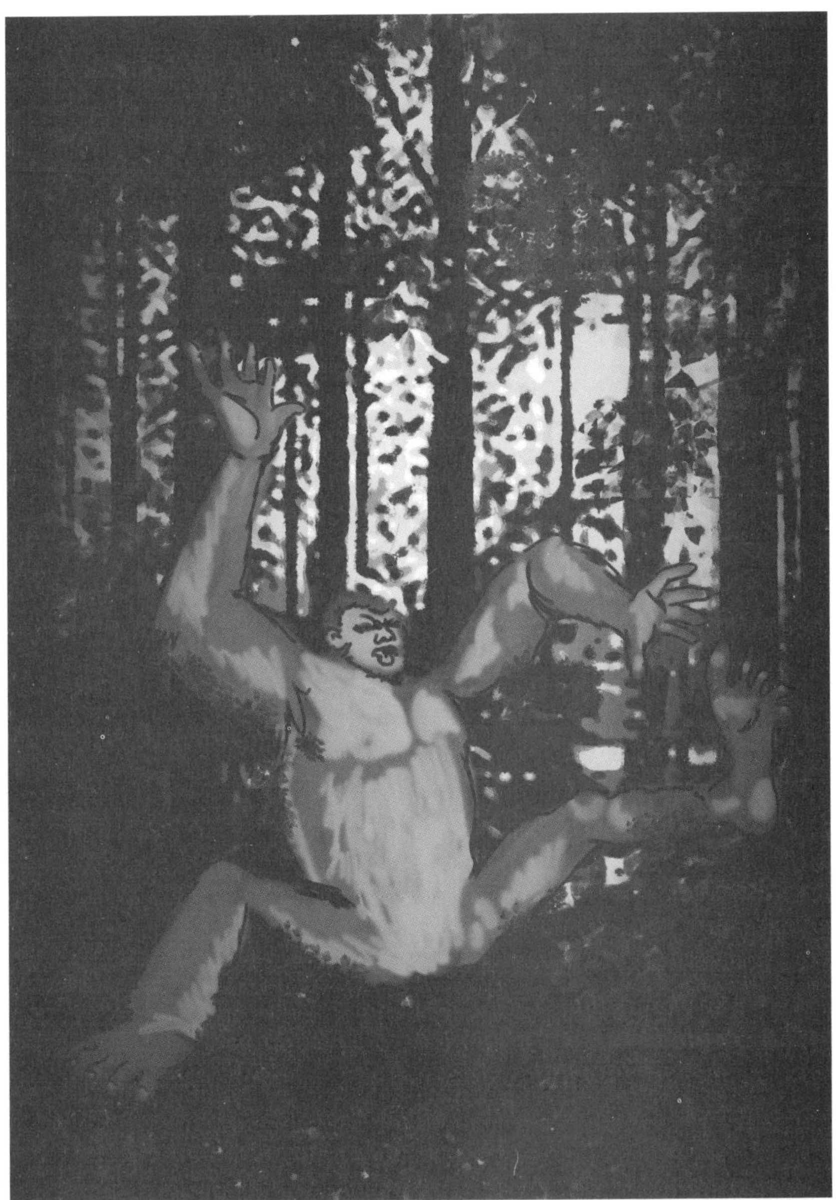

*"We observed him dancing wildly, jumping around and about, arms flinging in the air, a beam of a bright moonlight shining above him, like he was listening to his own music. It seemed like he was having a great time dancing, then he noticed us and quickly walked into the bush without making a sound."*
*Illustration: Rich Théroux*

found anywhere else in the Yukon would make plenty of food available for Sasquatch all year long.

**Investigation:** I had known the man who relayed this sighting to me for about five years before he mentioned this sighting, and I have no reason not to believe him. He told me that he was somewhat shaken after the incident and refused at first to admit what he saw. Then he stated that he was too scared of being labelled a fool and ridiculed, so he simply kept quiet about the sighting he had experienced. A few interesting points were brought forward; he first mentioned the Sasquatch being tall and skinny.

Queried about the possible height, he stated that he would judge it to have been about 245 cm (96 in or 8 ft) tall, but he was not totally sure; therefore, I cannot take that as a totally accurate measurement, but, rather, a workable measurement. Taking that information as the height measurement of 245 cm (96 in or 8 ft), the creature would probably weigh around 305 kg (672 lbs), although the witness did mention that the creature observed was skinny. Therefore, I would remove about 25 per cent of the stated weight to about 229 kg (504 lbs).

According to my calculation, a 245 cm tall creature (96 in or 8 ft) would have a footprint of about 40.6 cm (16 in) with a step of some 156.5 cm (61.5 in or 5 ft 1.5 in). A creature of that proportion would probably require about 6,960 calories per day to remain healthy. This proportion is well within the average range of Sasquatch according to many sighting reports.

By "skinny," I take it as being emaciated, possibly by a lack of food or by age, which would further fit the witness stating that its hairs were whiteish, although the reported sharp natural moonlight from the full moon could have caused a visual distortion. Such effects of light have been reported in other sightings.

As to the dancing sort of actions, similar activities have been reported in several reports before, as well as jumping on two legs, jumping from leg to leg, moving back and forth, moving from side to side, and that sort of thing, although in this report the witness also mentioned that it was waving its arms about in a comical sort of way.

The dancing, in this case, appeared to be deliberate in the view of the witness and somewhat coordinated with smooth leg and arms movements, and, as emphasized by my friend, directly within the beam of the bright moonlight, as it was shining within the small clearing amongst the trees. I would have liked to investigate the area more closely, but the road access was restricted to company workers at the time for good reason.

The latest information about the area is that the gas operation has ceased, and the site has been cleaned up and reclaimed. Even the old access road has been removed.

## *The 1990s*

**Report #11**
**LIARD REGION**
**Sighting at the Nass River Bridge in 1990**
**Location: Coord. 56o 02'01 N 129O 08'13 W**
**(Map: BC Highway #37, South of Meziadin Junction)**

A TRUCK DRIVER contacted a colleague and friend of mine to report that he had observed a bipedal ambulating creature, which the driver described as a Sasquatch, standing on the bridge crossing the Nass River, then walking off the bridge onto the shore of the river to let the truck go by. This sighting occurred on BC Highway #37, the Cassiar Road, about 20 km (12 mi) south of Meziadin Junction, in the middle of March 1990 at about 1500 hours (3 pm).

The truck driver was a white male in his late 60s at the time who had resided in Whitehorse for over thirty years when the sighting occurred. At the time of the sighting, he was driving the route between Whitehorse, Yukon, and Prince Rupert, BC, on a regular basis. He has since retired from driving trucks and has moved out of the Yukon. That day he was on his regular run, driving from Prince Rupert back to Whitehorse with a load of goods that he had loaded at the Prince Rupert docks.

**Local History:** The Cassiar Road had been originally constructed in the 1970s, connecting the town of Watson Lake, in the Yukon, to the community of Cassiar and the Cassiar Mine site in Northern BC. The road was later extended in the early 1980s, in a southern direction connecting it to the community of Kitwanga, at the junction of BC Highway #16, the Yellowhead Highway.

**Geography:** The Nass River is in a deep valley. The surrounding hills have a good forest of white pine and some spruce, although one can notice the devastation caused by the pine beetles in recent years. There are numerous mountains in this area as well as very few roads. There is a large population of moose in this area with bears, cougars, deer, elk, and a large number of smaller animals. Every waterway would have a mix of fish ready for the picking.

There has been another reported sighting close by about 50 km (31 mi) further north in 2000. It was a few kilometres north of Meziadin Junction, this one involved a triple Sasquatch sighting with, according to the witness, a telepathic message passed on to him (check Report #27). As well, vocal occurrence took place 80 km (50 mi) further north of that sighting at the Bell-Irving River Rest Area in 2006, report #35.

**Investigation:** The witness was actually interviewed by my friend and colleague, who is a Manitoba Métis. My friend had known the truck driver who experienced the sighting for many years, as they both used to be in the trucking business together.

Actually, they were working for the same employer, the White Pass & Yukon Route, Highway Division, for a number of years. According to my colleague, the witness was very credible, and knowing of his honesty, he believes that his truck driver friend has presented a true account of the sighting. I had the occasion to meet this witness a couple of years later and referred to his sighting. He once-more explained what he had encountered without any changes to the written report of my colleague. Therefore, in a way, the witness was interviewed by two different people, my colleague and me.

**Encounter:** The witness was driving back to Whitehorse with a load of goods unloaded from a cargo ship in Prince Rupert. I should mention that the driver has seen just about everything through the years he had been driving, and nothing surprised him anymore. When I later talked with him, he pointed out, on a number of occasions, that he is absolutely sure that what he saw was a Sasquatch and nothing else. Just before one gets on that particular bridge driving from the south, a driver would make a gradual right turn to get on the bridge. The witness had just completed this turn and was now on the long bridge crossing the Nass River when he noticed something standing just about in the middle of the road at the far end of the bridge.

He assumed it was a human being, which had to be about 100 m (330 ft) away according to the driver. He then beeped his horn in a warning, and the entity slowly walked off the bridge onto the far end of the bridge, where it stood for a while.

As the driver approached and got closer, now about halfway across the bridge, he then noticed that whatever was standing there was not a human being as he had originally thought but a Sasquatch with a bit of snow on its dark brown hair. When the truck was about 10 m (33 ft) away, the Sasquatch slowly walked up the snowbank on his left, the right-hand side of the driver, and then walked down the ditch to the riverbank. And that was the last the driver saw of him, as his vision was blocked by the snowbank on his right-hand side of the road as he drove by.

Unfortunately, he could not provide any further details, as he stated that from that distance, he could not judge the actual height except that it was tall, bulky, and large. Nothing more specific, other than the creature was walking on two legs, not a human for sure, and it certainly was not a bear of any kind.

## Report #12
## TATCHUN REGION
## Sighting close to Yukon Crossing in 1990
## Location: Coord. 62o 21'21 N 136o 28'37 W
## (Map: Yukon Crossing 115 I/8: GR 233 143)

IN MID-JULY OF 1990, two First Nations boys in their early teens were riding an ATV after having completed their daily chores while at a fish camp. This fish camp is located just upriver from Yukon Crossing, on the right-hand side of the Yukon River as it flows. At around 1800 hours (6 pm), they reached a gravel pit located about 2 km (1.3 mi) north from the fish camp. They stopped and were smoking cigarettes in the middle and the deepest part of the gravel pit, whose gravel was used to maintain the nearby roadways, when they experienced the visit of a strange entity.

**Encounter:** They were in the gravel pit for a few minutes when they heard a loud noise, like a branch breaking, coming from the nearby tree line. Looking up towards the tree line where the noise came from, they noticed a tall, dark, bipedal creature walking out of the forest from the south side of the gravel pit, descending a sharp incline into the gravel pit. For a moment, it stopped about halfway down when it apparently noticed the two young lads. First, they thought that it was a black bear, but they soon realized that a bear does not ambulate on two legs like a human being as this creature was presently doing. The bipedal figure continued walking towards the two boys. The boys were getting afraid by then and decided to return to the fish camp.

After trying to start the ATV without success on a few occasions due to their nervousness, it finally started on the third try. By that time, the large bipedal entity was about 10 m (34 ft) from the teens, according to the witnesses. As they took off, they kept looking at the dark creature which, in turn, was looking back at the two them.

They drove down the trail which took them onto the North Klondike Highway's ditch, Yukon Highway #2. Turning right onto it, in the direction of their aunt's fish camp, they drove as fast as they could until coming to the side road leading to the fish camp. These two young fellows were quite surprised, somewhat in shock, and did not really know what to think of this bipedal creature. Somewhat confused, they returned to their aunt's fish camp located on the north side of the Yukon River, a couple of kilometres away from the gravel pit. It was getting dark by then, and they were really frightened.

On arriving at the fish camp, they explained their adventure to the people present, but none of the adults seemed to believe them, stating they must have come across a black bear.

It was only in November of 2014 that one of these young fellows came upon a colleague of mine, a Sasquatch enthusiast as well, and decided to tell his story. My colleague and I talked to one of the witnesses, a First Nation man, now in his 30s, who is a member of the Kwanlin Dün First Nation here in Whitehorse, on Saturday, November 29, 2014, and I recorded the story regarding his sighting.

**Local History:** Yukon Crossing was the site of a roadhouse on the old Dawson Overland Trail, which was known simply as the Dawson Trail. Actually, the roadhouse is still standing to this day, now being maintained by the Yukon Government's Heritage Branch and is located directly across the Yukon River from where the encounter took place. The Dawson Overland Trail was constructed to connect the gold rush town of Dawson City to Whitehorse, which became the centre of transportation for the Yukon when the White Pass and Yukon Route (WP&YR) completed the construction of the railway line connecting Skagway, Alaska, to Whitehorse in the Yukon in 1900. WP&YR constructed a shipyard in Whitehorse as well, where many paddle wheelers were built during the years. These would transport goods and people to Dawson City in the summer but as soon as the Yukon River froze, the boats were taken out of service and these same goods, as well as people, had to be transported overland. In 1901 White Pass & Yukon Route acquired a smaller company called the Canadian Development Company, which at the time delivered the goods to Dawson City by dog teams and improved the

*The creature stopped when it noticed the two young lads. First, they thought that it was a black bear, but they realized that a bear does not ambulate on two legs like a human being as this creature was presently doing. It continued walking towards them... Illustration: Rich Théroux*

same trail used by that company to make it feasible to be used with horses to connect both towns. To achieve this, the White Pass & Yukon Route started another company called the Yukon Stage Line, which would carry goods, people, and mail between Whitehorse and Dawson City.

The Dawson Overland Trail came alive with a number of roadhouses located at every 30 to 50 km (20 to 30 mi) along the way. These roadhouses provided food and overnight sleeping accommodations for the travellers. As well, horses were kept at each roadhouse and they would be exchanged whenever a horse team with their sleigh full of people and goods would arrive for the night. Route: From Whitehorse the Dawson Overland Trail roughly followed what is today the Alaska Highway, Yukon Highway #1, to Takhini Crossing. Once across the Takhini River, it would follow the low ground of the Klusha Creek and Little Rivers valleys to Braeburn Lake, where the present-day Braeburn Lodge stands. Then the Dawson Trail roughly followed what is today the North Klondike Highway, Yukon Highway #2, better known as the Mayo Road by most Yukoners, to the community of Carmacks. From Carmacks, the Dawson Trail then continued on the west shores of the Yukon River to what was then known as Mackay's Roadhouse, named after its original owner operator, which was later renamed Yukon Crossing. At this location, the Dawson Overland Trail crossed the Yukon River and then would follow the very same trail crossing the site of the gravel pit where our two young fellows observed a Sasquatch back in 1990, and this trail would join the present route of the North Klondike Highway roughly following the Yukon River on the east side of the river from this point on to Dawson City.

**Investigation:** As I conducted the interview, I was trying to get details about specific facial features of the large creature they observed, but all he could provide me with was that the large ambulating entity was dark, tall and big, walking on two legs just like a human being, slightly hunched forward, long arms and seemingly not paying particular attention to the two young fellows, only some 10 m (34 ft) away, until the very last minute and kept looking at the young lads until they were out of sight.

Interestingly though, the KDFN man remembers that a bit later, during the early evening of the same day he experienced the sighting, he was in his aunt's cabin at the fish camp after returning from the gravel pit, when the four dogs they had with them, started barking loudly and retreating into their dog houses, scared and whimpering. A reaction they had never shown before.

The reporter stated that his cousin's boyfriend tried to get the dogs out of their dog houses, but the dogs totally refused to leave, seemingly too scared of whatever was in the close by forest. Which is much the same animal reaction as all the other animal reaction occurrences that are presented in this book.

Upon witnessing this reaction by the dogs, one of the adults got his rifle out figuring that something was wrong and wanting the group to be safe. Others threw a more logs on the campfire to make it bigger, while everyone stood by the fire for a period of time before going to bed. During the rest of the night, the adults took turns guarding the fish camp, as there were quite a few Chinook salmons hanging in the smokers, being smoked and dried.

They heard noises coming from the bush as if something or someone was walking about watching them, but the people guarding the camp did not see anything specific except for the odd shadows. The next morning some of the adults went down the hill from the cabin at the fish camp on the shores of the Yukon River to check on a cache of salmon, and sure enough, something had taken a few salmon.

A bit further down river on a small trail that follows the Yukon River, our witness noticed a pile of fish bones neatly stacked in one spot. In my view, those bones having been placed in one neat, organized pile would be indicative of a behaviour trait usually connected to human nature and showing some degree of intelligence.

A bear for example would have scattered all the bones wherever they would drop them after eating the fish and actually eating some of the bones.

The reporter experienced another sighting in 2010, explained in Report #43.

## Report #13
## TATCHUN REGION
## Sighting close to Crooked Creek, along with large footprints in 1991
## Location: Coord. 62o 59'40 N 136o 29'59 W
## (Map: McQuesten 115 P; GR 022 016)

IN MAY OF 2006, I was investigating the discovery of a number of large human-like footprints around the community of Pelly Crossing, when a member of the Selkirk First Nation (SFN) mentioned to me that in April 1991, three members of SFN had observed what was described by them as a Sasquatch standing on the side of the road on the North Klondike Highway, Yukon Highway #2. This is located about 1.5 km (1 mi) before Crooked Creek, about halfway between Pelly Crossing and Stewart Crossing.

**Encounter:** The three members of the SFN were travelling the highway on their way to Stewart Crossing to visit friends when they noticed a Sasquatch standing on the bank of the road, on their right-hand side. When the creature saw the pickup truck, it raised its arms above its head and then turned around to walk into the forest. The driver stopped the truck and, along with his two passengers, got out of the truck in order to look around. They found a few large human-like footprints, each measuring some 38.1 cm (15 in), according to their rough measurements, on the soft soil of the bank.

They had planned to follow the foot track when after about ten minutes they experienced an odd feeling, akin to not being wanted in the area. This is when the driver suggested they return to the truck, which they did and soon departed. They shared their encounter with a few other members of SFN who simply acknowledged these encounters being an occurrence that happens fairly often in the area.

**Geography:** The area around the sighting location is a low rolling type of terrain, with mostly bare, small hill tops, with a few aspens and poplar trees, along with low black spruces and willows. Large rocks were noted, which would appear to have rolled from the higher hills located further away, and a few small lakes were noticed around the immediate area, in mostly swampy ground, which was home to water plants.

**Investigation:** A few days later, I drove the road taken by these SFN witnesses and found the sighting location. I walked about looking for possible activity signs, but nothing obvious could be observed. The encounter location is fairly close to the Ddhaw Ghro Habitat Protection area, formerly known as McArthur Wildlife Sanctuary.

This habitat is home to a large number of sheep, goats, and many other types of animals. It is also a host to a number of hot springs, which assist in the growing of warmer-weather plants not found anywhere else in the Yukon. This area is one of the few areas protected from any type of hunting activities, even from members of various Yukon First Nations.

The access to the area is limited to helicopters only. See the related story of "The Guardians of the Ddhaw Ghro Hot Springs" in the "Sasquatch Stories from Across the Yukon" section of this book.

An Elder of SFN once mentioned to me that Keecho, a local name for Sasquatch, would spend most of the time in the Ddhaw Ghro Habitat Protection Area.

A 38.1 cm (15 in) large human-like footprint would indicate the print-maker to be about 231 cm 7.5 ft) in height, would weigh around 286 kg (630 lbs), and have a step of some 147 cm (5 ft). Such a bipedal ambulating entity would require about 6,500 calories per day to remain healthy.

## Report #14
## SQUANGA REGION
## Vocals and Tree Thrashing along Hall Creek in 1992
## Location: Coord. 60o 30'50 N 132o 48'57 W (Map: McClintock 105 C/12: GR 727 093)

I WAS CONTACTED by a man who reported that he had experienced very loud screams, scary vocals, thrashing sounds of trees being banged together, and a deep feeling of not being wanted in the area while exploring the land around Hall Creek in the search for a downed airplane in July of 1992.

**Occurrence:** Our witness landed his boat at the mouth of Hall Creek and because of the dense foliage along the creek bed he climbed up to the open ground about 10 m (33 ft) to the north of the creek from where he still could see the creek flowing. He experienced those occurrences after walking about 2 km (1.2 mi) in a north-northeast direction on the ground above the creek.

**Local History:** Hall Creek is located on the northeast side of Squanga Lake, some 6 km (4 mi) from the Yukon Government Campground, which is located on the Alaska Highway, Yukon Highway #1, 23 km (14 mi) east of Jakes Corner and about 2 km (1.5 mi) directly east of Summit Lake.

The man in question who was in his mid-60s at the time is a member of the Whitehorse Transportation Museum and was conducting a search for an old World War II US Air Force aircraft that went down in the vicinity of Squanga Lake while on its way to Russia as part of the US Air Force lend/lease program with Russia during the Second World War. Information received by the museum from the US War Department stated that the aircraft went down close to Hall Creek by Squanga Lake; therefore, the man was conducting his search in the vicinity of the lake and the creek in question.

**Investigation:** Through my research and talking with members of the Whitehorse Transportation Museum, I eventually found out that the aircraft in question actually went down by the Hall Residence close to Squanga Creek, and not by Hall Creek, as previously and mistakenly mentioned in the US Air Force documents. The residence in question is actually the home of the Hall family, a local Carcross Tagish First Nation (CTFN) family who had been residing by Squanga Creek and on the shores of Squanga Lake for as long as anyone can remember.

**Occurrence continues:** When our history buff went on his adventure and started searching in the area of Hall Creek, he first came across a strange smell, which he did not pay much attention to at first—then the noise of trees banging and thrashing and the screeching started. As the vocals progressed louder and louder, our history buff became very scared and started feeling a sense of deep anxiety, which forced him to leave the area as quickly as he could. He reported the incident to his museum friends who did not really know what to think of it. The witness refused to go back to that location again.

The lend/lease program in question was a program whereby the US Government had an agreement with the Russian Government of the time to acquire a large number of US Air Force aircraft to beef up the Russian Air Force and fight the Nazis on Europe's eastern front during the Second World War. In order to move the planes, airfields were constructed every 100 km (60 mi) or so along the Alaska Highway from Dawson Creek in British Columbia to Alaska and onto the Aleutian Islands.

The aircraft remains were eventually located close to the Hall Residence by another group of people, also from the Whitehorse Transportation Museum. But after sixty years of being in the swampy ground, there was hardly anything useable left and no signs of the pilot. The remains were covered over and buried forever where the plane and its pilot went down, very close to Squanga Creek, which empties Squanga Lake in a southern direction and the water of which eventually reaches the Teslin River.

There have been a number of Sasquatch activities reported to have taken place around this lake, Reports #29, #31, and #38.

## Report #15
## TAKHINI REGION
## Sighting in the Area of the Copper Ridge Subdivision in 1992
## Location: Coord. 60o 41'55 N 134o 07'03 W
## (Map: Whitehorse 105 D/11: GR 935 292)

On a sunny day in August of 1992, a man was taking a leisurely mid-afternoon stroll with his mother, who was some 60 years old at the time, along an old and twisting logging road. His mother was occupied picking wildflowers, so he ended up walking alone some 15 m (50 ft) or so ahead when he noticed what he first thought to be a large person wearing black coveralls standing by a tree some 20 m (65 ft) further down the trail.

**Encounter:** He described the figure as being very tall and huge with a great mop of black hair sticking way out above its head and down its shoulders. The report continues by mentioning that the witness could not make out the details of the entity's face no matter how hard he was trying; the face being too fuzzy and the entity being in the shadow-side of a tree with the sun shining brightly behind the same tree. The report then mentions they were both looking at each other for what seemed to be close to three minutes before the witness turned around and started to walk away with the intention of rejoining his mother.

After walking for about a minute, he turned his head to look back, and the creature had moved closer and was now standing only 6 m (20 ft) away or so from him, although he had not heard any walking sound. But then, as the reporter fully turned around, the creature took one look at him and walked across the trail in two steps, then "glided away"as if its feet were not be touching the ground—as if levitating away.

This trail is a single-lane vehicle trail and would have been about 3 m (10 ft) wide. The reporter mentioned that while this was going on, he could not hear any of the usual sounds that one would encounter in a forest, no squirrels moving about, no birds flying nor chirping, no wind, simply total silence. The report then states that he realized he was probably staring down at what he

*Report #15. It "glided away"— its feet appeared to not be touching the ground as if levitating away.*
*Report #47. It started to becoming transparent.I could see right through him...then puff...like magic he was gone."*
*Report #50. The Sasquatch became gradually transparent. After a minute, it became totally invisible.*
*Illustration, Rich Théroux.*

describes as a Sasquatch, and a weird sense of fear came upon him, which made him turn around to rejoin his mother, and the same feeling remained with him until they both returned home.

**Investigation:** This sighting occurred in the area known today as the Copper Ridge subdivision, directly west of Whitehorse, about 3 km (2 mi) from the Whitehorse International Airport, as the raven flies, and well within city limits.

The area at the time was crisscrossed by numerous small logging roads and trails. Nowadays, three additional subdivisions have been erected in neighbouring areas with about two thousand people living in these subdivisions.

At the time of the sighting, the witness would have been looking mostly in a west-southwest direction, as he states that it was mid-afternoon and the sun was fairly high and shone from behind a tree, near which stood the creature.

Therefore, the sun would have been partially in the eyes of the witness and blurring his vision to some extent, probably enough that he could not make out the details of the face he was looking at. The reporter, 39 years of age at the time, was a resident of Whitehorse. In the report, he mentioned that he likes the outdoors and taking walks in the woods, mostly off the beaten tracks to explore around. He also mentioned being a serious rock hound and somewhat of a local history buff. Therefore, he would feel at ease in the forest but probably not be bush-wise.

**Local History:** The area where the sighting occurred is part of the Kwanlin Dün First Nation traditional territory, and KDFN actually has a residential development called McIntyre subdivision some 2 km (1.2 mi) north-northeast from where the sighting is described to have occurred. Starting in the early 1920s and up until about 1970, this area and surrounding area was the site of many small copper mining operations, as well as a large copper mine called Whitehorse Copper, which operated until 1982. To this day, one can still find remains of old cabins and old mining equipment scattered about and now mostly covered by moss and various types of vegetation.

**Interesting Note:** In 1973, a woman, then a Yukon resident, took a group of youth for an outing by an old copper mine, close to this sighting location, and found some interesting bone fragments, which she bagged up. In 2014 she showed those bone fragments to a Yukon paleontologist by the name of Grant Zazula who after studying the fragments, identified one of them as being from a rhinoceros and the other one from a turtle and dated them to be some eight million years of age. Rhinos and turtles in the Yukon, you say! There are still many open mine pits to be found across the area to this day, and one has to be extremely careful when venturing around the bush or one may well end up falling into one of those open mine pits, which were completely abandoned without any signs or warnings close by.

**Geography:** The area in question is part of the northern boreal forest with a very dense bush of tall black spruce and lodgepole pine upon a rocky rolling ground with a few small pounds, vintage of the last ice age, and the odd openings in the forest. Some 3 km (2 mi) north of the reported sighting is the Mount McIntyre cross-country ski area, on a rolling high ground. I know the area well as there are numerous cross-country ski trails around the area that I have used to hike and ski on.

The Report mentions the trail the witness was on kept turning every which way. I take it that he was actually on a logging road. Further west is a large low ground area with a stream called McIntyre Creek and some swampy grounds. Behind that is pure wilderness for days of travelling.

Varied sources of plant food can be found in the area; one would find kinnikinnick, high-bush and low-bush cranberries, mushrooms, rose hips, and raspberries on the high ground. Blueberries, swamp grass, wild onions, skunk cabbage, and tubers would be plentiful on the low grounds around this area, along with a variety of other plants.

As for animals, one can find hares, grouse, and all kinds of birds along with bears, caribou, coyotes, deer, elk, foxes, lynx, moose, and porcupines. Besides the tall black spruces, one would see aspens, birch, lodgepole pines, white pines, and willows.

**Further Investigation Notes:** There have been a number of Sasquatch activities from the general area although actual written reports are few, except for those in this book. The reporter said that he was not able to make out facial details. Usually, one can pick up general facial details up to about 50 m (164 ft) without a problem when the face is entirely visible. The fact that the sun was directly behind the creature identified as a Sasquatch could account for the lack of clarity. He also said the entity was moving slightly from side to side, sort of swaying, that could indicate the creature was also trying to concentrate on what it was seeing. Mention was made of there being no movement or noise from small animals; that is quite common in many other reports where all the small animals sort of have disappeared. I have experienced strange smell events back in 2003 and again in 2010 where all the small animals, birds, squirrels, and so on had totally disappeared during the event.

He mentioned that the observed creature sort of "glided away"—that its feet appeared to not be touching the ground as if levitating away. Similar activities came to light in other reports, including three more from the Yukon that I know of: one in the subdivision of Crestview, about 5 km (3 mi) directly north of this sighting, and two more sightings with similar gliding or levitating activities in the Keno Region. I cannot speculate as to the meaning of such action. However, as I conducted more research on the matter of Sasquatch, many reports have come to light mentioning some sort of levitation process and simple visual disappearances.

Unfortunately, the reporter did not make any mention of the possible height of the creature, except that it was tall and huge, which does not really mean much as tall and huge may be taken differently by different people.

For the record, the average Sasquatch height, calculated from numerous sighting reports, would be some 238 cm tall (94 in or 7 ft 10 in) and would weigh between 295 kg (651 lbs) & 370 kg (815.5 lbs) according to its size. It would also have a footprint of some 39 cm (15.5 in) with a step of 152 cm (60 in or 5 ft). Such a Sasquatch would need about 6,688 calories per day or so.

## Report #16
## KENO REGION
## Sighting by Elsa in 1995
## Location: Coord. 63o 56'34 N 135o 34'06 W
## (Map: Keno Hill 105 M/14: GR 807 906)

In July of 2000, a First Nations couple reported that in mid-April of 1995 they had observed a huge and tall bipedal ambulating creature eating raw meat from an animal's carcass in a small clearing beside the road. This road is called the Silver Trail, Yukon Highway #11, the sighting location is about halfway between the communities of Keno City and Elsa on the left-hand side of the road, driving in the direction of Elsa from Keno City, roughly across the road from Crystal Creek. The man in question is of Mi'kmaq First Nations descent. The Mi'kmaq are from the provinces of New Brunswick and Nova Scotia in Eastern Canada. Our witness was in his 60s at the time of the sighting, while his wife is a Northern Tutchone from the First Nation of Na-Cho Nyak Dun (FNNND), and she was about the same age at the time. Both resided in Keno City at the time and had been married for a number of years.

**Encounter:** The couple was on their way to Whitehorse on a shopping trip to replenish food as well as to visit relatives and friends. A few kilometres after leaving Keno City, the husband realized that he had left their thermos of coffee in the box of the pickup truck that he was driving. So he found a place to pull over, stopped the pickup truck, and got out to retrieve the thermos of coffee, which he then placed on the left-hand rear bumper of the truck. He then realized he had to answer the call of nature. He stepped off the left-hand side of the road and crossed the ditch towards a small clearing to relieve himself, which is when he experienced his sighting.

**Geography:** As previously mentioned in the Region introduction, The Silver Trail, Yukon Highway #11, is the name of the road connecting Stewart Crossing at the junction with the North

Klondike Highway, Yukon Highway #2, to Mayo, Elsa, and then Keno City. The sighting location, which was on the left-hand side of the road driving from Keno City to Elsa, is on the lower slopes of Galena Hill, which has an elevation of 1,580 m (5,184 ft). The lower portion of the hill is now covered with alders, black spruce, shrubs, and willow trees, while the top portion is mostly bare, with many mine openings, road networks, caves, and tailings.

On the opposite side of the road, the north side or the right-hand side, the terrain is quite wet and swampy with many small creeks emptying into a large swamp with many alders, dwarf spruce trees, willows, birch trees, shrubs, and aspen trees.

The area is well-known for its deer, elk, and moose population, as well as other smaller animals. There are plenty of edible wild plants along with wildflowers, tubers, skunk cabbage, and so on.

**Encounter Continues:** When the witness walked into the clearing, after taking six steps or so, he noticed what he first thought to be a bear crouching over an animal's carcass about 10 m away (33 ft). The meat-eater then must have noticed the man as well and stooped up. This is when the witness realized that he was face-to-face with what he identified as a Sasquatch. The Sasquatch at that moment started jumping up and down, stomping, with its arms waving about, still clenching a piece of bone with raw meat in its right hand.

The man in question immediately ran back to his pickup truck and took off in a hurry, forgetting all about the thermos of coffee, which by then had fallen off the truck's bumper right in the middle of the road.

He did not stop until reaching the old Stewart Crossing Lodge, which is now closed, at the roadside community of Stewart Crossing, located at the junction of the Silver Trail and the North Klondike Highway, Yukon Highway #2, some 83 km (52 mi) further down the road.

**Investigation:** The man described the Sasquatch as huge, very muscular, bulky, very big, being somewhere between 244 cm to 305 cm tall (8 to 10 ft) and weighing what he said to be at least 417 kg (480 lbs). That stated weight by itself is somewhat confusing, but then again, it is extremely difficult for a normal human to judge the weight of someone else, even though they may see that person on a daily basis, as they only have their own weight to make a comparison with, let alone judging the weight of a Sasquatch, which one does not see every day. Besides that, a witness usually experiences some form of shock when coming face-to-face with such a creature.

I would challenge readers to try to judge the weight of their friends and see what the results would be. Then take it into consideration when comparing it to the witness's ability to judge the weight of a creature such as a Sasquatch. For comparison and to set our mind, a Sasquatch with a height of 244 cm (96 in or 8 ft) would have a footprint measuring about 40.6 cm (16 in), would have a step of 156 cm (61.5 in or 5 ft 1.5 in) and would weigh about 305 kg (672 lbs) if of a medium size. And it would weigh closer to 382 kg (842 lbs) if on the heavier size for such a creature. Such a Sasquatch would need about 6,945 calories per day to stay healthy.

A Sasquatch with a height of 274 cm (108 in or 9 ft) would have a footprint measuring some 46 cm (18 in) with a step of 176 cm (69 in or 5 ft 9 in) and a medium-size one would weigh some 343 kg (756 lbs) while the heavy-set one would be around 430 kg (948 lbs). The daily calorie requirement for such a creature would be some 7,890 calories to remain healthy.

A Sasquatch with a height of 305 cm (112 in or 10 ft) would have a footprint of about 51 cm (20 in) with a step of about 195.5 cm (77 in or 6 ft 5 in) and if of medium build would have a weight of about 381 kg, (840 lbs) while the heavier, larger size would be about 477.5 kg (1,053 lbs). Its daily food requirement would be at least 8,746 calories to remain healthy.

Another interesting comment was made by the witness in that the hair over the creature's body was black, short, and somewhat spotty, making the Sasquatch look like he was partly naked in some locations, and that the hair was unkempt in appearance with long black hair on the back of its head and upper back/lower shoulder side, along with a scraggly moustache. That would indicate to me a somewhat older Sasquatch, who had been losing its hair to some extent, much as human males do after a certain age.

The man called the creature by the name of Sasquatch, while his wife first called it a Bocq and later referred to the creature as a Wild Man. These names, Bocq and Wild Man, along with Bushman, are common names used by the Yukon First Nations Peoples to describe the Sasquatch.

I have been to the area of Mayo, Elsa, and Keno City a number of times investigating this report as well as other reports from the Keno Region.

The exact location of this report has been very difficult to pinpoint due to the extreme brush overgrowth around that area since 1995, as the Elsa and Calumet silver mines have been out of operation since the early 1990s and not many people use the area except in the summer.

Although with the recent opening of a few new silver mines and re-opening of older ones, as well as a new large gold mine in the area of Keno City, the road traffic has increased drastically along the Silver Trail.

Other Sasquatch-related activities around the area occur in Reports #24, #37, #50, and #65.

## Report #17
## SQUANGA REGION
## Vocals by Brooks Brook in 1995
## Location: Coord. 60o 25'01 N 133o 11'39 W
## (Map: Brooks Brook 105 C/6: GR 996 991)

A GOOD FRIEND from the Teslin Tlingit Council reported being subjected to extremely loud vocals, screams, and shrieks while camping at Brooks Brook in early June of 1995. These vocals were coming from a short distance outside of the tent she and her husband were sleeping in, at about 0400 hours (4 am).

**Occurrence:** They had been out fishing on Teslin Lake with another First Nations couple and were camping by Brooks Brook when this occurrence took place. Brooks Brook is a small creek emptying into Teslin Lake from its north shores and is located about 10 km (6 mi) east of the Johnson Crossing Bridge on the Alaska Highway, Yukon Highway #1.

This site is presently used by the members of the Teslin Tlingit First Council for gatherings and meetings. Also, it is often used by boaters and canoeists, as it offers a very good, protected campsite.

The woman who first reported this incident to me was born and raised on the shores of Teslin Lake and is a member of the Teslin Tlingit Council. She was accompanied by her husband at the time of the occurrence. This is the same couple who experienced an animal behaviour occurrence by the Northwestel microwave tower west of the community of Teslin in 1984, Report #9.

**Local History:** Brooks Brook was the location of a construction camp during the construction of the Alaska Highway in 1942, in the middle of World War II, and remained open as a highway maintenance camp for many years. This camp was named after the Commanding Officer of the US Army Engineer Company, Lt. Brooks.

**Geography:** The area where this small creek joins Teslin Lake is mostly flat and the soil is mostly clay mixed with soft sand, often becoming muddy as a result of rain. A few aspens, balsam poplar, and shrubs are scattered around the immediate area. Further away from the open area of the creek and on both sides of Brooks Brook as well as across the Alaska Highway one finds an almost impassable dense forest of black spruce.

**Occurrence Continues:** In this vocal occurrence, both couples were awoken by these strange, unidentified, extremely loud and scary screams early in the morning, at about 0400 hours (4 am). The dog they had with them was then trying to hide wherever it could, as it was frightened as well. The source location of these screams appeared to be fairly close to the campsite and as far as they could make it out, the vocals originated from across the Alaska Highway, directly north of Brooks Brook and within a distance of about 300 m (984 ft) or so away, in dense black spruce forest. The couples in question did leave soon thereafter, as they could not go back to sleep and at one point became uneasy with what was going on. They packed their gear back in the boat and left the area, deciding to camp somewhere else.

**Investigation:** Vocals are intriguing in the maker of the vocals must have been very large to project such intense shrieks and screams. I would venture to say that to express itself in such a way is probably to frighten people away from a certain location. In my view, it reflects a protection against a territorial trespassing as if conveying a message that whomever the intruders are, they are not wanted at that specific area and should depart.

As described to me by the witnesses, the types of shrieks and screams would have been similar to those experienced by the Ross River Dena Council's First Nation couple from the community of Faro, when explaining their vocal occurrences to me: first in the canyon by the Magundy River during the winter of 2010, then a second vocal occurrence on the trail leading to Swim Lake in the spring of 2010, Report #42.

## Report #18
## TATCHUN REGION
## Sighting and Rock Throwing close to the Nordenskiold River Bridge, in Carmacks in 1995
## Location: Coord. 62o 06'03 N 136o 19'00 W
## (Map: Carmacks 115 I; GR 032 005)

WHILE DISCUSSING the subject of Sasquatch with my Selkirk First Nation's contact, he relayed a sighting that he became aware of, and after talking with members of the Little Salmon/Carmacks First Nation (LCFN); he reported the following encounter to me.

**Encounter:** In mid-afternoon on Wednesday, June 14, 1995, two teenage girls were hiding from their mother in a small bush area close to the Nordenskiold River just past the bridge, smoking a cigarette. They were sitting on a log, side by side, one facing one way and the second girl the other way. One girl faced a small trail while the other faced the bush area. They had been there for a few minutes when a strange smell was noticed, something like a smell similar to when someone burns damp garbage. One girl jokingly told the other one that she should have taken a shower. Then the smell became stronger, and the other girl yelled loudly, "Look, there is a Sasquatch!" She then stood up and told her friend that she was going home. The one girl still sitting, then noticed a huge hairy man-like entity coming out of the bush onto the trail about 3 m (10 ft) from where she was sitting. Then she in turn got up and started running back home.

My contact further stated that after talking with some of his cousins in Carmacks, he found out that many activities, probably related to Sasquatch, had taken place around this part of the forest during the summer of 1995. Some of these occurrences consisted of people walking in the trails hearing some bipedal entity walking close by them, following them step by step, then stopping whenever they would stop. One time, a LCFN man was walking the same trail when he heard some noise close by. Thinking it was a bear, he threw a rock in that direction, just to have the same rock thrown back at him, although he did not observe the "rock thrower."

**Investigation:** I have visited the area on many occasions, most often stopping for lunch when travelling to locations further north. I found that most people were reluctant to talk about the subject of Sasquatch for whatever reason. However, one First Nations member did mention that Sasquatch occurrences would often take place, but most people would simply shrug it off as if it was just a regular happening like there was "nothing to see here."

My contact person further said that he has heard of Sasquatch often mimicking the voice of young girls, as if trying to make contact with them. I have investigated six other Sasquatch-related activities from the Tatchun Region.

## Report #19
## TAKHINI REGION
## Strange Unusual Tree Structure Discovered at Ben-My-Chree in 1995
## Location: Coord. 59o 24'50 N 134o 27'10 W (Map: Edgar Lake 105 M/8: GR 317 851)

A good friend of mine of Dutch descent reported that he had located an unusual tree structure.

**Occurrence:** My friend, now in his mid-80s, was visiting Ben-My-Chree in 1995 when he discovered a large, unusual tree structure. He had been wandering around Ben-My-Chree while visiting a friend during a period of about a week, during the summer of 1995, when he came upon this unusual structure, located about 1.5 km (1 mi) southwest from the main residence, across a small bay.

**Local History:** The name "Ben-My-Chree" means "Girl of My Hearth" in the Manx Gaelic language spoken by the inhabitants of the Isle of Man, located in the Irish Sea. A man by the name of Otto Partridge, originally from Hertfordshire, England, had arrived in the Yukon during the famous Klondike Gold Rush. But rather than moving on to the goldfields, he decided to stay around the Southern Lakes region of the Yukon, getting involved mostly in boat and ship building.

He and his wife Kate had been mining along the west shores of Taku Arm of Tagish Lake when, in 1911, they decided to build a home by the Swanson River outlet not far from their Engineer Mine. The soil upon which they built their home was very rich and provided them with bounty full vegetable and flowers.

As entrepreneurs, they realized the "bit of paradise" they acquired could become a successful business and constructed a few more cabins to start a summer visitors destination which operated successfully until the great market crash of 1929.

Today, Ben-My-Chree is privately owned and sees very few visitors.

Sketch Drawn by John Nystad, in 1995

*Takhini Region: Unusual Tree Structure Discovered at Ben-My-Chree in July 1995.*

**Investigation:** During my last visit to the area in July 2015, during "Expedition Ben-My-Chree," my friend and I tried to locate the structure in question but without any luck as dense and deep, impenetrable vegetation has taken over the entire area.

However, my friend described the structure as being 1.5 m high (4ft 10in), 4 m long (13 ft), and 4 m wide (13 ft), located in a ground depression surrounded by large white spruce trees and willows. The structure itself was composed of a large number of spruce branches, about 15 cm (6 in) at the base and gradually tapering off.

They were bent in such a manner as to form a canopy resting on larger branches with many tree branches crossing over each other. The entranceway was about one m wide (3 ft) and 60 cm high (2 ft).

My friend also noticed a bed of dead grass with pine and spruce needles spread about inside of the structure. He also reported that he found the structure unusual because the branches were broken off, without the use of any saw or axe as there were no marks revealing the use of such tools.

One would conclude that the structure was not human-made, as in a shelter for example.

On the opposite page is a sketch that John Nystad drew of the structure.

**Report #20**
**LIARD REGION**
**Footprints Discovered by Simpson Lake in 1995**
**Location: Coord. 60o 42'13 N 129o 12'50 W**
**(Map: False Canyon 105 A/11: GR 884 293)**

WHILE DISCUSSING the subject of Sasquatch, a man of Dutch descent, same friend as Report #19, mentioned to me that while on a camping trip, he had come across two large human-like footprints, each measuring some 38 cm (15 in).

**Occurrence:** The footprints were located on the grounds of a Yukon Government Campground located on the shores of Simpson Lake, some 20 m (65 ft) from shore. The lake is located on the Robert Campbell Highway, Yukon Highway #4, at about 100 km (60 mi) north of Watson Lake. This fellow who, at the time of this writing, is in his late 70s, is still working in the building maintenance and repair fields.

I have known this fellow since 1987, when he first arrived in the Yukon upon retirement from the Canadian Army. He and I became good friends, and he shared his experience only after he found out about my interests in the Sasquatch phenomenon. This is the same man who reported a strange structure by Ben-My-Chree on the shores of Tagish Lake in the province of British Columbia, which he discovered in 1995 as well as reported in the Takhini Region part of this book. He was taking a vacation at the time, travelling the Robert Campbell Highway, and had just pulled into the Simpson Lake Campground for the night with his pickup truck and camper at about 1600 hours (4 pm) in mid-July of 1995 when he discovered these large human-like footprints.

**Local History:** Simpson Lake has been named after the then Governor of the Hudson Bay Company, Sir George Simpson (1787–1860), by its Chief Factor John McLeod (1795–1842) in the summer of 1854. Simpson was exploring this region of Northwest Canada, which at that time was totally unknown except by the original inhabitants of the region. Interestingly the southern portion of the present-day Robert Campbell Highway, from Watson Lake to Tuchitua, now at the junction of the Nahanni Range Road, was first named the Cantung Road as it leads to the mining community of Tungsten, Northwest Territories. The road had originally been built and operated by the Canadian Tungsten Company to reach their new mine site.

In the 1960s the road was extended to reach the community of Ross River and named the Robert Campbell Highway, while the old Cantung Road was re-named the Nahanni Range Road.

**Geography:** The land around Simpson Lake is an area of low ground type of terrain, with willow trees growing in the vicinity of the lake. The land gives way first to gentle rolling hills with mostly lodgepole pine trees and then steeper and rather rocky mountains the further away from the lake one ventures.

**Investigation:** These footprints were found in soft soil and measured at 38 cm (15 in), the print-maker would be about 231 cm (91 in or 7 ft 7 in) tall with a medium weight of some 286 kg (630 lbs) while the heavy-set print-maker would be at about 358 kg (789 lbs) the step distance of such creature would be some 146.6 cm (57.8 in or 4 ft 9.8 in) which is close to the 153.9 cm (60 in or 5 ft), as reported to me by the finder who had actually measured the distance between the two large human-like footprints, according to my calculations.

A footprint-maker of that size would need about 6,517 calories per day to remain healthy. This size is very close to the average size of the Sasquatch as presented in my Proportion Table, resulting from various measurements taken through the years by several Sasquatch researchers.

As I have mentioned, he reported his finding to me only in 2005, after he found out about my interests in the matter.

He has not reported his discovery to anyone else for fear of being ridiculed and taken as a fool. Which, sad to say, is a very common reaction from closed-minded people when such findings are described to them. I last visited this location in 2017.

## Report #21
## TATCHUN REGION
## Sighting at the Outlet of Tatchun Lake in 1995
## Location: Coord. 62o 17'12 N 136o 13'58 W
## (Map: Carmacks 115 I; GR 036 006)

This sighting was relayed to me by a member of the Kwanlin Dün First Nation (KDFN) in 2005 when talking about my interest in the Sasquatch phenomena.

**Encounter:** In August of 1995, a friend of my KDFN contact was on his way to fish for chinook salmon at Tatchun Lake. When driving on the Frenchman Lake Road, at around 1630 hours (4:30 pm) that day, he observed a tall and huge entity, which he called a Sasquatch, squatting or sitting in the water by the lake's outlet into Tatchun Creek. He stopped his truck and watched this entity catch a couple of salmon, stand up, kill the fish, and throw it on the opposite shore of the creek.

The Sasquatch was judged to be about 2.5 m (7 ft) tall, dark, and muscular. He watched the Sasquatch fishing for a few minutes. The creature seemed to be unaware of his presence, and he then moved on to the boat landing site, about one kilometre away from this location.

**History:** The Frenchman Lake Road was originally built in the 1970s as a basic trail connecting the North Klondike Highway, Yukon highway #2, to the Robert Campbell Highway, Yukon Highway #7, by way of Tatchun and Frenchman Lakes. In the mid-1980s, a number of campgrounds were constructed by these lakes, and the road was improved for easier access by RV and trailer.

**Geography:** Close to these lakes, one finds a low, rolling, hilly terrain with gradually taller mountains further to the northwest. The vegetation consists mostly of willow trees, aspen, poplar trees, with the odd black spruce and lodgepole pine. Many large rocks have tumbled down from the mountains, probably carried by the iceflow thousands of years ago.

**Investigation:** I have been on this road many times since residing in the Yukon; actually, I was subjected to an odd smell occurrence on Frenchman Lake in 2003 while fishing with a close Tr'ondëk Hwëch'in First Nation female friend, in Report #30. I would usually stop at the same location where this Sasquatch was observed in 1995 and try to catch a few fish. I did not get any salmon but caught many Arctic graylings.

Unfortunately, there is no mention of any facial or other specific details in what my contact told me.

See Report #8 for another occurrence that has taken place close by at the site of the Tatchun Lake Campground.

## Report #22
## Liard Region
## Sighting on the Silver Hart Project Road in 1995
## Location: Coord.60o 18'40 N 130o 43'43 W
## (Map: Sab Lake 105 B/7 GR 044 872)

A MAN contacted me by email in October 2020 to report that he had experienced two Sasquatch sightings along the access road leading to the Silver Hart Project exploration area: one in 1995, and the other in 1997. Additionally, the witness reports discovering a dead tree stuck in the ground with the roots up in the air, an "upside down or inverted tree" along the same road. This report deals with the first sighting only.

**Encounter:** The witness was working at the Swift River Lodge at the time and was riding an ATV on the Silver Hart Project access road on his day off. The first sighting encounter occurred in the late afternoon of Thursday, September 7, 1995. He remembers the date quite well, as it was his 25th birthday, and he was spending a bit of time exploring on his day off as he had done many times before.

When he reached Km 40 (Mile 24) or so of the Silver Hart Road, which is the distance from its intersection with the Alaska Highway, Yukon Hwy #1, he heard a loud "snap," like the sound of a large branch being broken in the nearby bush on the left-hand side of the road, about one kilometre north of the end of Edgar Lake. Focusing on the area where he heard the sound, he then observed a large creature, judging it to have been about 213 cm (7 ft) tall, sort of trying to hide behind a couple of large trees, about 30 m (30 yards) away.

The creature in question just stood still at that time, not moving at all. The witness mentions that it was a "big guy" 190.5 cm (6 ft 3 in) tall and then weighed some 113 kg (250 lbs), and he guessed the creature he was observing at the time of the sighting to have been somewhere around 272 kg (600 lbs), in his opinion, with dark unkempt shaggy hair. They stood sort of looking at each other for a few seconds and the witness then reports: "I got scared big time and peeled out" returning to the Swift River Lodge.

He mentioned that he was not armed at the time. It was only later on, a few days later actually, that it dawned on him that he had seen a Sasquatch, but he never told anyone about his experience, frightened of being ridiculed until he contacted me in October 2020.

**Local History:** The Silver Hart Project is an area just east of the Alaska Highway Continental Divide in southeast Yukon. It is located in the area of GS 0489 on the Sab Lake map 105 B/7. The Alaska Highway Divide is the divide between the water flowing westerly to the Bering Sea, which connects the Pacific Ocean to the Arctic Ocean.

The water first flows out of Pine Lake via the Swift River which empties into the Morley River; in turn, the Morley flows into Teslin Lake, then the Teslin River joins the Yukon River at Hootalinqua and continues by way of the Yukon River system to the Bering Sea.

The water flows to the Arctic Ocean originally in a southeast direction from Daughney Lake, then by way of the Rancheria River flowing mostly east and then to the north via the Liard River, then the Mackenzie River system to the Beaufort Sea. MCM Metals Ltd. has been exploring the area for gold, silver, lead, and zinc since the early 1980s close to that location and still is for that matter.

The Silver Hart access road is located some 5 km (3 mi) west of the Divide Lodge on the Alaska Highway and about 50 km (32 mi) east of the small roadside community of Swift River. Swift River had a population of about fifteen people at the time and was about 15.5 km (10 mi) west of the roadside lodge of Rancheria by the Rancheria River. Whitehorse is located 250 km (155 mi) west and Watson Lake 132 km (82 mi) east of the access road.

A Yukon Government Highway Maintenance Camp is in operation at Swift River, and during the period of time when the witness experienced this sighting, Swift River was the location of a popular truck stop with a lodge, restaurant, fuel pumps, and a small repair shop. It closed down in 2009; however, the many buildings are still standing to these days although they are now in a sad condition.

**Geography:** The exploration project is located on the southwest slope of a tall mountain called Meister Mountain with a height of 1,892 m (6,209 ft) in a very mountainous part of southeast Yukon called the Cassiar Mountain Range. The access road to the exploration project location, a distance of 43 km (29 mi), meanders through the low ground east of the Rancheria River and one kilometre east of Pine Lake, which empties into Swift River on the west side of the Alaska Highway Continental Divide. Then skirting Daughney Lake and crossing the Rancheria River, by the northeast end of North Wind Lake, it continues on the west side of North Wind, Roy and Edgard Lakes, on the eastern slopes of the Alaska Highway Continental Divide.

In turn, the Rancheria River empties into the Liard River farther to the east. A few cabins are located around Pine Lake and Daughney Lake, used mostly by members of the Teslin Tlingit Council. A small airstrip is located on the Pine Lake Road, as well as docking facilities at Daughney Lake, just west of the exploration project access road. Those can be accessed by using the Pine Lake Road. In its 2020 annual report, MCM Metals Ltd. reported that it has completed the upgrading of 12 km (7 mi) of the access road in 2020 and will continue an upgrading program in 2021 and 2022 in preparation to set up a milling operation at the exploration site by 2023.

**Investigation:** The witness was working at the Swift River Lodge at the time, usually working from 1800 hours (6 pm) till 0200 hours (2 am). He later married the lodge-owner's daughter. He had been at the lodge for a few years and had explored most of the nearby area when he experienced his sightings. I am familiar with the area as in the 1980s, 1990s, and 2000s, I had stopped at the lodge for lunch a few times on my way to and from Watson Lake.

Unfortunately, I have not had the chance to explore the specific area of the Silver Hart Project where these sightings occurred. At the time of this writing, there is a lodge called the Continental Divide Lodge, with a campground operating in the summertime only, by the Divide and just before the access road to the Silver Hart Project. I have stopped at this place on a number of occasions through the years as well, and at a roadside lodge at Rancheria.

For the record, a 213 cm (7 ft or 84 in) tall Sasquatch would have a footprint in the vicinity of 35 cm (13.75 in) and would weigh around 262.5 kg (579 lbs) with a step of some 134.4 cm (53 in).

The witness's rough judgment is a bit off but well within the range when one looks at a person or creature and tries to state the exact height or weight.

The witness experienced another sighting on the same road in 1997, see Report #23.

## Report #23
## Liard Region
## Sighting on the Silver Hart Project Road in 1997
## Location: Coord. 60o 08'58 N 130o 52'51 W (Map: Daughney Lake 105 B/2 GR 957 694)

THE SAME MAN who reported a sighting on the Silver Hart Project Road in 1995 further stated that in late September 1997, he had a second Sasquatch sighting on the very same Silver Hart Project access road, although at a different location.

**Encounter:** He had been riding an ATV on the same road as the other sighting encounter on his birthday in 1995, although this time he was hunting for moose. On his way back to the Swift River Lodge in the late afternoon, he observed another Sasquatch at a distance of some 100 m (105 yd) on his left-hand side, the east side of the road, some 11 km (6.8 mi) from the Alaska Highway intersection, while driving in that direction.

**Investigation:** As this one had a smaller body size, the witness figured it was a female, although he could not see any observable breasts. The witness judged the height to be about 213 cm (7 ft) and the weight to be somewhere between 180 to 230 kg (400 to 500 lbs). Our reporter states he stood still for close to two minutes. The Sasquatch, meanwhile, was not moving much either, just trying to hide in the close by foliage. The witness had a rifle with him this time, but it never crossed his mind to take a shot at it. After a couple of minutes, the witness states that the Sasquatch moved into the forest, and he simply drove back to the lodge, and again he did not mention his experience with anyone.

Details on local history and geography were presented in the first report, Report #22.

## Report #24
## KENO REGION
## Sighting in Mayo in 1998
## Location: Coord. 62o 35'29 N 136o 53'53 W
## (Map: Mayo 105 M/12; GR 557 518)

WHILE DISCUSSING Sasquatch with a man of the Na-Cho Nyak Dun, he said that in late June of 1998, a woman of the First Nation of Na-Cho Nyak Dun (FNNND) told him that she had once observed a Sasquatch.

**Encounter:** She had gotten out of bed at around 0300 hours (3 am) to get a drink of water. As she was pouring water in her glass, standing by her kitchen window, she happened to look outside and observed a tall, large Sasquatch picking carrots from her garden. He ate a couple and carried a few more with him while crossing the street in the direction of the Stewart River.

**History:** The town of Mayo came about when a Paddle Wheeler's Captain, by the name of Mayo, set-up a storage site by the river in early 1900, where his boat would be loaded with silver from the nearby mines. He named this new site Mayo Landing. A trading post was built a short while later, and today the small town is located around the bend of the Stewart River. The FNNND, known as "The Big River People," have been around these parts for about 10,000 years. Originally, they had set up a village of their own, located across the river and north of the present location. This village was flooded in 1921, the members of the FNNND moved to the east side of Mayo Landing. Recently, a new residential townsite was erected north of town, and most First Nation members have moved to that townsite. Silver, galena, and gold mining have taken place since the early 1900s. Two large mining operations have opened up in recent years, one for silver and one for gold, from which some 200,000 ounces of gold reach the market each year.

**Investigation:** The witness has mentioned the Sasquatch being "tall and large," which could mean many things to different people. She obviously had a good look at the creature, at three o'clock in the morning in that part of the Yukon is almost like noon in the southern parts of Canada. I visit Mayo regularly in the summer, as I have friends living there.

There are another three reports from the area. Check out Report #16, a sighting; Report #37, a double sighting; Report #50, another sighting; and Report #65, a vocal and fleeting movements report.

## Report #25
## TAKHINI REGION
## Sighting North of Fox Lake in 1998
## Location: Coord. 61o 18'40 N 135o 33'55 W (Map: Lake Laberge 105 E: GR 070 097)

In the early evening of Sunday, July 26, 1998, I was contacted by a Dene woman who told me a group of people she was riding in a car with had observed what they identified as a large Sasquatch, just north of Fox Lake.

**Encounter:** This group consisted of two Dene couples who were driving back home to Fort McPherson, Northwest Territories, (Teetl'it Zheh) after shopping in Whitehorse. At about 1500 hours (3 pm) on Thursday, July 23, 1998, they observed what they reported to be a tall and big Sasquatch, climbing over the side of a ditch and onto the steep adjoining hill on their right-hand side, east side of the road. She reported that the Sasquatch in question was leaving tracks on the soft ground of the bank as it was climbing out of the ditch using both feet and hands while doing so; the height of the creature was estimated at being at least 213 cm (7 ft) tall.

The sighting occurred at about 1.6 km (1 mi) past the north end of Fox Lake, in the direction of the community of Carmacks, on the North Klondike Highway, Yukon Highway #2. This paved highway connects the city of Whitehorse to Carmacks, 177 km (110 mi) away, and other communities located in central and northern Yukon as well as to the Dempster Highway, Yukon Highway #5, which leads to the Dene community of Fort McPherson in the Northwest Territories some 430 km (267 mi) north of Dawson City, Yukon.

**Local History:** This area is part of the traditional lands of the Ta'an Kwäch'än Council (TKC) and the KDFN people, where they have been hunting and living ever since they arrived in this part of the Yukon. Their route took them from farther west in what is now the state of Alaska, 8 to 7.5 Kya at the melting of the last ice formations and glaciers in the area, to their present location, according to archaeological research recently conducted in the general area of Whitehorse.

During the days of the paddle wheelers, which took place from 1897 to 1954, most of the large trees in the area were cut and used to operate the paddle wheelers, also called steamboats, as they would burn wood in their furnaces to provide steam by which the paddle wheel would be operated.

A winter stagecoach road, called the Overland Trail, some 531 km (330 mi) long, came across this part of the Takhini Region connecting the city of Whitehorse to Dawson City and locations along the way. The Overland Trail was originally built in 1902 and is a winter sleigh trip to Dawson City from Whitehorse.

And the other way around, of course, would take about five days on average, with a number of roadhouses located every 30 to 40 km (20 to 25 mi) along the way where passengers would be fed, would sleep overnight, and where horses would be exchanged for fresh ones in the morning. There would be on average of three departures per week from each location, but each one departing every other day from each point so as not to cause the problem of sharing the same roadhouses mid-way through.

From Whitehorse, the Overland Trail first went north roughly to Takhini Crossing, covering 35 km (23 mi), where it would cross the Takhini River. The present-day Alaska Highway roughly follows the same route to Takhini Crossing. The winter stage road would then follow the Little River Valley and the Klusha Creek Valley to present-day Braeburn Lodge on the North Klondike Highway, located close to Braeburn Lake and a little distance from Fox Lake. From Braeburn, the trail would then roughly follow the Nordenskiold River Valley. Actually, the North Klondike Highway follows just about the very same route to the community of Carmacks, and then the Overland Trail would carry on to Yukon Crossing following the west side of the Yukon River, which is located some 50 km (31 mi) downriver from Carmacks.

The Overland Trail stagecoach road would then cross the Yukon River at this point and mostly follow the eastern side of the river. It would cross the Pelly River near its confluence with the Yukon River, at a location known as Pelly Farm today, some 430 km (266 mi) downstream from Whitehorse.

It would then climb to higher elevations away from the Yukon River, continuing to a location just west of Grizzly Dome where it would cross the Stewart River, which became known as Stewart Crossing. (However, please note: it is *not* the Stewart Crossing that is today located on the North Klondike Highway, Yukon Highway #2, at the intersection of the Silver Road, Yukon Highway #8 and as indicated by such name on travel maps.) From this river crossing, the winter stage road would navigate further inland crossing the Indian River roughly 50 km (31 mi) southwest of King Solomon Dome, then it would join established trails by Eldorado Creek and Bonanza Creek and finally reach Dawson City by following those established trails.

The Overland Trail was used exclusively by horses until the winter of 1914–1915, when tracked Caterpillars began to replace all the horses. Then in the mid-1920s, the airplanes took over from these tracked machines with a number of airfields located at prominent settlement locations between Whitehorse and Dawson City. The North Klondike Highway was built in 1954 and has since been open all year round.

**Geography:** Later during the summer of 1998, a wild forest fire had gone through the area where the sighting took place, burning everything in sight and leaving a mess of tangled burned trees and devastation. As a result, the terrain at the time of the sighting was mostly bare with dead trees, some standing and some falling down every which way, covering the entire area. Surprisingly, a few black spruce that escaped the fire devastation were located close to the sighting location, as I discovered during my initial investigation of the area the day after I received the report by email on Monday, July 27, 1998.

The terrain on the right-hand side of the road, where the sighting occurred, is elevated, and this trend continues eastward with mostly rolling sand hills with a few pothole lakes, remnant of the last ice age, then mostly sharp rocky formations as far as the shores of Lake Laberge, some 50 km (31 mi) to the east.

The area to the west, left-hand side of the road driving north, is mostly low land with a small lake and swampy area. Past that wet, swampy, low-lying area, the ground gradually increases in height with numerous rocky out-crops joining the slopes of Kingston Mountain, at an elevation of 1,265 m (4,150 ft). The ground is somewhat soft around these parts and is mostly a mix of sand and volcanic ash, dating to the volcanic eruptions that had occurred around 845 CE in the general area of Mount Churchill in the middle of the Wrangell-St. Elias Mountains, as well as gravel with a few rocky formations to the east and west of the sighting location. Due to the wild forest fire that occurred in June of 1998, there would not have been many sources of food readily available in the immediate area at the time of the sighting, but past the burn areas, one could find wild grasses and plants with balsam poplar, black spruce, lodgepole pine, paper birch, and all sorts of willow trees.

There are plenty of gophers (Arctic ground squirrels) in the general area, although they would have all gone underground during the fire. However, by the time these people went through the area, these gophers would have been everywhere, thus providing a good source of food. Prior to the fire, the land would have been alive with bears, caribou, deer, elk, lynx, moose, and porcupines. Both Fox Lake and Little Fox Lake, another 4 km (2.5 mi) down the road in the direction of Braeburn Lake, have plenty of fish like Arctic grayling, lake trout, and white fish. An elk herd would usually hang around these hills as well but would have gone away due to the forest fire, probably in a northern direction, as the fire actually started very close to the sighting location.

According to investigations conducted by the Wildfire Management Staff at the Yukon Department of Renewable Resources, this fire started as a result of careless campers leaving their roadside campsite without totally extinguishing their campfire after cooking breakfast.

There has been another Sasquatch sighting recently reported on the west shore of Fox Lake, reported to have occurred at about 2100 hours (9 pm) on Saturday, August 16, 2014. As well, strange unidentified vocals were reported to have been heard at around 0300 hours (3 am) on Sunday, August 17, 2014. It was located just a few kilometres north of Fox Lake on the west shores of Little Fox Lake.

**Investigation:** There were four people in the car: the first person to notice the ambulating entity was the front passenger, the Dene woman who contacted me, sitting in the right-hand side seat. She had originally thought the creature to be a bear. The woman pointed this out to the other passengers, who then exclaimed that it was actually a Sasquatch. There was absolutely no doubt whatsoever in their mind as to the creature being a full-size healthy Sasquatch, according to the reporter. A 213 cm tall (84 in or 7 ft) Sasquatch, as stated by the reporter, would have a footprint of just about 35.5 cm (14 in), a step of 137 cm (54 in 4 ft 6 in) on average.

A medium-sized Sasquatch would weigh on average about 267 kg (588 lbs), while a larger and heavier-sized one could be up to 364 kg (802 lbs). A Sasquatch of this size would need approximately 6,112 calories per day to remain healthy, which is only about twice the number of calories required by the average 183 cm (6 ft) tall human being.

Unfortunately, the witnesses and the reporter did not pay much attention to details concerning the creature, as they were somewhat in a state of shock and were surprised by such a sighting. So not much else is available, except that they mentioned the Sasquatch to be very large (which, of course, could mean different things to different people) and with mostly dark brown hair.

I visited the location the day after receiving the report on Monday, July 27, 1998. The reporter contacted me three days after the sighting occurred, on Sunday, July 26, 1998. During my first investigation visit to the sighting location, I could not find any tracks or signs of any footprints. It should be noted that it had been raining during the two previous days prior to receiving the report. I have explored the immediate area up to a radius of about 5 km (3 mi) around the reported sighting location during the following years for further traces of possible Sasquatch activities with no conclusive results. My last visit was in the summer of 2020. I did not notice anything out of the ordinary during that visit, except for the carcass of a deer, which could have been taken down by wolves or even maybe by a grizzly bear, just days before my visit to the area. Most of the burned trees have been salvaged during the last few years, and the wood cutting activities would have kept large animals away in any case.

Following newly made trails used to extract the wood, I have been able to investigate the major portion of the area, and nothing of importance has been found. Obviously, I will be returning to the area as often as I can, especially now that I have received two more reports about Sasquatch activities in the immediate area. Many Whitehorse residents, including my family, use the Yukon Government Campground at Fox Lake on a regular basis, as it is fairly close to Whitehorse and the lake offers good fishing opportunities.

## *The 2000s*

### Report #26
### SQUANGA REGION
### Sighting at Summit Lake in 2000
### Location: 60o 26'18 N 133o 39'36 W
### (Map: Squanga Lake 105 C/5: GR 739 011)

A First Nation woman of the Carcross Tagish First Nation reported to have observed what she described as a Sasquatch, for about ten minutes, in July of 2000.

**Encounter:** The ambulating bipedal creature is described as being dark brown or black, with long arms and broad shoulders, and huge in stature with no visible neck. The entity was sighted on the northwest shores of Summit Lake. (One of many lakes called "Summit.") This small lake is located on the north side of the Alaska Highway, Yukon Highway #1, some 2 km (1.5 mi) directly west of Squanga Lake, which in turn is located 23 km (14 mi) east of Jakes Corner.

The woman in question was camping with friends on the east shore of the lake. At around 0400 hours (4 am) she got up to answer the call of nature and while walking in the direction of the toilet facilities, she noticed a Sasquatch across the lake, who was in the water pulling some stuff out of the water, probably tubers or such, to eat.

**Local History:** The location where the witness was camping is a private camping location on the Carcross/Tagish First Nation traditional land, where members of this First Nation often set up camp by the lake and fish, mostly with nets for whitefish.

**Geography:** Summit Lake is surrounded by mostly black spruces and lodgepole pines upon gently rolling hills with the odd rocky formation here and there. Summit Lake empties into Squanga Lake via a very small creek flowing in an easterly direction. The grounds around the creek route are very swampy with low bush of alders, willows, and shrubs, while the ground around the private unorganized campground is mostly dry and flat with large white pine trees and moss.

A truck-only trail takes drivers from the Alaska Highway to the shores of the lake a distance of about 400 m (1,220 ft). The usual array of large and small animals is found around these two lakes; hunters enjoy the chase for moose in the fall and a medium-size herd of elk, which are protected from hunting, roam the area mostly in between Squanga Lake and Summit Lake. Both lakes are known for whitefish and northern pike.

**Investigation:** I have spent some time at the very spot where this woman was camping and know the area quite well, having walked the area on a few occasions and fished the lake for northern pike. The campsite where the woman in question was camped is on the east shore of Summit Lake.

The Sasquatch was on the west shore directly across the lake, a distance of about 600 m (615 yards). This is what could be called an unorganized wilderness campground, used mostly by the members of the Carcross/Tagish First Nation (CTFN). Most people are not aware of this location nor of the trail leading to it. The time of the sighting was about 0400 hours (4 am). Up this way in the summer it is quite light at 0400 hours, and the visibility would be very good when it is not raining.

In the report, the woman states that it was a cool, calm, and clear morning with good visibility. According to the witness, the Sasquatch was walking in the lake, close to shore, at about knee-high in the water, and grasping plants and various vegetation, probably to eat I would venture, but that is not stated by the witness. It should be remembered that grasses and wild plants, especially tubers and aquatic plants would make up a good portion of a Sasquatch diet. The witnessed entity is described as dark brown or black, which is quite consistent with other reports.

Unfortunately, there is no indication of height, size, stature, or girth from which an assessment of its size could be made, except that it had long arms and broad shoulders, which again would be consistent with other descriptions.

Check out the numerous Sasquatch-related activities that have taken place around close-by Squanga Lake

## Report #27
## LIARD REGION
## Sightings by Meziadin Junction in 2000
## Location: Coord. 56o 07'06 N 129o 16'56 W
## (Map: BC Highway #37, North of Meziadin Junction)

A MAN CONTACTED ME by phone to report that while driving the Cassiar Road he had to swerve in order to miss a family group of ambulating bipedal entities, which he described as Sasquatch. This sighting took place at about 0400 hours (4 am) on Monday, July 3, 2000, at a location about 30 km (21 mi) north of Meziadin Junction, on BC Highway #37, close to the junction of BC Highways #37 and #37A, which lead to the community of Stewart, BC.

This highway is known as the Cassiar Road by long-time residents of northern BC and Yukon, as at one time, it was the only road connecting the mining community of Cassiar, in northern BC, which had an asbestos mine located just outside of town.

**Encounter:** The man who reported the sighting is a Métis, aged 35 then, who, at the time of the sighting, was working at a sawmill in the vicinity of the First Nation community of Kitwanga, located at the junction of Highways #37, the Cassiar Road, and Highway #16, the Yellowhead Highway, in Northern BC. He was a resident of Whitehorse at the time. He contacted me in 2006 to report the sighting after reading an article written about my research work in the field of Sasquatch in the *Yukon News*, a regional newspaper. When he contacted me, he was working at Yukon College (Now Yukon University) in Whitehorse, as the overall supervisor of the College's cleaning crew, for the building maintenance department.

The witness originally came from the province of Quebec and had moved to the Yukon in the late 1990s. As he mentioned to me, the reasons he moved to the Yukon were the vastness of the territory, its fishing and hunting opportunities, and the overall wilderness of the Yukon. I would consider the witness as being bush-wise. He had come to Whitehorse on his days off to visit his family and enjoy Canada Day. He had driven from Whitehorse all day on Sunday, July 2, 2000, stopping at Dease Lake on the Cassiar Road for dinner and continuing on in the direction of Kitwanga after dinner.

At some time in the evening, he had become tired of driving and around midnight decided to take a nap. He awoke at about 0330 hours (3:30 am) and decided to carry on driving. He had driven only a short distance when he came upon the Sasquatch family group in the middle of the road.

**Local History:** The area of Cassiar is well-known for its minerals: asbestos, copper, gold, jade, silver, lead, zinc, and a few others. It has experienced prospecting booms since the 1880s, with miners gradually moving farther north each year. There have been a number of First Nations trails connecting the region with the outside world, mostly through sea access at the community of Stewart, BC, and there have been people in the region for quite a while.

**Geography:** The land around these parts is full of lakes, mountains, and valleys, and it is very rocky and hard to navigate. In the northern portion of the region, most rivers empty into the Liard River system. However, in the area where the sighting occurred, all the rivers find their way into the nearby Pacific Ocean.

Trees common to the area are alpine fir, aspen, balsam poplar, birch, black spruce, cedars, cottonwood, Douglas fir, lodgepole pine, white spruce, and the odd white pine closer to the ocean. There are numerous wild plants, especially in the valleys, and they are noticeably larger the closer they are to the warmer water of the Pacific. One would call the area where the sighting occurred a jungle due to the number of trees and its density, which makes it very difficult to enter and walk about. The area abounds with wild animals and wild plants, providing unlimited access to a large variety of food, although the access would be a bit more limited in winter due to the large amount of snow falling in the region.

**Encounter continues:** The witness was driving at about 90 kph (55 mph) when he entered a right-hand curve in the road. Even though it was almost daylight, the sky was still greyish at the time, but the visibility was good on the road. As he was about halfway through the curve, he noticed two very large bipedal ambulating entities in the middle of the road right in front of him and no more than 3 m (10 ft) away; he immediately moved onto the left-hand lane of the road so as not to hit them and applied the brakes.

This was when he realized that he was looking at two mature Sasquatch: a male on the right-hand side of a female Sasquatch with his left arm on the shoulder of the female. He noticed the female holding "something" in her arms, which he did not clearly see. However, a bit later on, when he reviewed the encounter in his mind, he took the "something" as being a newborn baby, an infant. During this time, the creatures continued walking slowly across the road and reached the forest into which they disappeared.

The most important factor of this sighting, which he repeated a number of times, is the look given to him by the female Sasquatch and the impression it left on the witness; she looked directly and intensely into the witness's eyes, and her eyes seemed to pass or convey a message which he clearly understood the meaning to be "do not hurt me."

The man in question then stated that by that time he was totally in shock, and he pulled over to the side of the road a few metres ahead, just past the curve.

Although he had a camera on the passenger seat, he did not make an attempt to take a photograph; actually, the witness mentioned that the idea never occurred to him—it never even crossed his mind until much later.

The witness cannot recall exactly how tall the two Sasquatch were. He only could say that they were tall, huge, stocky, and big, which may be the result of him being in shock. He remembered them to be greyish brown, which may be due to the time of the morning and the lack of good light. It should be remembered that most Sasquatch have been reported to be in some shade of brown, usually dark brown. This was the first time he had ever seen a Sasquatch, but he had read about them, and he came forward only after reading an article about me in the local newspaper. He is absolutely certain they were a couple of Sasquatch. During the three interviews that I conducted with him, he mentioned a number of times the look given to him by the female, and he stated that in his mind it was as if she was talking to him, saying: "do not hurt me."

**Investigation:** In some of the many sighting reports that I have read from the Pacific Northwest, it is pointed out that some of the witnesses received a telepathic message of some sort. This idea is mentioned by a number of people, and some researchers have advanced the theory that some form of telepathy is being used to transmit a message. I really do not know what to think of that theory. However, when a witness says that a message was somehow transmitted to him, and the message was clear in his mind, I have no other choice but to accept what the witness is telling me.

If I had better knowledge of the ability of the human mind to receive such messages, I could possibly try to interpret this point of a message being non-verbally transmitted in a better manner. However, as a regular guy conducting Sasquatch research, even though I conduct the research on almost a full-time basis, I really do not feel qualified to state the reasons why this witness was able to understand or interpret the meaning of the look given to him by the female Sasquatch. Therefore, I will leave this interpreting work to someone else who may have better knowledge of such things.

There are two other reports along the Cassiar Road, one was a sighting at the Nass River Bridge in 1990, Report #11, and the other was a vocal occurrence in 2006 at the Bell-Irving River Rest Stop, Report #35.

## Report #28
## SQUANGA REGION
## Knuckle Print Discovered by the Morley River Bridge in July 2000
## Location: Coord. 60o 00'34 N 132o 09'24 W (Map: Teslin 105 C; GR 059 055)

I RECEIVED A REPORT from a former colleague, who resided in Red Deer, Alberta. He had a photo of a very large knuckle print, embedded in the mud, with information mentioning that it had been taken close to a bridge, about 50 km (31 mi) past the community of Teslin in the Yukon, just beside the Alaska Highway, Yukon Highway #1.

**Encounter:** A motorcyclist was on his way back to Alberta in mid-July 2000. At one point, his helmet's visor became quite dirty, with multiple mosquitoes stuck to it, so he decided to stop and clean it up at the first chance he could get. Shortly thereafter, he noticed an old, abandoned highway lodge with a decent parking area by a river, so he pulled in. He then noticed what would have been a campground at some time in the distant past, beside the old lodge. He parked his bike and made his way to the water's edge, cleaned up his visor, and as he was getting ready to climb back up the riverbank, he noticed an unusually large knuckle print that looked like a human knuckle but much larger. So, he took a photo of it.

**Investigation:** On his return to Alberta, he contacted a local Sasquatch research group and forwarded his photo to this group. One of the members of this group knew of me and contacted me with the story, sending me the photo in an email.

I examined the photo in detail. It was very human-like and had four clearly shown finger knuckles, although no indication of a thumb, clearly from a left hand. It showed the proximal phalanges from the metacarpophalangeal joints to the proximal interphalangeal joints of the four fingers. I judged the length of the proximal phalange of the middle-finger to be about 15 cm (6 in) long, with an approximate width of about 6 cm (2.5 in). No other prints or signs were visible according to the motorcyclist.

Upon further observations and reading the report, I gathered that the motorcyclist had driven some 50 km (31 mi) past Teslin, a route that would take him to the Morley River, and indeed there is an old highway lodge at that location: the Morley River Lodge and an attached campground.

I have driven past this location on many occasions. After receiving the report. I went to the location, but there was no sign of the knuckle print. Everything else matched the description provided, though.

Unfortunately, my former colleague would not give me permission to use the knuckle print photo in this book.

Footprints were discovered close by in 2015 by a hunting party, see Report #61.

## Report #29
## SQUANGA REGION
## Animal Reaction and Strange Smell at Hall Creek on Squanga Lake in 2002
## Location: Coord. 60o 29'49 N 133o 41'18 W (Map: Squanga Lake 105 C/5; GR 737 671)

I WAS CONTACTED by a man reporting that his dog had been acting very strangely after going off into the bush and returning to its master's location.

**Occurrence:** The dog appeared extremely frightened when he came back from venturing into the nearby bush, whimpering at the owner's feet and shaking with its tail between its legs and refusing to return to the bush. The dog had jumped back in the boat and was trying to hide under the seats.

The fellow in question reports going into the bush to investigate the reason why his dog was acting so strangely, thinking that perhaps the dog had fought with a bear. As soon as he entered the bush, accompanied by his wife, they noticed a very odd smell, sort of like strong rotten eggs and a lot of unusual movement in the bush—types of movements that were not related to the usual known animals such as bears, elk, or moose, but they could not clearly see what was moving about.

The location of this occurrence is by Hall Creek at the northeast end of Squanga Lake. This lake is next to Summit Lake which is about 2 km (1.5 mi) farther west, where there was a reported Sasquatch sighting in 2000, Report #26. Squanga Lake is located on the Alaska Highway, Yukon Highway #1, 23 km (14 mi) east of Jakes Corner, where there was another reported Sasquatch sighting in 1975, Report #5. The married couple resides in Whitehorse.

The man is a carpenter by trade as well as a member of the Canadian Rangers, Whitehorse Patrol, and his spouse is a member of the Kwanlin Dün First Nation. They were both in their mid-30s at the time of the occurrence. They are both quite at ease in the bush, enjoying hiking, camping, canoeing, hunting, fishing, and ATV and snowmobile riding—the usual stuff that most Yukoners do around these parts. The witnesses were out fishing on Squanga Lake that July day in 2002 and had stopped for lunch and to stretch their legs by Hall Creek around noon when this occurrence took place. Of note, there have been at least four other occurrences reported on Squanga Lake and Little Squanga Lake.

**Geography:** The immediate area around Hall Creek has a fairly swampy shoreline on the southeast side, and the area where the creek empties into the lake with mostly lodgepole pine trees, although the trees closer to the lake on that side are mostly alders, aspens, balsam poplars, and low bush willows. The rolling ground in the immediate area eventually gave way to rocky formations and then a few small mountains further inland before reaching the high peaks.

Bears, elk, moose, woodland caribou, a few deer, along with the usual smaller animals, are found in this area. In the close-by swamp, one finds a fairly large number of muskrats with many types of wild berries, wild plants, and swamp grasses. The beavers, quite numerous as well in the area, were busy building a dam at the beginning of Squanga Lake at the time, actually where the Squanga River joins the lake. This lake is well known for its large whitefish population and northern pike, along with Arctic grayling and Chinook salmon.

There are three other reports directly related to the lake itself and a few others for the general area. One is about a very similar experience by the same couple but a year later, Report #31, while another involves strange unidentified mimicking vocals and a deep feeling of uneasiness that I experienced in September of 2008, Report #38, and another report from the very same location in 1992 by a member of the Whitehorse Transportation Museum, Report #14.

**Investigation:** The reporter further mentioned that there was no significant wind that day, which would have carried the smell of an animal kill, for example, so he doubts that the smell came from a dead or rotting animal. He also stated that the noise they heard was more like someone walking on two legs, ambulating, described as walking then stopping, then walking again, and making noise going through the bush, as if on purpose.

The dog's reaction and behaviour would be quite natural for when an animal of that size faces something much more intimidating. The dog owner had made mention that his dog had been running around in the bush since he was a pup and had never been afraid of bears, elk, moose, or any other types of animals usually found in these forests.

Whatever scared him off had to be something totally different and unusual. These types of animal behaviour and reaction to the presence of a bipedal ambulating entity, such as a Sasquatch, have been reported to have occurred at other locations as well.

I have conducted a number of boat trips on Squanga Lake, Squanga River, and Little Squanga Lake, and I have investigated the area on foot as well, camping at a few locations along the shores, at one of which I was subjected to a mimicking type of vocals, Report #38.

I was last at Hall Creek in 2020.

**Report #30**
**TATCHUN REGION**
**Foul Pungent Smell at Frenchman Lake in 2003**
**Location: Coord. 62o 08'20 N 135o 44'15 W (Map: Glenlyon 105 L: GR 559 936)**

A FIRST NATION WOMAN and I were canoeing and lazily fishing on a bright sunny, warm afternoon, on Friday, July 4, 2003, when we experienced an unidentified and extremely foul short-term pungent smell that lasted about one minute. The sickening smell appeared to be coming from the shores of Frenchman Lake, in a small bay about 8 km (5 mi) north of the Frenchman Lake Yukon Government Campground. My friend is originally of the Tr'ondëk Hwëch'in First Nation (THFN), and we had been camping at Frenchman Lake for a few days and were leisurely canoeing on the lake that day, fishing for northern pike.

**Local History:** This campground was the first to be open on Frenchman Lake. The access road was located on the Robert Campbell Highway, Yukon Highway #4, just past the access road to the First Nation village of Little Salmon and on the left-hand side, when driving from the community of Carmacks, some 50 km (31 mi) away. Another access road from the direction of Tatchun Lake some 30 km (21 mi) away was later opened. One would find the same type of terrain and vegetation like that of the location of the previous strange smell report from Tatchun Lake. A bit farther to the east, one would find the highest hill around the area, the Tatchun Hills, while the remainder of the area is comprised of gently rolling hills and valleys.

**Occurrence:** We had been on the lake for about four hours, just enjoying the scenery and the weather. It was a nice sunny day, about 25 degrees C (77 F) with a little breeze coming from the south. We had caught and released a few northern pike and were lazily trying to get some more; actually, we had noticed some huge ones in the small bay we had ventured into.

At one point, we were about 10 m (33 ft) away from shore

when a strong sickening smell hit us. I jokingly told my paddling companion to stop farting. Then, an even stronger stinking smell hit us. I would describe that pungent smell as day-old dirty baby diapers mixed with pig manure, dog excrements, and the spray of a skunk; something strong enough to make your eyes water.

We both looked at each other not really knowing what was happening and decided to head for shore to investigate and explore the possible cause of this stink.

It took us about two minutes to reach the shore at the location where we figured that smell came from; about a minute later, the smell suddenly disappeared, and the immediate area was completely still.

While on shore, we went looking for a dead animal as the possible cause of this smell, after searching around for a while, no dead animal was found. This is when we realized that the wind had died down prior to the smell occurrence, not a breeze, a totally dead calm as if we had been enveloped by an invisible bubble of some sort, something that I had never previously experienced.

We also noted that all the birds had stopped flying about and chirping before the stinky smell hit us. No squirrel movements either, total dead silence, and a weird feeling of not being wanted, a scary feeling.

We probably spent only eight to ten minutes investigating and exploring on shore before deciding to return to the safety of our campsite, still wondering what that smell was all about.

It was a few weeks later when I put it all together that I realized that this occurrence we had experienced was very similar to many other similar smell occurrences involving an unknown source of a short-term foul and pungent smell understood to be related to the possible presence of a Sasquatch.

Recent research work on the subject has been undertaken by John Green, former journalist and presently involved in Sasquatch research, and Dr. W. Fahrenbach, a retired biologist from the Oregon Primate Center. They both claim that the biped creature, widely known as Sasquatch, could very well have an ability to release a pungent smell in order to defuse unwanted encounters or situations with other animals and humans. This is similar to the ability of mountain gorillas to do the same thing, as studied and reported by anthropologist Diane Fossey.

We did not see or observe any creature that day, nor did we find any dead animal on shore. The smell lasted for only two to three minutes, and there were no winds whatsoever at the time the stink came upon us. Whatever it was is not known for sure, but it sure smelled bad.

The reason I had mentioned pig manure is that when I was a youngster, I had worked on a pig farm one summer and part of my job was to clean the pig pens, a stink that I will always remember. Having raised three kids, I know what dirty baby diapers smell like, as most readers would know, and, of course, I had owned a dog at one time, and I know what their excrement smells like after walking onto it.

As well, one evening, when I was about 14 years of age, I hit a skunk with my bicycle and became the host of some skunk spray, so I know what that smell is. Therefore, it had been easy to make a similar identification with the four specific smells as a possible scent qualification of previous pungent smell occurrences.

I have returned to that campground on many occasions through the years and fished the lake quite a few times. Actually, that is where I take visitors on a quick fishing trip where one is guaranteed to get large-sized northern pike right from shore in a short period of time. I have never experienced another foul smell as I did that day.

My last visit to Frenchman Lake was in September of 2013 when I took another woman fishing for the day.

I have not noticed any possible activity signs that may be related to Sasquatch activities around this lake, although there are other reports from close-by locations to Tatchun Lake, Report #21, and the Tatchun and Frenchman Valley.

## Report #31
## SQUANGA REGION
## Animal Reactions and Vocals at Little Squanga Lake in 2003
## Location: Coord. 60o 30'13 N 133o 45'50 W (Map: McClintock 105 C/12; GR 680 080)

THE SAME MAN who had witnessed his dog acting strangely by Hall Creek in 2002, Report #29, reported to me during the same interview that he had witnessed his dog acting very strangely after going off in the bush on another occasion, this time on the shores of Little Squanga Lake.

**Occurrence:** When his dog returned from a run in the bush, the witness reports that the dog was shaking badly, acting very strangely and was frightened, refusing to go back into the bush. The witness further mentioned walking into the bush to investigate, only to be greeted by loud yells and various types of shrieks. The man then went back to his boat, where his wife was waiting, and they took off onto Little Squanga Lake.

This event occurred in mid-August of 2003 at the beginning of Little Squanga Lake, on the right-hand side. The same couple had a similar experience by Hall Creek on Squanga Lake in July of 2002, as previously reported. Again, they were out fishing and just enjoying themselves.

**Geography:** A short and small river by the name of Squanga River connects Little Squanga Lake to Squanga Lake. It has very swampy, low shorelines with dwarf spruce trees and shrubs with only a few limited places to stop on dry ground. Most of the banks, mostly away from the shorelines, are fairly high and made of clay and loose sand upon which there are nice white pine trees and very sharp drops, with a number of small lakes further away, which are the remnants of the last ice age.

The ground up on these rolling hills is fairly clear with good visibility for a good distance and is mostly covered in pine needles. The large branches of the white pine trees provide very good cover and shelter, bending all the way down to the soil.

During my last foray in the area, I noticed a large number of high bush cranberries and rose hips as well as mushrooms, lichen, and moss in addition to the usual food plants. Animal-wise, one would come across bears, deer, elk, lynx, moose, as well as the smaller types of animals, along with beavers, hares, and muskrats.

**Investigation:** This occurrence took place about 4 km (2.5 mi) farther west than the other similar occurrence, which had taken place in July 2002 at Hall Creek, Report #29, the close-by area on Squanga Lake.

Again, this couple observed a very unusual reaction by their dog, but this time when the reporter investigated the close-by area, he came under what could be considered verbal threats in the forms of yells and shrieks. These came from an unidentified source, which, by all indications, was not a regular type of animal, as they simply do not yell nor produce shrieks of the types they experienced.

I had travelled the same area in the late 1990s and early 2000s on a few occasions. In September 2008, I spent a week investigating these two occurrences along the small river and the shorelines, camping just about at the same location where this event reportedly occurred. No signs of activity were noticed at this location or the one by Hall Creek during my investigations.

However, I did experience a mimicking vocal occurrence, along with feelings of not being wanted, at another location just about 5 km (3 mi) farther south and west of this event location and directly across the lake from the animal reaction that had occurred at Hall Creek, Report #38.

This is the third animal behaviour-related occurrence reported from the Squanga Region, along with all the other incidents making the Squanga Region one of the more active Regions in the Yukon to date that I know of.

## Report #32
## SQUANGA REGION
### Sighting West of the Community of Teslin in 2004
### Location: Coord. 60o 10'24 N 132o 45'31 W
### (Map: Teslin 105 C/2: GR 245 727)

A HUSBAND AND WIFE, both from the Teslin Tlingit Council (TTC), reported having observed a large ambulating bipedal creature crossing the Alaska Highway, Yukon Highway #1, just across from the airport at the western edge of the community of Teslin, at about 0130 hours (1:30 am), on Thursday, June 10, 2004. It was reported that the creature observed was slightly hunched over with dark hair and identified by the man as a Sasquatch. The community of Teslin is located 183 km (114 mi) east of Whitehorse on the Alaska Highway. The witnesses are two respected members of the Teslin Tlingit Council (TTC), whose names have been widely publicized through CBC North radio and the local Whitehorse newspapers.

**Encounter:** At the time, they were riding an ATV on their way home, located west of town, travelling in a westerly direction in the right-hand ditch between the Alaska Highway and the airport when they noticed what they originally thought to be a person standing beside the Highway, on the lake side of the road, their left-hand side. As it was about 0130 hours (1:30 am) they thought this person might need a lift to town.

**Geography:** There is a open ground between the road and the lake (Teslin Lake) at the location of the sighting measuring about 5 m (16 ft), while on the opposite side of the road, one finds a few balsam poplars and willow trees between the road and the airport grounds, which are, of course, open ground for about 1 km (0.6 mi) width. Then a forest of aspen, balsam poplar, and black spruce mixed with lodgepole pine exists, creeping up the slopes of gently rolling hills, making way to fairly rocky and tall mountains.

**Investigation:** These two respected First Nation members from the Teslin Tlingit Council reported the incident to the local Conservation Officer (CO) and the RCMP on the morning of Thursday, June 10, 2004. The CO went to the sighting location to investigate, only to find a group of local residents looking around as well. Nothing was found to indicate the passage of any animal or otherwise—no footprints and no hair samples could be found. Because they actually reported the sighting to the authorities and obviously to many other residents, they were showing good faith.

They certainly were convinced of what they observed standing beside the road, and then observed it crossing the road in a bipedal fashion, directly in front of them.

They are both experienced hunters and bush-wise, as the great majority of the Yukon First Nations people are, and there is no way in the world they would have mistaken a Sasquatch for anything else. The witnesses reported that they had first stopped their ATV, then turned around and approached the creature to within about 6 m (20 ft) when the Sasquatch crossed the Alaska Highway in three steps, directly in front of them. As I have travelled the part of the highway where the sighting occurred many, many times. I know the highway is a two-lane highway at that specific location.

To be more specific, I took the time to do the following measurements: each lane is 3.7 m (12 ft) wide for a total of 7.4 m (24 ft), plus a curb of 1.2 m (4 ft) on each side of the road for a total road width from ditch to ditch of 9.7 m (32 ft). The ditch on the lakeside is about 1.5 m (60 in or 5 ft) deep, while the one on the airport side is about 1 m (39 in or 3 ft 3 in) deep. If the Sasquatch was standing at the edge of the paved portion on the lakeside, it would have to cover a distance of some 8.5 m (28 ft) in three steps to get into the ditch where the witnesses were originally travelling, or 2.83 m (9.3 ft) per step.

The Sasquatch was judged to be about 213 cm tall (84 in or 7 ft). My "Quick Calculation Method" would indicate that a 215 cm (84 in or 7 ft) tall Sasquatch would have an average step of 137 cm (54 in or 4 ft 6 in). That would indicate covering about

4.14 m (163 in or 13 ft 6 in) in three steps. That distance is somewhat less than the measured distance of 8.5 m (28 ft).

If we were to calculate the same 8.5 m (28 ft) in four steps instead, that would provide an average of 237cm (7 ft 8 in) per step, which would indicate a Sasquatch being about 370 cm (12 ft 1 in) tall, which is way over the average as well. Five steps would provide a distance of 190 cm (6 ft) per step, which would indicate a Sasquatch being 295 cm (9 ft 7 in) tall, still over the average. Six steps would indicate an average step of 158 cm (5 ft 2 in) per step, which would indicate a Sasquatch being 246 cm (8 ft 1 in) tall, much closer to what is generally accepted as the average height of a Sasquatch in the Yukon, which is 254 cm (8ft 5 in). If we were to take the average North American Sasquatch height of 238 cm (94 in, or 7 ft 10 in) for a calculated step of 152 cm (60 in or 5 ft), then it would have taken the average Sasquatch six steps or three strides to cover the distance between the edge of the pavement on one side of the road to the end of the curb side of the ditch on the other side of the highway.

Problems with judging height are quite common for most people in normal life. One could misjudge someone else's height quite often, especially if the person you are looking at is taller than you are, while the opposite will occur when what you are looking at is shorter.

In this instance, there are a number of factors making the problem worse. Visibility would be the first factor, as the time of the sighting is 0130 hours (1:30 am) on June 10.

The longest day of the year is the 21st of June, which is almost total daylight in the northern portion of the Yukon, at least above the 63rd parallel of latitude, but Teslin is just above the 60th parallel of latitude and does not really get to have 24 hours of true daylight even on the 21st of June.

So, the natural light would be what one would expect it to be at around 2130 hours (9:30 am) around the 50th parallel of latitude, for example.

The second factor would be the location of the witnesses compared to that of the Sasquatch; they were in the ditch on the opposite side of the road with a distance of at least 10.5 m

(34 ft) separating them. Sitting on an ATV, their eyes would be at about the same height as the lower legs of the Sasquatch; therefore, to judge the height of the creature, they would have to look up, which provides a false height observation as previously explained.

The third factor would be the speed they were travelling when they first noticed the creature; originally, they thought that it was a person standing beside the road. It was only when they had stopped and turned back that they recognized the creature to be a Sasquatch. The speed of travel is not mentioned, but it would be quite important in the height estimation process. But the witnesses stated that they had approached within 6 m (20 ft) before it started crossing the highway. One would think they would have been moving slowly by that time; therefore, the speed of the ATV may not be that important at that point.

The fourth factor, and probably the most important, is the common human reaction when coming face to face with a creature that is not immediately recognized, especially if the creature is one that many people actually think of as a simple figment of the imagination, a legend, a myth, a tall tale related to the First Nations folklore or even an illusion. It probably took them a minute or two to recognize what it was, to accept the reality that, indeed, a Sasquatch was right there in front of them.

Most people faced with the same thing would probably shake their heads and say, "I'm seeing things. . ." Considering the estimated 213 cm (84 in or 7 ft) tall Sasquatch, as stated in the report, its footprint would have been close to 35.5 cm (14 in), its step 137 cm (54 in or 4 ft 6 in), its weight about be about 267 kg (588 lbs) if medium-sized or about 334 kg (736 lbs) if heavy in stature. Such a creature would require about 6,088 calories per day to remain healthy.

However, I would take the Sasquatch as actually being 246 cm (97 in or 8 ft 1 in) tall, based on the factor of having taken six steps or three strides to completely cross the road. That creature would have a footprint of 40.64 cm (16 in) and a step of 158 cm (62 in or 5 ft 2 in), and the medium-sized creature would weigh about 305 kg (672 lbs), while the heavy-set creature would be about 382 kg (842 lbs). Such a creature would require some 6,970 calories per day to remain healthy.

One last point: by stating the Sasquatch crossed the road in three steps, they may also have meant that it crossed the portion of the road between the two white lines, which would be only 7.4 m (24 ft).

In any case, the number of steps taken is obviously wrong, but then again, who is counting when one comes face to face with one of these forest giants? I, for one, would be too excited to accurately count the steps taken and could easily mistake five steps for three steps, or maybe they considered and called a stride a step, although we should all know by now that a stride is two steps.

On Saturday, March 14, 2015, following an article about my Sasquatch research work in a local paper named the *Yukon News*, the younger brother of the man who was riding the ATV in question contacted me mentioning that he actually was driving a pickup truck in front of the ATV on the Alaska Highway and observed the same Sasquatch, a couple of minutes before his brother and his wife observed the Sasquatch crossing the road.

Undoubtedly, this latest report lends more credibility to the original report. This First Nations man also reported a few more sightings and occurrences from the immediate area of the community of Teslin. Most of them are presented in this book.

**Report #33**
**ANVIL REGION**
**Sighting by the Lapie River in 2004**
**Location: Coord. 61o 39'18 N 132o 36'59 W**
**(Map: Quiet Lake 105 F: GR 295 675)**

A KWANLIN DÜN FIRST NATIONS FRIEND told me that a male drive had come face to face with a bipedal creature, which he identified as a Sasquatch, in the early morning hours of Friday, September 29, 2004.

**Encounter:** He reported that the large bipedal creature was standing in a small clearing beside a roadside pull-off rest area, located about two hours away from the community of Carmacks, in an easterly direction on the Robert Campbell Highway, Yukon Highway #4.

The man was on his way outside (meaning "out of the Yukon" for us Yukoners) after having worked in Dawson City during the summer, when he decided to take the Robert Campbell Highway as a shortcut to Watson Lake and farther southern destinations. After about two hours of driving, he decided to take a rest at about midnight, after previously turning onto the Robert Campbell Highway at about 2200 hours (10 pm) at Carmacks.

**Investigation:** I would calculate that a person would have covered between 190 km (120 mi) and about 220 km (135 mi) or so during that period of time. That would place the location where he stopped as being a little distance before the community of Ross River, which is located 230 km (143 mi) east of the community of Carmacks.

Having driven the very same road many times in various road conditions, with and without snow, day and night, the last time being in the summer of 2015, I know of a pull-off about 10 km (6 mi) before the left-hand turn in the direction of Ross River. Therefore, I would consider that pull-off, which is just before the Lapie River Bridge, to be the location in question.

Reportedly, the man was on his way to some other location outside of the Yukon and was taking the Robert Campbell Highway as a shortcut, rather than driving the North Klondike Highway, Yukon Highway #2, to Whitehorse and then taking the Alaska Highway, Yukon Highway #1, in an eastern direction.

There is not much difference distance-wise, but this road is more scenic and has much less traffic, even though it is not paved all the way. The road conditions are usually pretty good; however, roadside services are very limited.

As previously reported, there was a sighting in Faro in the winter of 1970 and a sighting in Ross River (Takaden'I Tue) during the winter of 1970. There was another sighting by Dragon Lake (Tuetset'i) in 1975.

The driver had stopped at a pull-off for a short sleep. After a few hours, he woke up and was ready to carry on but first went out of the vehicle to answer the call of nature. As he approached a small clearing in the forest, he noticed a strange smell, similar to a dead animal. He then ventured into the bush for about 5 m (16 ft) in the general direction of the smell to explore the cause of this strange smell.

This is when he noticed what he first thought to be a bear, bending over and appearing to be eating an animal carcass. The bipedal meat-eater then stood up, most likely realizing it had company, and began walking on two legs in the direction of the driver, with its arms swinging.

This is when the driver realized that he was actually facing a Sasquatch and not a bear. The driver then quickly ran back to his car and took off in a hurry.

The sighting report mentioned the observed meat-eater, a Sasquatch, to be about 185 cm tall (72 in or 6 ft). A Sasquatch of such stature would indicate its weight at about 229 kg (504 lbs) for a medium-sized creature and at about 286 kg (630.5 lbs) for the larger heavy-set Sasquatch. Such a creature would have a footprint of some 30.5 cm (12 in) and a step of about 117cm (46 in or 3 ft 10 in).

This size of Sasquatch would have a daily requirement of about 5,230 calories to remain healthy. A Sasquatch stated to be only about 185 cm (72 in or 6 ft) tall is well below the calculated Pacific Northwest Sasquatch average of 238.7 cm (94 in or 7 ft 10 in) tall, according to Dr. Grover Krantz and many other Sasquatch researchers, and well below the Yukon Sasquatch average of 254 cm (99 in or 8 ft 3 in) that I calculated by using various reported sightings and a number large human-like footprints discovered in the Yukon.

There are other reports from the area, check Reports #1, #2, #4, #41, and #42.

### Report #34
### TAKHINI REGION
### Sighting by the Cowley Stretch in 2006
### Location: Coord. 60o 32'02 N 134o 52'32 W
### (Map: Robinson 105 D/7: GR 075 056)

On Saturday, January 7, 2006, a woman of the Kwanlin Dün First Nation (KDFN) in Whitehorse contacted me by email reporting to have observed what she identified as a Sasquatch the evening before.

**Encounter:** That evening, the woman was driving back to Whitehorse when she observed the creature, described as a tall Sasquatch with dark hair and a sort of bluish hue reflection, standing beside a power line pole on her left-hand side of the road (west), while driving back from Carcross on the South Klondike Highway, Yukon Highway #2, on her way home to Whitehorse. She was in her late 30s at the time of the sighting.

She had spent part of the day visiting friends and relatives in the community of Carcross, some 75 km (46 mi) south of Whitehorse and was returning home with her two young children. That specific stretch of road is known by the locals as the Cowley Stretch. It is so named due to being one of the few straight stretches on this road and being in the vicinity of the Cowley Lakes.

This is located some 10 km (6 mi) south of the Carcross cut-off, which is the name given to the intersection of the Alaska Highway, Yukon Highway #1, with the South Klondike Highway, Yukon Highway #2, by the local residents. The land on both sides of the road around the sighting location is Kwanlin Dün First Nation's settlement land. The actual sighting occurred on Friday, January 6, 2006, at about 2130 hours (9:30 pm).

**Local History:** The area where the sighting occurred is part of the KDFN traditional territory, with many of its members still residing at various locations across this land enjoying fishing, hunting, and trapping as well as their traditional type of living.

In 1942, the Alaska Highway came through this area connecting the community of Caribou Crossing, now called Carcross, to Whitehorse, mostly following the rail line, which was built in 1898 and which in turn was mostly following old transportation trails used by the various First Nations of the region, conducting trade in the area and exchanging goods, a practice dating back centuries.

That had been the traditional trade route between the Pacific Coast, Coastal Tlingit, and the inland First Nations of the area, mostly Tutchone, Tagish, and Tlingit.

The South Klondike Highway was extended in the 1970s to connect the community of Carcross in a southern direction as far as the town of Skagway in Alaska, another 108 km (67 mi) farther south.

This has been the trailhead of the Chilkoot Trail, leading across the Chilkoot Pass since the First Nation Peoples came to this part of the land 8 to 7.5 Kya. The Chilkoot Trail became famous during the Klondike Gold Rush with thousands of people toiling to get over the mountains, many dying as a result on their way to the Klondike Gold Fields. The Chilkoot Trail is still in use today, as a hiker's challenge of 53 km (33 mi) with thousands of people crossing the Chilkoot Pass each summer.

The White Pass and Yukon Route Railway Company operated the rail line, between Whitehorse and Skagway, from 1899 until the closing of the Faro lead and zinc mine in 1982. Today, the rail line operates during the summer months as a visitor's attraction between Skagway, Alaska, and Carcross, Yukon, with the odd ventures to Whitehorse to maintain their railroad right of way.

**Geography:** This area is part of the northern boreal forest. The immediate area where the sighting occurred is mostly forested with black spruce and lodgepole pine, with the odd aspen and poplar tree on higher grounds, while alders and willows are found on the lower grounds. Overall, it's a rolling type of terrain with the odd depression and many fair-size rocks strewn around.

On the left-hand side, the west side of the road where the sighting took place, one finds a low-lying, swampy ground down by the small unnamed creek. The ground elevates on the right-hand side, the east side, with small but gradually larger rolling hills and eventually these hills join the northern slopes of Mount Lorne, which rises to an elevation of 2,021 m (6,630 ft).

There is a caribou herd along the slope of Mount Lorne, along with deer and moose. Other animals would include bears, coyotes, grouse, hares, foxes, lynx, wolves, wolverines, and other types of birds, along with gophers, squirrels, and other small animals of that type. The usual mountain slope types of wild plants would be found, although they were covered with snow at the time of the sighting. Food-wise at this time of the year, an animal would dig through the snow for rose hips, kinnikinnick, lichen, and moss, mostly on the south-facing slopes, while black spruce, lodgepole pine, and subalpine fir trees would present their needles, bark, and sap to chew on.

**Investigation:** There have been many reports of Sasquatch activities close by, as you will read further in the book. The person who made the report is a member of the Kwanlin Dün First Nation who has lived in the Yukon all of her life. She has relatives living in Whitehorse, Carcross, and many other locations around the Yukon. I am confident that she is a credible witness. She first contacted me by email the day following her sighting, but at the time, I was wintering in Mexico. We communicated by email through the winter, and when I returned to Whitehorse, I contacted her again, and she took me directly to the sighting location to explain the sighting one more time.

She had mentioned that it was snowing lightly at the time of the sighting. She had the wipers on, but her view was unobstructed, and she clearly saw a tall and large entity standing on two feet on the left-hand side of the road by a power line pole, identified as a Sasquatch. She stated that its left shoulder was against the pole and it was looking in the direction of her vehicle, although she could not remember the fine details of the face. However, she figured it had to be at least 213 cm (7 ft) tall.

The sighting was about ten seconds long, and I would venture to advance that the reported bluish hue observed was probably due to the headlight shining against the hairs, reflecting a light covering of snow upon it.

I would suggest readers experiment with such a reflection of light with any dark piece of fur in a dark environment. Readers would just need a slight layer of snow covering the fur and bright headlights shining directly on it from a distance of about 10 m (33 ft) or so to actually observe the effect of car lights shining on a dark piece fur while a light snow is falling.

While further communicating with the reporter, she mentioned that her uncle lives directly across the road, on the east side, where the sighting occurred. Interestingly, when she reached home, she phoned him to mention the sighting.

Her uncle told her that at about 2200 hours (10 pm) that evening, his dogs went crazy in their kennels, as he raises dogs, and he said to her that it lasted a while, and they were still barking when she called. She is definite about the sighting and has no doubt in her mind whatsoever as to the creature being a Sasquatch.

A 213 cm tall (84 in or 7 ft) Sasquatch would have footprints of about 35.5 cm (14 in) and would have a step of about 138 cm (54 in or 4 ft 6 in). A medium-sized average Sasquatch would weigh about 267 kg (588 lbs), while a larger more muscular and heavier one would weigh up to 334 kg (736 lbs). Such a Sasquatch would require approximately 6,000 calories per day to remain healthy.

I visited the location of the sighting a number of times to see if I could find any possible Sasquatch activity signs, but none were seen.

There was another sighting close to the Robinson Roadhouse in 2014, Report #59 and a vocal occurrence in 2010, Report #45.

## Report #35
## LIARD REGION
## Vocals at the Bell-Irving Rest Area in 2006
## Location: Coord, 56o 44'51 N 129o 48'08 W
## (Map: BC Highway #37, north of Meziadin Junction)

A MAN WHO WAS A TRUCK DRIVER BY TRADE contacted me by email to report that he had experienced a vocal occurrence after stopping at a roadside rest area, at around 1930 hours (7:30 pm) on Thursday, March 23, 2006.

**Local history:** This roadside rest area is located just before the Bell-Irving River Bridge, on the east side of the Cassiar Road, BC Highway #37, when driving in a southerly direction. The Cassiar Road connects the Alaska Highway, Yukon Highway #1, some 37 km (23 mi) west of the town of Watson Lake, in the Yukon, at the northern end to the Yellowhead Highway, BC, Highway #16 by the First Nation community of Kitwanga at the southern end.

This truck driver was on a regular haul, driving from the state of Alaska to the state of Washington. His route would take him on the Alaska Highway to the junction with the Cassiar Road down BC Highway #37 to the Yellowhead Highway #16, then on to the city of Prince George, where he would connect to BC Highway #97 driving south to connect with the Trans-Canada Highway at Cache Creek, BC. Then he would follow the Trans-Canada to his choice of US Border crossing along the 48th parallel of latitude into the state of Washington and onto his final destination.

Other reports from the area were previously mentioned; however, it should be noted that two sightings took place very close to this roadside rest stop: one in 1990 at the Nass River Bridge, located south of the Meziadin Junction, and another sighting in 2000, located just north of Meziadin Junction, just south from this rest stop.

As I have very limited information about the truck driver who made the report, as I did not interview him, only communicated by emails, I cannot make a judgment as to his credibility. Suffice to say that through my experience with truck drivers they are not a bunch to brag about what they have seen or experienced when on the road. Therefore, I would be inclined to accept this report as a true depiction of a vocal occurrence. This report is one of three Sasquatch-related occurrences that have occurred within a 100 km (60 mi) stretch of the Cassiar Road, all in the area of Meziadin Junction.

This road junction connects BC Highway #37 to the BC Highway #37A, which would take a person to the edge of the Pacific Ocean at the community of Stewart, BC, where the Portland Canal provides a water route through Portland Inlet to the Pacific Ocean. My last trip to Stewart was in 2011, and the land surrounding the wild area would provide a perfect home, with plenty of food for the "Wildmen" in a much warmer climate, closer to the Pacific Ocean.

**Occurrence:** The truck driver in question had stopped at the rest stop to have his dinner at about 1930 hours (7:30 pm). While his meal was heating up alongside the truck's engine, he decided to walk about, stretching his legs. As he started walking, he immediately had a feeling of being watched for some reason—a very strong feeling of not being wanted, to such a point that he experienced a hirsute effect, where hairs on the back of his neck stood erect.

He then returned to his truck and climbed aboard, as his door window was down, and the truck engine had been shut off. He could hear some sort of howling from a distance but could not quite make out what it was.

He started to eat his dinner when, a few minutes later, he heard that howl again, but now closer and much louder, which made him quite nervous, not knowing what the source of the howling was. Then a stronger feeling of not being wanted came upon him. At this point, he decided to throw his dinner into a nearby garbage can and leave the area. To do so, he had to step out of his truck and walk to the garbage can some 5 m (16 ft) away. After disposing of his dinner, as he was making his way back to the truck, he heard another louder howl, this time very close.

By now, it had been about ten minutes since he heard the first vocal, which each time appeared to be longer and louder, obviously showing that the maker of the vocals was on the move and getting closer to his location. This is when he started his truck and departed the rest area. The truck driver further attests that he had been driving for many years and had never experienced anything close to that occurrence before.

**Investigation:** Upon returning home, he decided to check out what could be the source of all this howling, and he discovered that similar vocals had previously been reported at other locations in the US. This is when he contacted me, and we communicated on a regular basis so I could gather the needed information.

There was no mention of other types of vocals, except howls accompanied by hair rising and a sense of uneasiness, a feeling of not being wanted at a certain place—a deep feeling that one must go away.

These feelings have been reported many times before, and I can vouch about such weird feelings, as I have experienced the very same thing on a few occasions.

## Report #36
## TATCHUN REGION
## Footprints Discovered around Pelly Crossing in 2006
## Location: Coord. 62o 49'20 N 136o 24'32 W
## (Map: Carmacks 115 I: GR 199 664)

I RECEIVED A PHONE CALL from a schoolteacher at the Pelly Crossing School on Friday, May 5, 2006, requesting that I take a look and investigate a number of large human-like foot impressions that had been discovered at the outskirt of the community of Pelly Crossing. The small community is located on the North Klondike Highway, Yukon highway #2, some 90 km (55 mi) north of the community of Carmacks.

**Occurrence:** These large human-like foot impressions were discovered on Thursday, May 4, 2006, by a grade seven student member of the Selkirk First Nation (SFN) who attended the school and informed his teacher, who in turn contacted me. I was contacted the following day Friday, May 5, 2006, late in the afternoon and went to Pelly Crossing on Saturday, May 6, 2006.

**Local History:** The community of Pelly Crossing came to life when the North Klondike Highway was built in 1954, which marked the end of the paddle wheelers' day. About 90 percent of the current inhabitants of Pelly Crossing are members of the Selkirk First Nation, residing around Fort Selkirk, Minto, and other locations around the region. They facilitate the administration of the Nation's affairs. The federal government strongly encouraged members of the SFN to move to Pelly Crossing, named after the Pelly River, which runs through the village. A river barge originally crossed the river at that location.

**Investigation:** When I arrived in Pelly Crossing, I contacted the schoolteacher who had called me. She was a First Nations woman, a member of the SFN, and she took me to two locations. The first location consisted of a group of six human-like foot impressions located at the local paintball range.

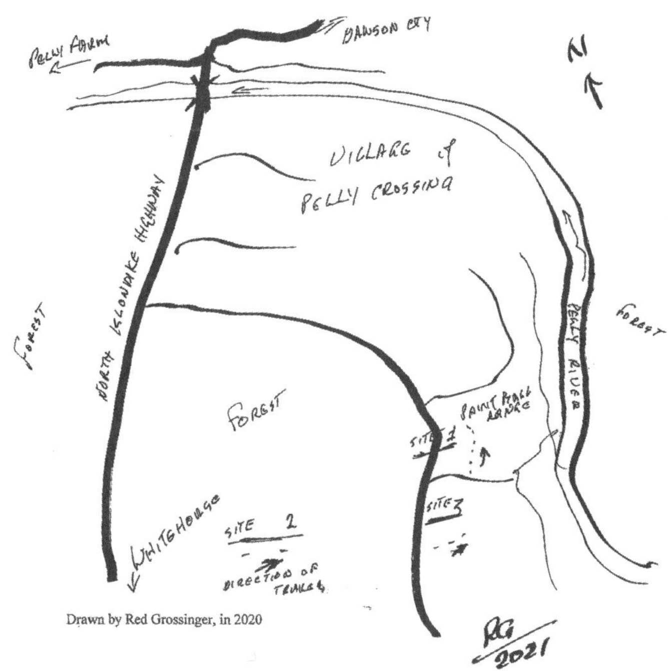


*Tatchun Region: Footprint discovery by Pelly Crossing,, May 5, 2006*

The second group of footprints, which consisted of two clear footprints, were located along a power line clearcut, about 1 km (0.6 mi) further west and had been discovered by a female member of the Selkirk First Nation Council.

While investigating around the area, I discovered another set of foot impressions about 100 m (330 ft) southeast of the original find.

The student in question was out checking his rabbit trapline (set with rabbit snares) first thing in the morning, as usual, before going to school on Thursday, May 4, 2006, when he first discovered the foot impressions around the local paintball range.

The first location consisted of a total of six large human-like foot impressions around the local paintball range. I consider these "foot impressions," as they were not clear footprints. The details of the toes were not clear enough to be considered footprints, but they were clearly done by large, human-like feet.

The foot impressions were calculated as follows: Impression number one, three, and five each measured 42.6 cm (16.75 in) and indicated a left foot, while impressions number two, four, and six measured 41.9 cm (16.5 in) and indicated a right foot. The distance of the step between foot impression number one and foot impression number two measured 147.4 cm (58 in or 4 ft 10 in). The distance of the step between foot impression number two and foot impression number three measured 158.8 cm (62.5 in or 5 ft 2.5 in). The distance of the step between foot impression number three and foot impression number four measured 160 cm (63 in or 5 ft 3 in). The distance of the step between foot impression number four and foot impression number five measured 160 cm as well (63 in or 5 ft 3 in) as well. The distance of the step between foot impression number five and foot impression number six measured 153.7 cm (60.5 in or 5 ft .5 in).

The average step distance for a 42.6 cm (16.75 in) long footprint would usually be about 164 cm (64.5 in or 5 ft 4.5 in) as calculated from my Proportion Table. This would make the print-maker about 258 cm tall (101 in or 8 ft 5 in) with an approximate medium-sized weight of 319 kg (703.5 lbs) and a heavier size print-maker of about 400 kg (882 lbs). Such a creature would need about 7,305 calories per day to remain healthy. As for the 41.9 cm (16.5 in) long footprint, the average step would be about 161 cm long (63.5 in or 5 ft 3.5 in), which makes the print-maker about 254 cm tall (100 in or 8 ft 4 in) and a weight of about 314 kg (693 lbs) for a medium-sized print-maker, while up to 394 kg (868.5 lbs) for the larger, heavier-set creature. The daily calories requirement for such a creature would be about 7,185 calories per day.

The differences from the average and the actual calculated distances can be explained due to the type of ground covering, which in this case, was moss and lichen. This type of ground covering does not provide the same accuracy of lengths or accuracy of step distances as one would expect in a sandy or muddy ground where the footprints are more detailed and better defined. Because these tracks were discovered in an area where the student had been setting rabbit snares, it would only make sense to think that the track maker would have been checking those snares as well for rabbits, expecting a free meal.

The second find consisted of a set of two large human-like footprints. They were discovered by the power line right away, and they consisted of two clear footprints a fair distance from each other, and not part of a continuous foot track, although they both pointed in the same direction.

They were in a mixed type of ground and muddy. It had been freezing at night and melting in the daytime for at least two days prior to the start of my investigation.

That would change the formation of the footprints somewhat and could not be calculated accurately as a result. They were, however, in the vicinity of 40.5 cm (16 in). A footprint of that size would indicate the print-maker to be about 247 cm tall (97 in or 8 ft 1 in) and would probably weigh about 305 kg (672 lbs) for a medium-sized creature and around 382 kg (842 lbs) for the heavy-set print-maker with a step of 156 cm (61.6 in or 5 ft 1.6 in).

Such a creature would require about 6,945 calories per day for sustaining its health. Such a measurement actually fits pretty well with the calculations made, although not quite exact.

The third set of foot impressions that I located consisted of three individual foot impressions I discovered at a distance of about 100 m (330 ft) from the paintball range. They were set in deep snow and at a depth of 30 cm (12 in) at least, and by all indications would have been made after the second set of foot impressions found and just before the first set of foot impressions found, as they were pointing towards the first set of foot impressions discovered.

These were measured at about 40.5 cm each (16 in) as well. However, this is not considered an accurate measure due to the snow and weather conditions. The measured distance of the steps was limited to about 110 cm (45 in or 3 ft 11 in), which, of course, is well below the average and other step distance measured here, again probably due to the snow condition. I should mention that I took all the measurements with the help of a local Selkirk First Nation woman.

I spent three days and two nights in the community of Pelly Crossing investigating this discovery and talked with a number of local people, most of them members of the Selkirk community. Each had some stories but nothing definitive, besides the foot impressions mentioned. During that period of time, I visited the community and walked many kilometres around town looking for further activity signs, but unfortunately, none were found. The annual general assembly meeting of the governing body for the Selkirk First Nation started on the day I was leaving town Monday, May 8, 2006, and one of the subjects of discussion was Keecho, which is the name given to Sasquatch in the region used by the local members of the Selkirk First Nation. Unfortunately, I was not invited to attend the assembly.

My investigation brought some interesting points. One of the Selkirk First Nation Elders I was talking with theorized that family groups of Keecho, another regional name for Sasquatch, actually live around the area of the Ddhaw Ghro Habitat Protection Area (formerly named the McArthur Wildlife Sanctuary) during the spring, summer, and fall, feasting on sheep and other animals. They would then migrate to the Pacific Coast area for the winter, crossing in the vicinity of the community of Pelly Crossing in the springtime and again in the fall. The Pacific coast would offer a much warmer climate and better weather conditions than that found around these parts of the Yukon.

Another Elder mentioned to me that "When the time is right. When Keecho is needed, he will come to us." The full meaning of this comment is somewhat ambiguous; the statement "... he will come to us" probably means that Kechoo will help the members of the community. But it could also be taken as expecting some rough times ahead and that Keecho will assist the community when they need him. Or I could be way off track, of course, and misinterpreting the possible meanings, as they were not actually explained to me.

Readers will note I had made mention of the Seven Secret Teachings in the "Introduction," and I mentioned the term Kietch Sa'be, whose pronunciation is very close to Keecho; however, the meaning is still the same.

## Report #37
## KENO REGION
## Sighting of Two Sasquatch by Duncan Creek Road in 2008
## Location: Coord. 63o 46'52 N 135o 29'57 W
## (Map: Keno Hill 105 D/14: GR 755 724)

I WAS CONTACTED by a Gitsegukla First Nation man who reported a sighting encounter with what he described as two Sasquatch: a male with a pregnant female.

**Encounter:** The sighting occurred on a short trail off the Duncan Creek Road, not far from Mayo Lake, located at a distance of some 20 km (12 mi) south of Keno City, at around 2000 hours (8 pm), on Tuesday, July 8, 2008. The witness was a male in his mid-60s at the time of the sighting. He was a self-employed hearing specialist, conducting hearing tests at various mine sites around the Yukon, on contract with the Yukon Workers' Compensation Health and Safety Board.

He had retired from full-time employment as a hearing technician in 2007 and then resided in New Hazelton, in Northern British Columbia, until his death in the summer of 2011. The witness was on his way to mine sites in the area of Keno City. As he was slightly ahead of schedule, he decided to stop on the Duncan Creek Road and set up camp for the night at a gravel pit before getting to the first mine site for his scheduled 1000 hours (10 am) appointment the next day, Wednesday, July 9, 2008.

**Local History:** The area around Keno has been prospected and mined since the turn of the twentieth century. First it was for silver, zinc, and lead. Now, it is mostly gold and silver, mined in the summertime with small family-type operations. Since the summer of 2010, a large-sized silver mine has been operating on a year-round basis by a mining company Alexco in the area just east and within the limits of Keno City. As of 2019, another large mining outfit, Victoria Gold, has opened a large mining operation in the area, with a residential camp for over two hundred and fifty miners. These workers are two weeks in-camp and two weeks out-of-camp (2IN-2OUT, as it is known). Since then, the Yukon's Air Line, Air North, has been providing regular flight service to the Mayo Airport from Whitehorse.

**Encounter continues:** This sighting location is just on the opposite side, southeast of a previous sighting close to the community of Elsa, which occurred in 1995 on the northwest side of Galena Hill. The location of this sighting is about 10 km (6 mi) away and directly over Galena Hill in a southeast direction as the raven flies.

The man in question reports that he had set up his three-ton truck fitted with his hearing testing equipment, a bedroom, and a kitchen/dining room, in a small clearing that had previously been a small gravel pit, ready to camp for the night. He had eaten dinner and at about 1900 hours (7 pm), decided to take a short walk along a small trail, which he later found out would lead to Duncan Creek. He reached the creek around 1910 hours (7:10 pm) or so and spent some time looking around for interesting rocks and that sort of thing. Around 1930 hours (7:30 pm) or shortly thereafter, he decided to return to his truck.

He mentioned that as he was making his way back to his truck, he was going up a small incline over mostly hard gravel soil with the odd sandy spots. The bush was quite dense, although the trees were not so large around the immediate area, mostly black spruce, white pines, willows, and occasionally birch trees. He then came to a slight right-hand bend in the trail, and as he proceeded, he suddenly came face-to-face with the two Sasquatch at a distance of about 3 m (10 ft) or so, directly in front of him, walking on the same trail in his direction.

He was surprised, to say the least. He then noticed the female Sasquatch, which was originally walking beside and mostly in front of the male. But, during the encounter, she immediately went behind the male, for protection it would appear, as soon as she noticed the the man in question. This is when the witness noticed that she was pregnant and was what he described as "ready to pop" (his words), meaning that she was just about ready to give birth.

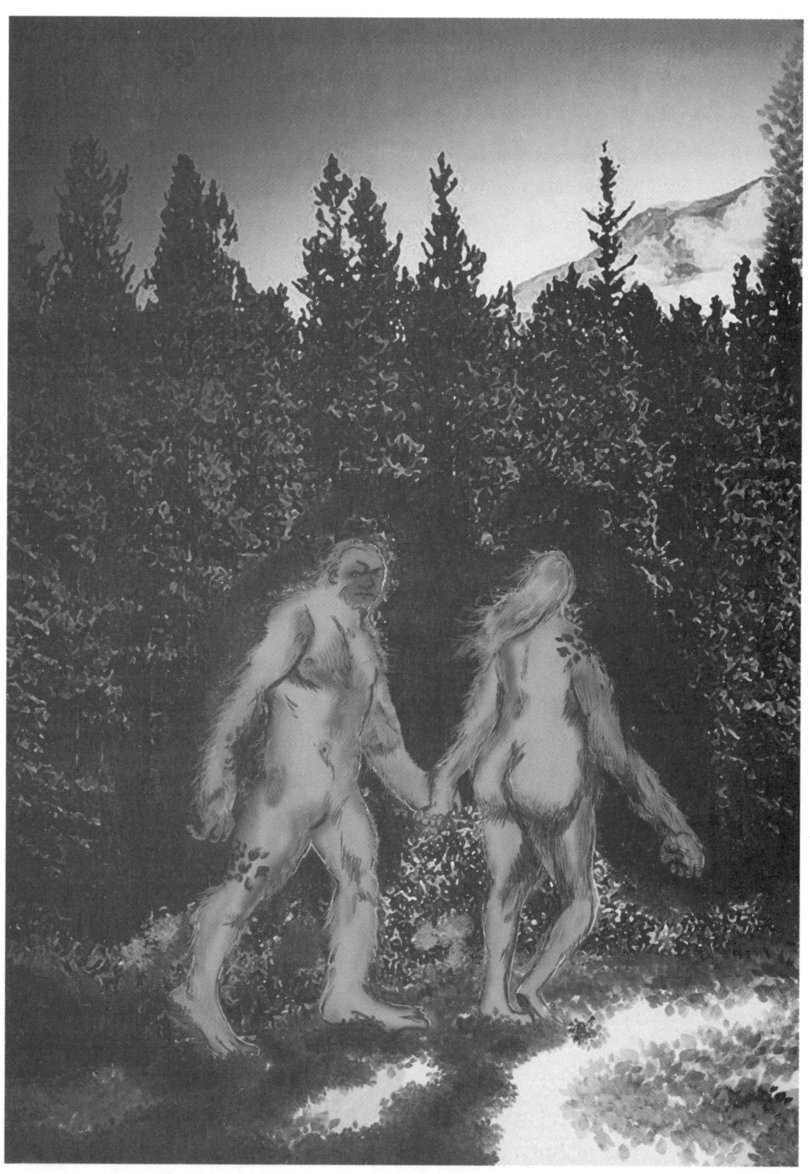

*"The gigantic male looked at me with a grimace…not happy to see me on the same trail, obviously. I then brought my right hand to my heart, then offered my hand to him, palm up…in a sign of friendship. They must have understood…the male's grimace was now gone, but he kept looking at me. They then silently walked into the forest and became invisible."*
*Illustration: Rich Théroux*

Both the male and female Sasquatch stopped walking at that moment as well. At first, the male showed teeth in a grimace of sort, as the witness reported, but made no sounds or vocals at all. The witness then stated that they all stood still for a moment, which seemed to him like minutes.

A few seconds later, while still facing the Sasquatch, the witness made hand gestures by first bringing his open right hand to his heart and presenting his open hand forward to the Sasquatch, palm up, in a sign of friendship. He did the same gesture about three or four times, as he recalled, and the male Sasquatch then became less agitated and no longer grimaced.

Then, the witness reports, he pointed to the sky with his right hand, as it was starting to cloud over and would probably rain in a few minutes, trying to send a message that it was going to rain soon. He then made another gesture with his left hand, showing that he would get out of their way by walking around them into the bush, to their right-hand side (his left) to let them have the trail. He communicated this by gesturing with his left hand and placing his right hand upon the left-hand side of his chest. Then, the reporter slowly started walking to his left, in an attempt to enter the bush.

All of sudden, both Sasquatch swiftly moved in the direction of the bush to their left and silently disappeared from view, without a single sound.

He mentions that specific point because he could no longer see them nor hear them walking in the bush: they made no noise whatsoever. Nothing like the sound a human being or a large animal would make while walking on soil covered with brush debris, broken branches, and dead leaves in a dense bush.

The reporter stated, at the time, that he thought the Sasquatch just sort of disappeared into thin air rather than walked away in a normal fashion and with the normal forest walking sounds. The man further mentioned that it took him a while to really and fully understand what had happened and realized that indeed he had come face-to-face with two Sasquatch.

He was obviously in shock for a while and had to first acknowledge the importance of the encounter in order to think clearly.

**Investigation:** The witness first contacted me through email the morning after the encounter on Wednesday, July 9, 2008, and we met at his campground site when he came back to Whitehorse the following weekend, on Saturday, July 13, 2008.

During the interview, the witness mentioned that the male Sasquatch would have been about 213 cm tall (84 in or 7 ft), big, very large, with a sturdy and very muscular physique. The male Sasquatch had long legs and very long, visibly muscular arms, hanging from huge shoulders, with the fingers sort of curled-in and facing to the rear. The hands were hanging just below their knees. Both Sasquatch were covered with long and dark shaded hair. The reporter did not venture any guess as to their possible weight, as he said that "I could not state a person's weight to save my own life."

As well, the reporter could not provide specific details of the skin around the face, other than it was dark, the eyes were rather small, and the shape of the nose like that of a boxer. He could not provide details as to the shape of the forehead nor the shape of the head, as the reporter stated that he did not even think about those features and details, probably due to his state of nervousness and possible shock.

He did notice the mouth of the male Sasquatch, however, as the Sasquatch made a sort of grimace while showing his teeth in a sort of facial distortion. The witness mentioned the lips being sort of greyish brown with dirty off-white greyish teeth, which were very human-looking. The mouth was elongated and large with what appeared to be prominent lips and a prominent chin, but the chin was not overly protruding in any way. There were no specific details concerning the female Sasquatch, except that she was pregnant and moved behind the male, as a movement of self-protection, I would think.

A few points are quite interesting in this encounter, such as the communication by the use of gestures and hand signals for example. It would appear that both Sasquatch understood the meaning of the hand gestures, as expressed by their responses to the gestures and their resulting calmness.

It would also appear that they understood that the witness

wished to move into the bush of his own accord, to give them the right of way, and they obviously meant to do no harm to the witness, as they actually gave him the trail.

The movement of the female Sasquatch is indicative of a human familiarity trait, as she was counting on the male Sasquatch for protection by moving behind him, away from the man on the same trail, directly in front of them.

As an investigator, these points demonstrate a certain amount of high intelligence on the part of the Sasquatch, such as understanding the meaning of the hand gestures, understanding that there was no danger from the witness, and sort of agreeing that the trail had to be shared by both parties.

This makes me wonder that if Sasquatch understands some simple things, such as hand gestures, they must then have an ability to communicate with each other and share ideas, thoughts, and other traits related to intelligence and sense of protection. The manner by which they disappeared is also interesting—in a swift silent type of movement not noticeable by the witness: "as if floating into thin air without making a sound," as the witness stated. Very few entities, if any, can move into our Yukon's forests without making sounds, due to the large amount of dead wood debris, loose broken branches lying on the ground, regular forest debris of dried-out plants, dead leaves, and grasses cracking under our feet with each footstep taken.

The manner in which the fingers were curled and faced to the rear, rather than to the side of the body as most humans would, is also significant, as the same thing was reported in a sighting which occurred in the Takhini Region in July of 2011 by Crestview.

The observed manner of disappearing, becoming invisible or moving out of sight is also presented in a sighting report from the Copper Ridge area of Whitehorse dating from 1992, Report #15, as well as the sighting report from the Crestview area of Whitehorse in 2011, Report #47. Also, another sighting in 2011 by Moose Creek, Report #50 mentions shape-shifting or invisibility while changing shape.

As for statistical details, a 213 cm (84 in or 7 ft) tall Sasquatch would have a footprint of about 35.56 cm (14 in) with a step calculated at about 137 cm (54 in or 4 ft 6 in) such a print-maker would have a weight of some 267 kg (588 lbs) on average for the medium size and some 334 kg (736 lbs) for the larger, heavier type. Such a creature would require about 6,100 calories per day to remain in good health.

**Report #38**
**SQUANGA REGION**
**Vocals on the Shores of Squanga Lake in 2008**
**Location: Coord. 60o 29'22 N 133o 42'28 W (Map: Squanga Lake 105 C/5: GR 723 060)**

IN MID-SEPTEMBER of 2008, I was out investigating a number of strange occurrences involving reported unusual behaviour and strange reactions from dogs, as well as vocals and tree-thrashing occurrences that had taken place around the area of Squanga Lake, Hall Creek, and Little Squanga Lake, Reports #29 & 31, when I experienced a series of mimicking sounds coming from the close-by forest on the western shores of Squanga Lake.

**Occurrence:** This activity took place on day eight of a planned ten-day expedition, Wednesday, September 17, 2008, when I had been investigating various occurrences reported to me. I was slowly making my way back to the Yukon Government Campground from the south end of the lake when I decided to camp on a high and dry point of land on the west shore of Squanga Lake for a couple of days. This location is well-protected from the wind by fair-sized lodgepole pines and black spruces. At this time of the year, I had noticed that the vegetation consisted mostly of lichen and thick moss, along with high bush and low bush cranberries and plenty of rose hips, with the usual assortment of Labrador tea and other small wild plants around the campsite.

Up until now, the weather had been quite decent, mostly sunny in the daytime with temperatures running between 8 to 10 degrees C (41 to 50 F), going down to between about -5 degrees C (23 F) and -10 degrees C (14 F) or so at night. It had rained a couple of times during the day, but not enough to cause any worries. However, I had noticed that around 1500 hours (3 pm) or so, just about every day, the wind would come up drastically and made navigating the lake a bit tricky. I was using a four-metre-long squared-stern Canadian Tire canoe with an electric trolling motor and two batteries, although most of the time, I had been paddling in order to save the limited energy provided by the batteries. I had arrived at this campsite at about 1600 hours (4 pm) on Tuesday, September 16, 2008, planning to stay here for a few days in order to explore a bit more around the area and generally keeping an eye out for any activities that take place around Hall Creek, which was located directly across the lake from this campsite at a distance of only 1.3 km (1 mi).

After a hot dinner of ham and beans, I got my pipe out relaxing by the lake for a while, then spent a bit of time catching a couple of northern pike, which I returned to the water as I had had my share of fish on this trip, pike, trout, and whitefish.

Around 1900 hours (7 pm), I started a campfire, lit another pipe, opened a beer, relaxed in the heat of the campfire, and just enjoyed the early evening sceneries for a couple of hours. With a clear sky, I knew that it was going to get cold that night. I just listened to the wilderness around me, to the birds chirping and the squirrels gathering food for the winter. I watched the numerous flocks of ducks, swans, geese, and loons gathering on the close by water, getting ready for their annual fall voyage south, flying away from the coming cold weather of the Yukon.

After gathering a good amount of firewood that I would need in the morning, I went to bed at about 2100 hours (9 pm). The tent was nice and warm, as I had lit a lantern about half an hour before to take the chill out of the air. Any fool could go to bed in a cold tent, so why not warm up the place first? At around 2330 hours (11:30 pm) and again at about 0300 hours (3 am), I had got up to answer the call of nature (as I usually do every night), and all was calm and quiet.

At 0600 hours (6 am) or so on the 17th, I got up again. As I got out of the tent this time, I noticed that it was about -10 degrees C (14 F) with frost everywhere. This is when I started coughing due to that cold air hitting my lungs.

To my surprise, out in the bush in a westerly direction and what seemed to be just a few metres away, I heard a loud coughing sound, much the same as the sound I made while coughing. For a moment or so, I just could not believe what I had heard. I knew for a fact that there was not any echo from this location, as

I had yelled a few times the evening before, something that most Sasquatch investigators would do to entice a possible Sasquatch reaction when out in the bush.

There had not been any echo returns at the time. There had not been any answer for that matter, so why would there be one in the morning? In any case, a few minutes later, I coughed again, and again, I heard a mimicking cough, this time though it was much more like mine, more refined, clearer, and the sound appeared to be a bit closer still.

Strange indeed. For the next few minutes, I got busy getting the campfire started and putting the coffee on. I coughed a few more times, and sure enough, the same mimicking sound was returned to me each time.

I was now convinced that some creature was in the bush trying to make contact with me or responding to my cough in some way. I tried to figure out if any large animals would make such a sound. Bears do not, for sure, as they would growl and would not stick around a human unless such a bear wanted the human out of the way, and then they would simply walk into the campsite to get whatever food odour had attracted them. Not a moose either, as they would grunt and call in a different manner but would not stay close by. An elk would make a grunting and huffing sound as well, but not as clear a mimicking sound as the one that I had heard, and they certainly would not stay around divulging their presence to a human. They simply do not share space with humans here.

I made a breakfast of toast with peanut butter and raspberry jam with a few cups of nice hot coffee. There were no further sounds, as I had stopped coughing.

After about an hour or so, for some unknown reason, a confusing feeling came upon me, a feeling of not being wanted, a sense of fear for no apparent reason, and hairs started to become erect on the back of my neck. Gradually, I acquired a strange deeper feeling of uneasiness, with the thought that I was no longer safe in this location, something that is very hard to explain. However, this type of feeling had been reported to me by other people who'd had a Sasquatch encounter at some time.

By about 0830 hours (8:30 am) I was not feeling well at all, with a sickening apprehension, dizziness and slow-moving decision making. I had a presentiment that something bad would happen soon. By now, I was totally confused, for whatever reason, and decided to start packing the camping gear and return to the safety of the YTG Campground just some 7 km (4.3 mi) away. This campground is located beside the Alaska Highway, Yukon Highway #1, and that is where I had left my travel trailer and my truck.

I departed at about 0900 hours (9 am), keeping close to the western shores, hoping to see something, hoping that my visitor would show up at the last minute. I had no such luck though; everything was calm. My only excitement was that my last battery soon died off, and I still had about five kilometres to paddle. Good thing there were no winds just yet.

Finally, just before noon, I arrived at the Yukon Government Campground and started unloading the gear off the boat. I left the boat at the dock, as I still had a couple of days left before having to return to Whitehorse, and my intention was to get back on the water after recharging the batteries and have another look around my last campsite location and Hall Creek.

I went back to my trailer, started the generator to charge up the batteries, and relaxed for most of the afternoon. I cooked a steak for dinner with a few glasses of wine and went to bed early, hoping to hit the water early the next morning. The following morning the snow started—completely changing my plans.

**Assessment:** Truthfully, I do not know what entity was trying to communicate with me, using what sounded to me like mimicking. I'm not sure what it was all about.

I had gone through the list of various big-game animals that make this forest home in my mind, and none would fit the sound made by that sound-maker that day. What I know for sure is that it was not a common animal; therefore, all I can only suggest is that indeed one of our Wild Men, a friendly Sasquatch, one of our forest-dwelling, gentle giants had made an attempt to communicate with me that day in September.

**Report #39**
**KLUANE REGION**
**Sighting at the Summit of the Chilkat Pass in 2008**
**Location: Coord. 59o 70'36 N 136o 60'67 W**
**(Map: Tatshenshini River 114P: GR 012 017)**

TWO MEN FROM ALASKA, on their way to catch a ferry at Haines, Alaska, reported to have observed two very tall human-like creatures, somewhere close to the "summit." At the time, they were digging their car out of the ditch along the British Columbia portion of the Haines Road, Yukon Highway #3, about 25 km (15 mi) before the Canada/USA Border at the top of the Chilkat Pass. This location is commonly referred to as "The Summit" by the locals from the Yukon and Alaska.

This sighting occurred in the early hours of Thursday, October 30, 2008. Readers will note that this is located inside British Columbia, but I decided to include it in the Kluane Region for ease of reading.

**Local History:** The Haines Road, Yukon Highway #3, was originally built in 1943 in order to connect the Alaska Highway, Yukon Highway #1, which was had been constructed in 1942, to the seaport of Haines, Alaska, in order to facilitate the transportation of required goods and ammunition to Alaska, which had been under attacks by the Japanese Forces. This area is part of the traditional land of the Champagne and Aishihik First Nation (CAFN) of the Yukon as well as the Klukwan Tlingit First Nation of Alaska.

**Geography:** The northwestern side of the Haines Road is part of the Kluane Wildlife Sanctuary in the Yukon, and then the Tatshenshini-Alsek Provincial Park from the Yukon/BC border as far as the BC/Alaska border, which is also the Canada/USA border, and then the Glacier Bay National Park on the Alaskan US side of the border. As the name indicates, the sighting location is the top of the summit of the Chilkat Pass at an elevation of some 1,065 m (3,493 ft).

Mostly void of significant trees, the area is covered with

small plants, dwarf trees, herbs, berries, and flowers in the summertime. The area abounds with blueberries in season as well as rose hips, cranberries, and similar low plants berries. There are millions of gophers as well and many smaller animals along with a healthy moose population and many roaming grizzly bears.

**Encounter:** The men reported they had driven from Tok, Alaska, through Beaver Creek, Yukon, arriving in Haines Junction late in the evening of Wednesday, October 29, 2008, around 2330 hours or so (11:30 pm). They decided to carry on driving to Haines, Alaska, in the dark and during a snowstorm. Not a wise decision, I might add.

At around 0200 hours (2 am) the snowstorm they had been fighting became more intense, and the visibility was so bad they had to slow down to a speed of about 25 kph or so (15 mph).

At about that time, their car went off the road, slowly slipping into the right-hand ditch. Throughout the night, they had make several attempts to get the car back on the road but without success. During one of these attempts, one of the men noticed a dark figure, standing and watching them from the top of a cliff, which was reported to be about 7 m (23 ft) high and just about 20 m (20 yds) away in an eastern direction.

The witness states that they had no idea how long this creature had been watching them: it just stood still, not moving, nor making any noise, just watching. One of the travellers decided to grab a machete from the trunk of the car and started waving it around in an attempt to scare away the creature watching them. That seemed to work, as the creature in question walked away after a few minutes.

However, about five minutes later, another ambulating creature appeared. This one was much taller than the first and judged to be about 275 cm (9 ft) tall and heavily built, according to the witness, with shoulders over 1 m (39 in) wide, with very dark long hair, probably about 25 cm (10 in) long, blowing in the wind. At this point the smaller creature came into view as well. It probably was the first creature observed, just behind the tall one. The tall creature stood there watching them, bobbing up and down, then going down in what would be a crouched-over position, just like a football linebacker, with his hand below his knees but not touching the snow.

The traveller who had scared off the first creature, so it would appear, mentioned that he should do the same thing again, but his partner persuaded him not to and they both got in the car, locking the doors. Some ten minutes or so later, both creatures departed and once again, they were alone in the ditch and the dark night.

About an hour later, having decided to try getting the car back on the road, they exited their car and started to shovel again, when a set of lights came up from behind them. That vehicle slowed down, just like they had done. That vehicle, a small red truck, slipped into the ditch as well, just behind them. This is when they noticed the driver: an elderly lady with white hair.

As they all worked trying to get the elderly lady's truck back on the road first, another set of lights became visible, and luckily it was a Yukon Department of Highways' snow plow this time.

As is the custom in these parts, the truck pulled both vehicles out of the ditch. The driver of the plow truck must have known the elderly lady, as he called her by name and mentioned that she should have known better than to drive in these conditions, according to the witnesses.

**Investigation:** Having driven the very same road on many occasions myself, in all seasons and often in the winter, I know how dangerous it can be. My last winter trip over that road took place in mid-December 2013. As well, in October each year, I would drive to Haines, Alaska to catch Coho salmon. So I know the road well.

In the fall of 2018, I conducted an investigation to locate the exact point where these gentlemen went into the ditch, and by using all available information, as well as the land, I concluded the location to be as mentioned above.

It just so happens that one of my friends, who is an Algonquin First Nation woman from an area close to Pembroke, Ontario, had been working at the Canada/USA Border Post of Pleasant

Camp, as a Canadian Border Agent for a ten-year period at the time, and she was there in October 2008 when this encounter took place. After being informed of this sighting by one of her friends in Haines, Alaska, she got the full story, which she later passed on to me.

The closest Highway Maintenance Camp, responsible for this stretch of the road and operated by the Yukon Government Department of Highways, is located at the Yukon/BC border at Camp Blanchard, about 55 km (32 mi), at Km 145, Haines Road.

Later, in Haines, Alaska, where they had stopped to get something to eat before catching the ferry, they overheard a conversation amongst local residents who were talking about Sasquatch, one saying that he had noticed Sasquatch in the vicinity of The Summit recently.

The two witnesses were totally convinced they had seen two Sasquatch at the Chilkat Pass Summit, a.k.a. the Haines Summit, certainly not bears out from hibernation or anything else, and both Sasquatch were in view for a good ten minutes.

The tallest Sasquatch reportedly was about 275 cm (9 ft or 108 in) tall. Such a creature is somewhat above the Pacific Northwest average of 238 cm (94 in or 7 ft 10 in) and a 275 cm (108 in or 9 ft) tall creature would have footprints of close to 45.72 cm (18 in). It would have a weight of about 343 kg (756 lbs) for a medium-built one and some 430 kg (948 lbs) for the heavier creature. Such a Sasquatch would have a step of some 176 cm (69 in or 5 ft 9 in) and would require about 7,876 calories per day to remain healthy.

The average medium-sized Sasquatch in the Pacific Northwest, as mentioned, is about 238 cm (94 in or 7 ft 10 in) tall and leaves footprints behind that are about 39 cm (15.5 in). A medium-sized creature weighs some 290 kg (640 lbs), while the heavier-set ones would weigh about 364 kg (803.5 lbs) and would have a step of about 151 cm (59 in). Such a print-maker would require about 6,714 calorie per day to be healthy.

How could a Sasquatch of that size survive in the area in question? Personally, I know there is plenty of food close by to not only survive, but to thrive on, as in this area one finds the

Kluane Wildlife Sanctuary, the Tatshenshini-Alsek Provincial Park and the Glacier Bay National Park. Each of these parks has strict no hunting regulations.

Therefore, plenty of large animals from deer to moose, in addition to smaller animals and fish close by, as well as various plants that provide food all year round. For many years this is the location where I would get my blueberries and some Saskatoon berries on my way to visit my friend at Pleasant Camp, the Canadian border post.

I still visit the community of Haines, Alaska, a couple of times a year to go fishing and keep looking for any possible signs of Sasquatch activities. This is the only report from the area of the Chilkat Summit.

**NOTE:** Readers should not confuse the "Chilkat Pass," located on Yukon Highway #3, where this sighting took place with the "Chilkoot Pass."

The latter is located further southeast, crossing the Alaska/ BC border on the famous Chilkoot Trail, the "Trail of '98" out of Skagway, Alaska.

## Report #40
## LIARD REGION
## Foot Track and Cave Discovered by Anderson Pass Creek in 2009
## Location: Coord. 61o 38'36 N 128o 34'16 W
## (Map: Ostensibility Creek 105 H/9: GR 308 290)

A MAN, who had been an acquaintance of mine for years, reported that he, along with his uncle, came across a series of footprints, described as a foot track, eventually leading to a small cave. The track is located on the southern and lower slopes of an unidentified mountain just north of Anderson Pass Creek and west of the Nahanni Range Road, starting about 3 km (2 mi) north of the Hyland River airstrip, beside the Nahanni Range Road close to where the largest bridge on that road is located.

**Occurrence:** This was reported to me by a young man, in his mid-20s at the time, who is a member of the Fort Selkirk First Nation (SFN) and who I have known for a number of years. He was on a hunting trip with his uncle, who is a member of the Liard First Nation, along the Nahanni Range Road in October of 2009 when they came upon fresh moose tracks on the road, about 5 km (3 mi) north of the airstrip.

They decided to follow the tracks which led them to cross the Hyland River in a generally westerly direction just north of the Anderson Pass Creek. A short distance later, they came across the track of a much different type of creature, with distances of some 152 cm (60 in or 5 ft) between steps.

This is when the First Nation Elder, the uncle of the reporter, identified the tracks as having been made by a Sasquatch. They decided to follow that track path instead of the moose track.

The track path they were following was located in a swampy area, frozen muskeg with numerous small creeks and waterways going every which way, with large mountains, up to 2,000 m (6,562 ft) in just about all directions around them. At the lower elevations, the types of trees were mostly black spruce with alders and willows mixed around the small bushes.

The witnesses informed me that it was a very difficult terrain to walk due to the multitude of dead trees found on the ground. After following the tracks for about three hours, he mentioned that he had actually lost track of the distance by that time, but they were going at a steady pace through mostly frozen muskeg, so the going was slow but steady as they ascended the lower slopes of a mountain.

From what I could gather from the young fellow in question, I would estimate a maximum distance of 8 km (5 mi) at the most was covered before they came upon a small cave entrance.

In a regular forested area in this part of the world, with the usual dead trees in the way, and mostly made of black spruce and lodgepole pine with the usual willows, a human being can usually walk at about 3 km (2 mi) an hour at a steady constant pace, without frequent long stops.

As the ground deteriorates, the speed of advance will be slower, and therefore, a shorter distance will be covered in the same period of time.

In this case, the ground was frozen muskeg covered with snow. It was frozen enough that they were not breaking through the frozen muskeg, but the snow impeded their advance to some degree making walking slower than usual, so the described distance may be a bit off.

As they arrived at the entrance of a small cave, they first noticed some bones of various sizes scattered about inside and outside of the entrance. They cautiously approached and noticed a strong smell, like rotten meat, but then the Elder mentioned that they were not safe there and stated they should not enter the cave.

They decided not to enter, and started to return to their truck instead, fearing for their safety. The young fellow mentioned that they were experiencing a feeling of anxiety when they were at the cave entrance, sort of not being wanted at the place—a feeling they must leave. When I asked him the reason for such a feeling, he could not explain what suddenly came upon them.

**Investigation:** A step of 152 cm (5 ft) would indicate a print-maker weighing about 295 kg (651 lbs), having a footprint of about 39 cm (15.5 in) and being about 238 cm (94 in or 7 ft 9 in) tall. Such an entity would probably require some 6,688 calories per day to remain alive.

This is one location that I wish to visit at the very first possible opportunity, as the witness confirmed that he would take me there. We had plans for the summer of 2011, but he was then employed at the old Faro mine site doing some recuperation work all summer long and we could not squeeze in enough free time to get there during that summer.

I was last on the Nahanni Range Road in August 2017 and did not notice anything out of the ordinary.

The reporter has since moved to British Columbia, and I have lost touch with him.

# *The 2010s*

## Report #41
## ANVIL REGION
## Vocals by the Magundy River in 2010
## Location: Coord. 62o 04'44 N 133o 21'26 W (Map: Faro 105 K/3: GR 859 838)

A WOMAN from the Ross River Dena Council (RRDC) contacted me to report that she and her husband had recently been subjected to extremely loud uneasy shrieks, scary yells, and debris thrown at them for a good ten minutes while they were out checking their trap line on the north shore of the Magundy River, deep in a restricted access canyon with high, rocky walls on both sides of the river, in mid-February 2010.

This spot is located about 16 km (10 mi) directly south of the community of Faro, across the Pelly River and across the Robert Campbell Highway, Yukon Highway #4. The Magundy River flows in a westerly direction from its source east of Fox Mountain to empty into the Little Salmon Lake.

This First Nations couple, in their late 20s at the time, are members of the Ross River Dena Council (RRDC) and have lived in the area of Ross River all their lives. They took up residence in the community of Faro shortly after they were married, and both were employed by a local air transport company in the summer. In the winter, they would make a living from trapping animals for their pelts.

**Geography:** This particular area of their trap line is extremely rugged and restricted, located in a deep rocky canyon with tall rock walls of some 12 to 15 m (35 to 50 ft) high on both sides of the trail, with a width of about 10 m (33 ft) between the walls at the bottom. These walls, forming a canyon, would go for about 30 m (100 ft) or so from where they experienced the vocals before opening again and getting wider. This area can only be accessed in the winter with snow machines, once the ground is properly covered with deep snow, or in the summer by helicopter.

The vegetation consists mostly of thick black spruce, some of them broken off and short willow brushes covering a mostly frozen swampy ground, although with a few open areas where the water flows faster, and which was not totally frozen at the time. There are plenty of small animals in the immediate area, such as foxes, hares, lynx, porcupines, wolverines, and others, which were the animals the couple were setting the traps for.

There are moose as well. On the higher grounds one finds deer, elk, woodland caribou, along with bears and cougars. (Bears would have been hibernating in dens at this time of the year.) Wild plants are plentiful as well, especially in the low grounds.

**Investigation:** I was contacted by the woman in question by email in May of 2010. She invited me to meet them in Faro whenever I could get there, which I managed to do in July of 2010 and conducted an interview with the woman, as her husband was away at a mining exploration camp.

She was very open during the interview and provided me with whatever details she could remember. There were actually two different vocal occurrences that she reported to me from two different locations around Faro. One of these experiences occurred along the Magundy River, this one and the other one, on a trail leading to Swim Lake, which is part of the next report. Because of the forwardness and the honesty shown by this First Nations woman, along with the minute details she provided me, I consider the witness to be very credible.

**Occurrence:** Here are the details of what took place. They had taken off from their Faro home early that cold February morning while it was still dark outside, each driving their own snow machine and each pulling a sleigh because they were off to check their trap lines across the Pelly River around the Magundy River Valley as they had done many times before in 2010 and in previous years.

They had arrived at the canyon from the east side and had to get through it in order to check their traps located on the other side of this canyon. The plan was to continue in a westerly direction and finally return home in the late afternoon. They would be covering about 100 km (60 mi) that day and hopefully fill their sleighs with all the animal pelts they could get.

As they entered the canyon, at about 1200 hours (noon), they were immediately greeted by extremely loud and scary yells, with shrieking guttural sounds, coming from both sides and above the walls of the canyon, from two specific and different locations at the same time, which simply "scared the hell out of us" (as she told me).

They had stopped by now, really confused and seriously scared; they could not see what was making all the racket, so they made the decision to turn around and get out of the canyon, as continuing seemed futile and possibly dangerous.

Because of the type of terrain they were in and the limited room provided to manoeuvre their snow machines, it took them a while to turn around, close to ten minutes, I was told. The entire time, they were subjected to yells, screams, shrieks, and then a few small logs and debris thrown over the canyon's walls by two or three entities fairly close to them, up on the canyon.

They finally managed to turn around and got out of the area as fast as they could, only stopping a couple of times to empty more traps before making it back home by late evening.

The following day they discussed what had happened to them with relatives, who were convinced they had come upon a family group of Sasquatch out hunting or possibly residing somewhere close to where this occurrence had taken place.

It was mentioned by the couple's relatives, all of them members of the Ross River Dena Council, that the Sasquatch were probably checking the couple's very own traps that they had set back in November and December of 2009, for the animals caught in them would have been an easy source of food and relatively plentiful.

This was not necessarily shocking news to the couple, as upon returning to the safety of their house they had figured out that the Wildmen of the forest were obviously the source of all the yelling and shrieking; however, hearing from family members did confirm what had evolved in their own minds.

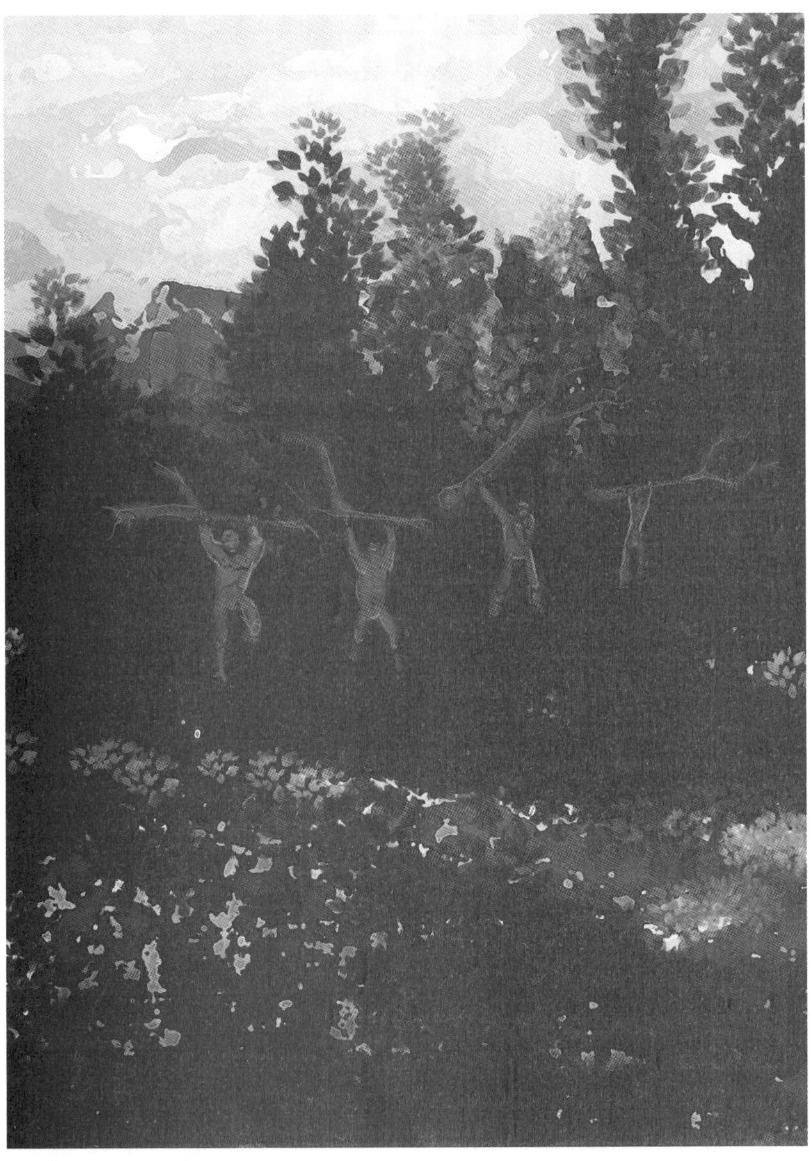

*"They were throwing dead trees, and other debris at us from high above the canyon walls. There seemed to be three or four of them. We were stuck in the Magundy River Canyon trying to turn our snow machines around. We were scared and they kept throwing stuff. So much for collecting other animals from our trap line on the other side of the canyon."*
*Illustration: Rich Théroux*

The couple have not returned to this canyon on the Magundy River since, abandoning their few traps they had on the west side of the canyon. The witness told me that they actually removed those on the east side during another trip a week or so later.

They have since moved a good portion of their trap line to a more friendly location further north and east and a bit closer to the Robert Campbell Highway as well as to their home in the community of Faro.

I was also informed of another vocal occurrence they had experienced in the spring of 2010 while on their way to fish at a small lake, named Swim Lake, Report #42.

This woman's father, who is a RRDC member as well, is the person who provided information concerning Reports #1 & 2.

## Report #42
## ANVIL REGION
## Vocals and Tree Thrashing beside the Swim Lake Trail in 2010
## Location: Coord. 62o 10'51 N 133o 04'24 W
## (Map: Faro 105 K/3: GR 004 957)

WHILE CONDUCTING an investigation concerning a vocal occurrence which consisted of strange loud and scary vocals, which a Ross River Dene Council (RRDC) couple were subjected to, along with loud shrieks for about ten minutes with logs thrown at them on the shores of the Magundy River, south of Faro, Report #41, the First Nations woman I was interviewing further mentioned the following occurrence to me.

**Occurrence:** On Thursday, April 15, 2010, she and her husband were on their way to Swim Lake to fish for whitefish, which are particularly delicious at that time of the year. They were walking on a small trail about 17 km (10.3 mi) east of the community of Faro. The trail is a bit further from Blind Creek and up a steep hill where a small unnamed creek crosses the trail. About 3 km (2 mi) before the west end of Swim Lake is where, once again, they were subjected to loud shrieks and yells.

**Geography:** The small trail in question is located on the slopes of an unnamed mountain on the east side of Blind Creek and immediately to the west of Swim Lake. The terrain is pretty soft with mostly clay and sandy type of soil covered with leaves and deadfalls. The trees are very dense in the immediate area, comprised mostly of aspen, birch, and poplar, with a few alders and willow trees at the lower elevation and along the creek bed.

The odd white spruce hang on the side of the mountain, and wild plants abound as well. Mount Mye, at an elevation of 2,061 m (6,762 ft), just across and west of Blind Creek, is well known for its large population of Dall sheep, and viewing points have been set-up at a number of locations. Blind Creek has a healthy population of chinook salmon, returning to spawn every spring and summer, and Swim Lake is well known as well for its white-fish, Arctic grayling and northern pike. The usual small and large animals are found in the nearby area with plenty of wild plants. As previously reported, this vocal occurrence is the second one experienced by this First Nation couple, who'd had another incident with unknown scary vocals in the immediate region around the community of Faro.

**Investigation:** What happened is as follows: the married couple in question had left their Faro home early this April morning with the intention of fishing for whitefish and northern pike at Swim Lake. They had driven their 4 x 4 pickup truck as far as they could on the small trail leading to Swim Lake and had parked it at the bottom of the sharp incline, where only ATVs could actually climb the steep hill. They were planning to hike the remaining 3 km (2 mi) or so to the lake. Upon reaching the first elevation at a height of some 1,000 m (3,280 ft), they came to a small creek that was crossing the trail flowing from their left-hand side and continued down the mountain on their right, which would eventually reach the Pelly River (Tu Desdes Tue).

They had stopped to get a fresh drink of creek water when they heard extremely loud screaming coming from their left, the general area leading to the top of the close-by mountain. However, the loud screams appeared to be quite close to them. The type of yells and shrieks reminded them of those very same types of vocals they had experienced earlier on in February while checking their trap line in the canyon by the Magundy River.

They froze in their tracks for a moment, trying to figure out what to do. They then heard crashing and thrashing in the bush to their left, fairly close to the creek bed and in a westerly direction, but could not see anything because the vegetation was so dense around that part of the trail, even in April. It was mostly covered with alders, tall willows, and large wild plants, although most of them were still without leaves at that time of the year. When they heard further thrashing coming from the same area of the forest, they immediately turned around and ran back to their truck, a distance of about 500 m (1,550 ft) downhill, and returned to town.

They contacted me soon after, in May of 2010, as I previously mentioned, and I went to Faro in early July to conduct the interview. In order to conduct an onsite investigation, I drove to the location of the occurrence the day after the interview, on Friday, July 16, 2010, with my own 4 x 4 pickup truck. I unloaded my Ruckus motorcycle at the same place they had stopped and parked their own truck, then went up the hill to where the creek crosses the trail to investigate the site.

The terrain was just as the witness had described to me: very dense woods through which one could not see more than a few metres or feet. I climbed partway up a sandy hill, only to slide back down. I later ventured around the creek bed for a short distance before being stopped by all the deadfalls and unsteady muddy terrain. It was very dangerous going where one could easily and seriously get injured.

I could not see any footprints or any possible signs of Sasquatch activities anywhere close by. I returned later that year in September 2010, again in July of 2011, and one last trip in July of 2012.

I have not experienced anything out of the norm, and I have not observed anything unusual during those visits.

However, I must admit that I did not feel at ease in the immediate area during my last visit in 2012, just a strange funny feeling that I was not alone and that I was not wanted for some unknown reason.

The last time I was there a grizzly bear checked my pickup truck while I was out riding my Ruckus motorcycle conducting the investigation. The grizzly bear followed my trail for a while, as its large tracks were evident, before going off into the bush after climbing about 10 m (33 ft) up the steep hill that I had climbed earlier. I still wonder if that grizzly was waiting for me at the bottom of the hill when I came by... One will never know for sure.

## Report #43
## TAKHINI REGION
## Sighting by Fish Creek in July 2010
## Location: Coord. 60o 43'20 N 135o 11'02 W
## (Map: Whitehorse 105 D/11; GR 098 318)

On Saturday, November 29, 2014, I was conducting an interview with a Kwanlin Dün First Nation man who was describing an encounter he had experienced close to Yukon Crossing in 1990, see report #12. After which, he described to me another sighting that took place in 2010 close to Pump House Lake.

**Encounter:** He described this encounter as follows: In mid-July of 2010, he and another member of KDFN, both in their 20s then, were returning home to Whitehorse from Fish Lake, where they had been fishing for a good part of the day. At around 1800 hours (6 pm) that day, they were approaching Fish Creek, just before the turn at the Yukon Electric flow control system, when they observed a large bipedal entity crossing the road just a few metres ahead of them. They identified this creature as a Sasquatch; it crossed the Fish Lake Road from the right-hand side to the left.

**Investigation:** The witness stated that the Sasquatch had climbed to the road from the right ditch, which I later measured to be 2 m (6.5 ft) high and fairly steep. The Sasquatch crossed the road in four steps. I measured the road width to be 5.5 m (18 ft) at that point, which means that each step would have been about 1.375 m (4.5 ft) in length. The KDFN man judged the Sasquatch to have been at least 215 m (7 ft) tall with long dark brown hair and very muscular. The Sasquatch climbed up to the the left-hand side of the road, which I measured at being some 4 m (13 ft) high and very steep with loose rock and gravel, walking in the direction of Mount Sumanik in a very dense forest.

A 215 cm (7 ft) tall Sasquatch would leave footprints of about 35.56 cm (14 in). Such a creature would have a step of some 137 cm (4.5 ft) on average, which is what I had calculated by measuring the width of the road. A Sasquatch of this height would weigh between 267 and 334 kg (588 to 736 lbs) and, on average, would require some 6,100 calories per day to stay healthy. There have been two other sighting reports close by: one in 1974, Report #3, and one in 1976, Report #6, all within a 1 km (0.6 mi) radius.

**Report #44**
**TAKHINI REGION**
**Foul Smell Occurrence by Grey Mountain in 2010**
**Location: Coord. 60o 45'49 N 135o 01'31 W**
**(Map: Upper Laberge 105 D/14: GR 986 356)**

ON TUESDAY, JULY 20, 2010, a close friend of mine and I came across a strange, unidentified, short-term foul and pungent smell while walking on a small bush trail some 500 m (1,700 ft) north of a foot track location, in Report #46.

**Occurrence:** We were exploring the area by Grey Mountain, north of Whitehorse, looking for any possible Sasquatch activity signs, following various reports of possible Sasquatch activities in the immediate area; actually, there have been some ten reports within a radius of 10 km (6 mi). My friend was walking 5 m (16 ft) or so ahead of me on a small trail used by bikers and hikers, while I was preoccupied looking at various plants. Then he noticed the smell.

We had crossed Croucher Creek onto the east side of the creek, across a small narrow wooden bridge. White spruce abounds in this area, quite tall and conquering, along with numerous fireweeds, low bush cranberries, and wild roses. There are quite a few walking trails crossing through this area, although I have not seen may people walking on this side of Croucher Creek.

My friend is from Calgary, Alberta. I had known him for some thirty years at the time, ever since we both served in the Canadian Army. He was walking ahead of me at the time and was the first person to notice a smell, which he described to be somewhat similar to that of a skunk stink.

He called up to me, inquiring if we had skunk in the Yukon, which we do not have.

**Investigation:** I then walked up to his location, and sure enough, a strong skunk-like and pungent smell was upon us. It lasted for another fifteen or so seconds before dissipating. I should also mention there was no wind at all during that period of time, and I could not hear any birds chirping or squirrels moving about, which was very unusual around these parts.

I know that some plants, such as skunk cabbage and some decaying trees may, on occasion, project a smell similar to a skunk. Evaporating methane gas as well. But these odours are at a much lower intensity level and not as pungent.

The smell in question was very strong. Although, not as strong as the smell that I experienced at Frenchman Lake in 2003 Report #30, and more like that of a skunk.

I mention this point as I have had bad experiences with skunks when I was residing in New Glasgow, Quebec, as a young lad, and I do know exactly what that awful smell is like.

I know that it was not from any of the ten species of skunk found in North America. Skunks are not found this far north in the Pacific Northwest Region, as the general limit of their habitat is the east side of the Cordillera Mountain Range. They are only found east and south of these mountains, while the Yukon is located north and west of the Cordillera Mountain Range, therefore, out of their presently known range

## Report #45
## TAKHINI REGION
## Vocals, Animal Reaction, and Tree Banging along the Annie Lake Road in 2010
## Location: Coord. 60o 23'47 N 134o 54'48 W
## (Map: Robinson 105 D/7: GR 049 954)

IN EARLY MARCH OF 2019, a Sasquatch enthusiast colleague from British Columbia contacted me, forwarding an email she had received from a fellow Yukoner who had had a possible Sasquatch experience. I contacted this person, a man in his early 30s, and set up a meeting to get his story.

**Occurrence:** The witness stated that at the time, he was residing with his parents on a nine-acre property on the Annie Lake Road, located some 50 km (30 mi) south of Whitehorse. One early fall morning in October of 2010, he got up at 0600 hours (6 am) to walk his five dogs and have a smoke. As soon as they were out of the house, he noticed his dogs taking a particular and unusual interest in the woods on their left-hand side. At first, they were just staring.

Being a fall day, the valley was covered with a thick fog. The temperature was a bit chilly with high humidity, which impaired the witness's ability to clearly see the close-by forest. Then, a loud indistinguishable "roaring" sound came from the same general location.

This sound "spooked me," the witness mentioned; at first, he thought it could be a moose or possibly a bear. His dogs then started barking and soon thereafter, other dogs in the vicinity, as there are many dog kennels close by, all started to howl and bark.

At that moment, an extremely loud and incredibly long bellow of a howl could be heard from the woods with a mixture of scream and yells being blasted. This went on for, it seemed, a couple of minutes, the witness stated.

Moments later, all the dogs quieted down, and the howling originating from the forest stopped as well. By that time, his dogs were sort of crying, ears flat to their head, tails low between their legs. They looked at the witness then towards the house and scuttled to the door. Just before he opened the door, there was another extremely loud whoop, followed by the sound of what seemed like trees being bashed against each another. At that time, the witness and his dogs entered the house.

**Local History:** The Annie Lake Road was constructed years ago to allow access to a number of quartz mining operations and placer gold mining, closer to the mountains along the Coast Mountains Boundary Range and those along the Gray Ridge. As time went on, there was a demand for country residential lots in the region, especially to allow people to raise dogs away from the city.

Because of the demand, the Yukon Government made a large number of residential lots available around what soon became the small community of Mount Lorne. Back in 1900, the White Pass and Yukon Railway had built a railway through the same valley, the Watson River Valley, and had a train station at the Robinson Roadhouse, which is still standing today as a Yukon Heritage site.

The Annie Lake Road starts by the same roadhouse and goes on for some fifty kilometres to the now-closed gold mine site at Mount Skukum. Other mining operations are currently operating around the area.

**Geography:** The valley's ground is mostly sandy and covered with a thick forest of white pine trees, black spruce, poplar trees, and willows of many varieties. The usual large game animals are found as well as smaller types of animals. The flora is that of ordinary river valleys with the usual plants and flowers. Unfortunately, the Watson River no longer has any fish due to a railway accident a number of years ago that resulted in spilling some unknown contaminants into the river and killing all the fish at that time. Arctic graylings are now slowly returning after all these years.

**Investigation:** I have interviewed the witness and have visited the area a number of times in the past but never noticed anything out of the ordinary. I visited the area again in the summer of 2021 to see if I could gain any more information; however, nothing interesting was noted.

**Note of Interest:** There was a sighting encounter at the close-by Robinson Roadhouse, some 8 km (5 mi) away, report #59 in 2014, and another sighting encounter by the Cowley Stretch, some 13 km (8 mi) away, Report #34 in 2008.

## Report #46
## TAKHINI REGION
## Foot Track Discovered by Grey Mountain in 2011
## Location: Coord, 60o 45'46 N 135o 01'19 W
## (Map: Whitehorse 105 D/11: GR 986 362)

WHILE CONDUCTING an observation expedition by Grey Mountain in 2011, I discovered a number of large human-like foot impressions each measuring 35 cm (14 in) in length, in the vicinity of a broken tree that I had noticed in the morning of Thursday, April 7, 2011, where I had camped overnight at the expedition location.

**Occurrence:** I made the discovery at about 0430 hours (4:30 am) on Thursday, April 7, 2011, close to the location of two sightings that had occurred in 2009 and 2010, (not in this book) along the southwest slopes of Grey Mountain, some 4 km (2.4 mi) north-northeast from downtown Whitehorse and 6 km (3.7 mi) directly north from my residence in Riverdale.

I was conducting an observation expedition as well as conducting an investigation into the two sightings that had occurred in the area.

That night, I decided to sit in my truck a short distance from the spot where the reporter had pointed out to me that a Sasquatch had climbed up an incline and disappeared in the dense lodgepole pine forest.

**Investigation:** I arrived at the observation location at 1900 hours (7 pm) or so and walked for about thirty minutes before selecting the most advantageous site to park my truck for the night. Shortly before 0200 hours (2 am) I took a stroll around the area and I must have fallen asleep some time after that.

When I woke up at 0430 hours (4:30 am), I noticed the broken tree branch on the left-hand side first, and upon further investigation, I noticed the foot impressions beside my truck. It was still fairly dark at that time, and I had not originally noticed anything new or anything that had changed since the other previous foot patrols when it was still light out and when I had taken a good look around at around 2045 hours (8:45 pm) and again around 2300 hours (11 pm).

Therefore, I know there were not any foot impressions in the vicinity of where I had parked my truck and the tree branch in question was very much intact on the willow tree.

These large foot impressions were very similar to those I had noted when investigating the previous sighting reports at that spot but much clearer, better defined, and freshly made. I was able to measure them at being about 35 cm long (14 in); however, they could have been slightly longer, as the thick moss covering the ground would not permit a more accurate measurement.

There were a number of steps forming a foot track, and I counted forty-five such foot impressions, each just about the same length, some covered with plants and moss debris, thus making an accurate measurement a bit more difficult.

The average distance between these steps, foot impressions actually, were measured to be around 135 cm (53 in or 4 ft 4 in). They started at a distance of about 14 m (45 ft) from behind my truck at the edge of a forest lined with a hard dirt flooring. The track-maker made its way past my truck on the driver side, by the broken tree branch (which they probably broke), then across a trail some 6 m (20 ft) ahead of my truck, across moss and low bush-covered hard, dry ground for about 50 m (160 ft), then up the very same incline that was mentioned in previous sighting reports into another forested area of hard dirt covered by pine needles, moss, lichens, and low bushes, which made further tracking impossible.

A 35 cm (14 in) footprint would indicate the print-maker to be about 216 cm (85 in or 7 ft 1 in) tall with an approximate weight of around 267 kg (588 lbs) for a medium-built print-maker. The larger heavy-set print-maker of a bigger build would probably be in the vicinity of 334 kg (736 lbs). By my calculations the length of the steps taken by such a print-maker would be about 137 cm (54 in or 4 ft 5 in), which is pretty close to the actual measurements of about 135 cm (53 in or 4 ft 4 in) that I had taken at the time.

This would indicate that an ambulating creature of such size would most probably need some 6,000 calories of food per day to remain healthy.

I have returned to the area a number of times since, the last being in June of 2018, but unfortunately, I have not come across any recent activity signs that may have been made by the creature known as Sasquatch. Since that time, members of the Ta'an Kwach'an Council (TKC) have returned to the area and constructed a few cabins; therefore, I do not venture in these parts any longer.

A smell occurrence took place nearby in 2010, Report #44.

## Report #47
## TAKHINI REGION
## Sighting by Crestview in 2011
## Location: Coord. 60o 45'53 N 135o 09'49 W
## (Map: Upper Laberge 105 D/14: GR 911 384)

A MAN CONTACTED ME through his daughter, whom I have known for many years, to report that he had observed a creature which he identifies as a Sasquatch, fairly close to his home while driving to Whitehorse at about 1430 hours (2:30 pm) on Tuesday, July 12, 2011.

**Encounter:** The man in question was driving downtown from his residence, located in the Crestview subdivision of Whitehorse, when he observed a bipedal, ambulating entity walking in the ditch, on his right-hand side, just about 1 km (0.6 mi) away from his home.

He slowed down to just about a crawling speed to have a better look at the creature and observed what he identified as a Sasquatch, while it covered a distance of about 90 m (200 ft) in about two minutes. He was sitting in the driver's seat of his car, just 2 m (6 ft) away from the Sasquatch in question until the creature gradually became translucent for a while, then transparent and then simply disappeared in thin air, vanished from sight, right in front of his eyes.

The sighting took place close by the city of Whitehorse water pumping station on Azure Road, which connects the subdivision of Crestview to the Alaska Highway, Yukon Highway #1. The entity was originally observed standing beside a water hydrant and then walking in a southerly direction.

This particular water hydrant has two cement protection pillars painted in yellow beside it. The creature disappeared by the first lamppost down Azure Road (south) from that location, a distance of about 90 m (200 ft) away from the spot he was first observed standing and close to the water hydrant.

The man first noticed the creature as his car completed a right-hand bend on Azure Road and the water hydrant in question came into view. The witness who reported the sighting to me is a long-time resident of Whitehorse married to a Carcross/Tagish First Nation woman.

He is a of German descent and was in his early 70s at the time. He reported the sighting to me in 2014. He had been working for the city of Whitehorse's Parks and Recreation Department for many years as a park maintenance and park upkeep employee.

He enjoys the outdoors and is experienced in all aspects of the Yukon wilderness. I have known the man since 2005 as he works at Shipyards Park, which is the park used to present the Canada Day Celebrations on the 1st of July, which I organized each year as the event coordinator for the Canada Day Celebrations. I know him to be a hard-working dedicated person and responsible in all aspects.

The reporter had heard of my interest in Sasquatch through his daughter, whom I have known for many years. That day was a day off for him, and he was on his way downtown to do a bit of shopping at the time of the sighting.

**Local History:** The Crestview subdivision was built on a knob hill with a good view of the surrounding area and is one of the original subdivisions within the city of Whitehorse. It was built in the 1960s and 1970s and is overlooking another subdivision called Porter Creek on the southwest side of the Yukon River, about 2 km (1.2 mi) away to the east and northeast sides of Crestview. Large green belts are on its immediate south, west, and north, with Hackle Hill and Mount Sumanik on its west.

It is considered one of the calmest residential subdivisions in the city. There are presently two wind turbines atop Hackle Hill, installed in the 1990s, along with a fire observation tower. It has been at the location since the devastating wild forest fire of 1956, which burned its way from across the Takhini River to the north and west of Whitehorse, to as far south as Snafu Lake and Tarfu Lake, barely sparing the city of Whitehorse, although encircling it for a few days.

Another wild forest fire occurred in 1998, originating from the slope of Hackle Hill, the result of a person who had camped in the area overnight and left his campfire burning when deciding to leave the area in the morning. That fire almost reached the subdivision of Crestview before being brought under control. The immediate geographic area is of rolling hills and high mountains, with the Ibex, Takhini, and Yukon Rivers making their way through the region and numerous small lakes.

**Investigation:** There are several sighting reports from the general area, one being some 8 km (5 mi) away on the east side of the Yukon River on the Long Lake Road, which occurred at about 0800 hours (8 am) in mid-August 1978.

Another report by Copper Ridge, which occurred some 8 km (5 mi) directly south of this sighting in August of 1992, Report #15 in mid-afternoon as well. Two more by Fox Lake, some 90 km (56 mi) north, one which took place at around noon in July 1998, Report #25, and another one in August of 2014, Report #55.

There is another sighting report which took place some 40 km (24 mi) southeast, on the Cowley Stretch in January 2006 at about 2130 hours (9:30 pm), Report #34.

**Now for the good part:** The witness noticed the bipedal ambulating entity on his right-hand side, walking in a southerly direction in the ditch. The witness was about 10 m (32.8 ft) away from the ambulating entity when he first noticed the Sasquatch. The creature kept on walking at a steady speed, in a dedicated fashion that can be described as a "man on a mission," according to the witness, which would indicate an entity with a purposeful and determined walk. Which means the creature he was observing at the time appeared to have something on their mind and was walking with a specific determined purpose.

The witness continued on driving, catching up with the entity and actually followed it at a distance of some 2 m (6 ft) away for a couple of minutes, while the creature slowly walked

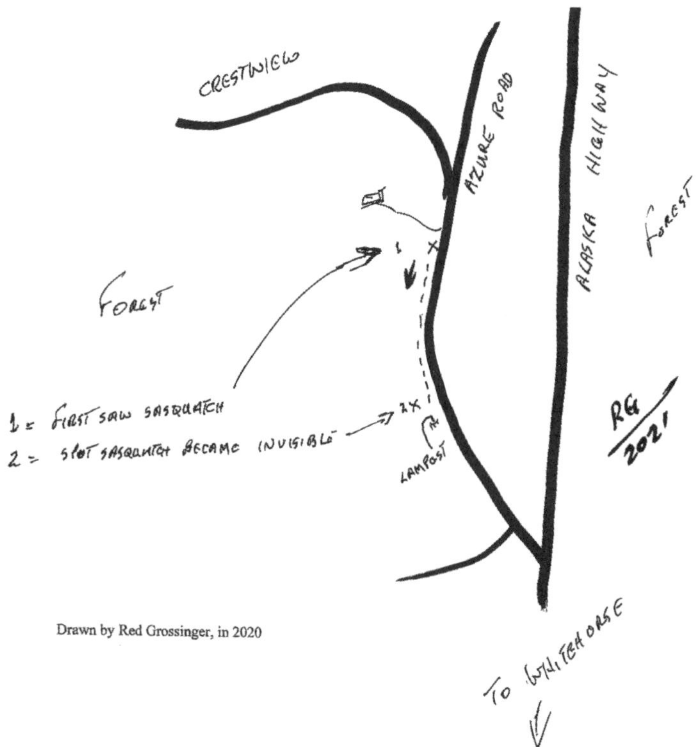


Drawn by Red Grossinger, in 2020

*Takhini Region: Sighting by Crestview on Tuesday July 12, 2011*

for a total distance of about 90 m (200 ft), according to the spots pointed out to me by the witness from where the creature was first seen and to where he was last observed.

The reporter had no hesitation in calling the creature beside him a Sasquatch, as he stated to me the identity was immediately clear in his mind.

His Sasquatch was walking in the ditch, standing fully erect at all times, much like a young healthy human, with the palms of its hands turned somewhat backward. Meaning the hands were towards its back or behind him, much like Patty ("Patty" is the name given to the Sasquatch filmed by Roger Patterson in California in 1967) as opposed to facing inward or towards the body as a human would. The creature also had the exact arm swinging fashion that we humans would use while walking in a determined fashion and with a purpose in mind.

The Sasquatch stood at about 213 cm (84 in or 7 ft). This was measured against a specific spot marked on the lamppost by which it disappeared, as shown to me by the witness.

The witness said that its head was somewhat rounded, as opposed to the stated "cone-headed" description as reported to have been observed on "Patty." The hairs were of a dark brownish shade, surprisingly very well groomed according to the witness, with a length of about 15 cm (6 in) around its head and somewhat longer around the shoulder and about 10 cm (4 in) along its entire body, mostly straight and without any knots.

Its ears were not visible due to the long hair, and it did not appear to have a neck, or it was a really short one and not discernible at all, again due to the long hair.

The ambulating entity's arms reached just slightly below its knees, although its knees were slightly bent when it was walking, and therefore, the length of the legs could not be specified, as it was walking in a ditch with fairly tall grass.

The arms were very muscular, with large well-developed forearms and biceps. The shoulders were described as being big, huge actually, about 70 to 75 cm (28 to 30 in) wide according to the witness.

The creature's build is described by the witness as solid, strong, powerful, big and very muscular with a deep, broad chest, at a side looking width of at least 60 cm (2 ft) and a very hard-looking stomach with plenty of muscles, although not fat in any way.

Its upper legs were reported to be muscular and strong-looking. The feet were not visible, due to where it was walking, in the ditch with grass about 30 cm (1 ft) tall.

The witness mentioned that he did not see the full face, only a partial view of about three-quarters of the face, because he never overtook the bipedal ambulating entity but rather stayed with it, almost in line with it, at a distance of some 2 m (6 ft). The skin was clearly visible on the left side of its face, which was dark brown.

The nose was more like that of a boxer, somewhat flat with large nostrils, as much as he could see. The jaw was protruding, but not that much, and the lips were closed and a darker shade than the rest of the skin.

The shade of the skin was described as dark brownish, much the same as a Yukon First Nations person. The forehead was sort of square to the hair line with a noticeable brow ridge, although not that protruding at all as far as the witness could see.

The hairs were massive and long, looking like they were well-kept and not tangled at all, as is often reported. The overall expression on its face, as much as the witness could see, would be similar to that of a person dedicated to a specific task and walking with a purpose.

The Sasquatch never paid attention to the car at all, at any time, as far as the witness can remember, even though he was right beside the creature at a distance of some 3 m (10 ft) for a good two minutes and never turned its head in the driver's direction.

No sexual organs or genitalia were visible due to its sideway view, and there were no visible breasts. Therefore, it is taken that the identified Sasquatch observed was a male, and again according to the witness, "he was a young one." The witness stated that he thinks that the entity observed weighed about 110 to 120 kg (240 to 260 lbs). However, according to my calculation chart, a Sasquatch of 213 cm (84 in or 7 ft) would weigh approximately 262 kg (577.5 lbs) with a footprint of just over 34.994 cm (13.75 in) and a step of 134 cm (53 in or 4 ft 5 in). The man stated that he believes the distance of the steps taken by this young Sasquatch was around 90 cm (36 in or 3 ft), which is somewhat less, by 44 cm (1 ft 5 in) than what I have calculated in my Proportion Table.

But then again, the reporter's view of its legs was somewhat limited as he was sitting behind the steering wheel of his car and could not fully, nor accurately, observe the leg movements or the length of the steps at all times.

Keep in mind as well that the creature was walking approximately 40 cm (16 in) lower than the pavement where the car was, as the Sasquatch was walking in the right-hand side ditch. This would provide an observation angle which would place the witness's eyes at about the same height as the ambulating entity's eyes.

The top of the witness's head would have been at about 134.6 cm (53 in or 4 ft 5 in) from the pavement. In this area, the ground is very hard packed and covered with gravel consisting of small rocks and grass, and therefore, it would not leave any footprints behind. To check out this point, I actually tried to make any type of footprints or marks with my feet and also with a walking stick while I was investigating, without any results.

However, the one aspect that has me puzzled is the creature's method of disappearance. About three steps away from and before the lamppost in question, a distance of 3 m (10 ft) or so, the witness states that the body of the creature, identified as a Sasquatch, became gradually translucent and then transparent, to the point of losing more and more of its overall natural visible shape, shade, density, details, and body structure, the closer it got to the lamppost.

And then, as the Sasquatch reached the lamppost, it became totally invisible, "poof" gone, no longer visible to the human eye, as if having walked into a portal that transported it somewhere else, like into another universe or into another dimension and becoming totally invisible to us poor humans.

Now there are three other sighting reports which mention some sort of levitation and a similar type of disappearance. The sighting by Copper Ridge in August 1992, Report #15 in the Takhini Region as well, some 8 km (5 mi) south of this location and which occurred at a distance of about 20 m (65 ft) from the witness of that sighting. Yet, not quite a similarly quick disappearance but rather a gliding motion and then disappearing in a sort of levitation, according to the reporter of that sighting.

One other sighting report is from the Keno Region at Duncan Creek Road in July 2008, Report #37, close to the community of Keno City, where two Sasquatch, one a pregnant female ready to give birth and the other a large male, similarly disappeared in front of the witness about 10 m (35 ft) away in a swift, silent and undetectable movement, according to the reporter.

Another sighting report is from the Keno Region also. There was a sighting by Moose Creek in mid-August 2011, Report #50, where a two-legged entity, described as a Sasquatch by the witnesses, disappeared. Three ravens, not previously noted by the witnesses, flew from the very same spot where the Sasquatch had been standing just seconds before, as reported to me by a First Nation female and her companion, a First Nation male.

I will be first to admit that I really do not know what to think of these reported disappearing phenomena.

There are not enough data in my possession to make a knowledgeable assessment of the meaning and to conduct proper analyses, as I have only three examples to work with.

To be noted, however, similar activities are reported by Raymond Yakeleya in the foreword of this book, and, as well, in one of the latest and most recent books by Chris Murphy and Thomas Steenburg: *Sasquatch in British Columbia*. I have recently read about various and numerous theories regarding the phenomenon of levitation, transparency, translucency, disappearances, and similar activities.

Members of various Yukon First Nations have presented me with their beliefs of spirituality and that of Sasquatch changing forms at will in a cloaking fashion or at times simply becoming invisible.

I also know of some sort of experiments by the US Military where a product made of cloth is used to cloak a person and even some material being used for cloaking planes in flight as well as ships sailing on the water—making them invisible to the human eyes.

How is that done, how could that be achieved? As I have yet to study the matter in more depth, I am not ready to make a knowledgeable statement on the subject at the moment.

Of interest to some readers, the witness of this sighting and I have recently (in 2015) been interviewed by a television production company from Montreal, Quebec, on contract with the Discovery Channel. The documentary is being aired on various television channels under *Boogeyman* with a mention of "Sasquatch in Yukon."

The last time I was at this location was in June of 2021, as my youngest son presently resides some 500 m (1,640 ft) away from this sighting location.

## Report #48
## TAKHINI REGION
## Tree Thrashing and Vocal Activities by Steamboat Slough on Livingstone Trail in 2011
## Location: Coord. 60o 55'34 N 135o 04'15 W
## (Map: Upper Laberge 105 D/14 GR: 957 545)

WHILE TAKING A LUNCH BREAK during an exploration expedition of the area of Steamboat Slough on Friday, July 22, 2011, I was subjected to threatening actions from the nearby forest.

**Occurrence:** This threatening action consisted of large trees being thrashed about by an entity of some sort, with low guttural growls, seemingly in an attempt to chase me away. (And it worked . . .)

The occurrence took place close to an area known as Steamboat Slough, which is located about 2 km north from the occurrence location. Steamboat Slough is located on the Yukon River, some 32 km (21 mi) downstream from the Robert Campbell Bridge in downtown Whitehorse, a distance of about 35 km (23 mi) from my residence in Riverdale, using the back trails on my Ruckus motorcycle, which I was doing that day and had been doing on a regular basis.

On that beautiful sunny July day, I was exploring the Livingstone Trail, which runs off the Long Lake Road roughly following the eastern shores of the Yukon River and of Lake Laberge for a while, then the trail goes across the mountains in an eastern direction, to eventually cross the Teslin River and reach the Big Salmon River where the abandoned gold mining camp of Livingstone Creek is located.

My intention was to follow the trail as far as I could. At the time that I experienced the occurrence, I had stopped by a flooded area and was trying to figure out a route around the flooded area when I decided to have a bite to eat, and soon thereafter, the threatening actions began.

**Local History:** Steamboat Slough is a swampy area on the east side of the Yukon River, with a number of shallow waterways well protected by large trees where paddle wheelers would be anchored for the winter months during the Second World War.

This was done because of the possibility that Japanese airplanes would reach Whitehorse as they could easily bomb the ships pulled out of the water for the winter months at the White Pass Shipyards in Whitehorse.

Therefore, wherever there were sloughs big enough to accommodate various paddle wheelers during the winter months, ships would be moved away from Whitehorse and anchored there.

At one time there were seven paddle wheelers anchored at Steamboat Slough, with a cabin where keepers would stay over the winter and connected by a telegraph line to the White Pass Shipyards in Whitehorse.

**Occurrence continues:** About ten minutes after stopping at the flooded creek area, at about 1315 hours (1:15 pm), having explored upstream of the creek from where the bridge had been removed as a result of water overflow, I was trying to figure out a way to get across this flooded area. That is when I heard something walking heavily in the bush from across the creek on my left and downstream from my location.

Figuring it was a moose, I originally did not pay much attention and started eating my lunch. While doing so, the sounds became much louder, and at this time, trees were being shaken and thrashed about. I could hear some of them breaking, starting at a distance of about 30 m (100 ft) or so to my left and downstream of the creek, and then gradually getting closer, at a distance I would judge to have been about 10 m (33 ft) or so from my location.

From where I stood, I could easily see the tops of the tall trees being shaken about every which way, but I could not see the tree shaker due to the thickness of the forest. There was not a bit of wind on that day, totally calm.

A bear could not have done all that shaking, as they simply do not move trees in that fashion. They do not act that way. Yet, I could not see how a moose or an elk would move trees in that fashion either. Usually, they would grunt and would hit the trees with their antlers creating an audible thump. This was not the case at all: something else was grasping the trees and moving them, shaking and thrashing them about, and obviously breaking some. By "grasping," I mean by using hands.

That lasted a good ten minutes or even longer. At one point, I could hear some sort of low guttural growl, which increased in intensity, becoming louder and more acute. I did not detect any type of smell, although I could observe some movement by what appeared to be a bipedal entity of sorts, but I could not clearly see what it was. Meanwhile, I just stayed on the trail by the flooded creek hoping and expecting to see the culprit.

Was it a Sasquatch or some other similar entity? I would advance the former. Then an odd yet familiar feeling came upon me: a feeling of not being wanted in that specific area—a strange feeling much like the one I had previously experienced on Squanga Lake in September of 2008, in Report #38.

I took one last bite of my sandwich, finished eating my lunch in a hurry, got on my Ruckus motorbike, started travelling back onto the trail, and went some 30 m (60 ft or so) in a westerly direction before stopping for a few minutes to look around. Maybe the thrashing maker would approach in my direction? No such luck.

Not seeing anything unusual, I waited a while longer, and everything got quiet. I did not find a way to cross the flooded area so I decided to explore other parts of the area.

Being alone and not armed, except for a knife, walking stick, bear spray, and air horn, I simply did not feel safe. I did not see what or who was making all that racket, but whatever it was must have been serious, did not like me being there, and wanted me to leave the immediate area.

I had a plan to return to the location during the summer of 2012 with some other people, as there is safety in numbers, but could not make it happen for various reasons. I have returned to the location in the summer of 2013, but all was calm with only a few moose tracks in the immediate area and a group of deer a bit further. along

I have thought of the possibility of a large black or grizzly bear but rejected the idea, as a bear would have come out of the bush to make its presence known as part of their usual behaviour.

In addition, bears do not usually shake trees in the manner those were being shaken and thrashed, because, in order to shake those trees, the shaker would have had to actually grasp the trees while moving them back and forth as well as from side to side.

I returned to the area of Steamboat Slough by boat in August of 2014 with my youngest son, and we experienced two strange calls that were very similar to Sasquatch calls recorded in British Columbia during that same summer.

See vocal occurrence by Steamboat Slough dated Saturday, August 30, 2014, in Report #57.

**Report # 49**
**KLUANE REGION**
**Rock-throwing Incident South of Beaver Creek in 2011**
**Location: Coord. 61o 51'05 N 140o 08'33 W**
**(Map: Kluane Lake 115 G & 115 F: GR 509 579)**

BETWEEN 1900 AND 2000 HOURS (7 and 8 pm), on Monday, August 8, 2011, an elderly couple from Montana experienced a rock-throwing incident at a highway rest area south of Pickhandle Lake, on the Alaska Highway, Yukon Highway #1.

This couple were returning home to Montana after visiting Alaska and had originally stopped at that location hoping to stay for the night but soon departed in search of another more pleasant and welcoming location to spend the night.

This report was sent to me by my good friend, a colleague Sasquatch researcher and fellow writer from Alaska, Dr. J. Robert Alley, the author of *Raincoast Sasquatch* and *Brushes with Bigfoot.*

**Occurrence:** The following is a previously unpublished account of the incident, as written by the witness and is presented here with the kind permission of Robert Alley, to whom my appreciation is forwarded.

> We left Tok, Alaska, headed for Haines, Alaska, around the 8th of August, after touring Alaska since June. We decided to pull our fifth-wheel camper over and spend the night along the Alaska Highway shortly after going through Beaver Creek in the Yukon. The spot we pulled into was just across a bridge. We can't remember the name of the river or stream, but there was a nice turn-around area on the left side of the road, just after crossing the bridge, heading east, that looked like a good place to have dinner, get some sleep, and continue on to Haines, Alaska the following day. We do know that the area was just before the Kluane Wilderness Village and Burwash Landing. I left the pickup hooked up to the camper, as we were going to leave first thing in the morning.

After dinner (I believe it was around 7 or 8 pm), we took our dogs to the river's edge so they could get a drink and stretch their legs before we called it a day. As we turned to walk back to the camper, there was a loud splash, like someone threw a very large stone at us, and it landed in the river. At first, my wife thought I did it, and as I told her, 'no way, it wasn't me'. Just at the same moment, I turned to look at the river, and a second very large rock/stone hit the water on our side, as if whoever threw it at us was clear across the river up on the ridge. I told my wife: 'Get to the camper and be quick about it.'

I shouted out in the direction of where I thought the stones came from, including the bridge and upstream. 'Whoever that is knock it off! There are people down here! Who are you? What do you want? Show yourselves!' There was no reply. No response of any kind.

That sort of put fear and concern in me, thinking of our safety. So I went to the camper, and I happened to have legally checked and declared my 12-gauge shotgun through Canada for bear protection while in Alaska.

So I uncased it, plus the ammunition, loaded it up, and went outside to further investigate as to who or what it was that could be hurling rocks at us. I hurriedly put the stabilizer jacks up on the camper, pulled in the slide, and instructed my wife to get in the driver's seat and if I wasn't back in fifteen minutes, or if someone approached, start the truck immediately and get to the next town and report what happened just as fast as she could. I didn't want to take any chances, not this day and age anyway. We at first considered just getting the heck out of there, but I was pretty mad and upset over why someone would be throwing rocks at us for whatever reason and I felt more confident with my shotgun loaded, and at the ready.

I went to investigate. The area is very remote, no other rigs were coming down the highway at this time and I went upstream, no sign of anyone or anything and looked under the bridge. Nothing. All this time I continued to shout the command, 'Show yourselves! I am armed and this isn't one bit funny'. Nothing. I went across the bridge and went up on the ridge across from where we were parked, the area I assumed the rocks were hurled from.

There was a sort of old skid-trail or logging road that had grown over that headed up that way. I walked past the area across from the camper but there was no sign of anything. I happened upon a governmental-looking sign that read Tribal Land Settlement Area, and it gave a number to call if any questions. At any rate, after finding no sign of anyone, the more I thought about it the more I thought it would be wise to just leave the area and proceed further down the highway. *If they, or them, or whatever it was, were throwing rocks before dark, Lord knows what they would be doing to us after dark* was my thought.

And I knew we wouldn't be getting much sleep. Whoever it was that threw stones had to have one heck of a strong arm, as it was a long way from the ridge to where we were standing, twenty more feet, and they possibly would have hit us. So we went further down the road. There were two other fifth-wheel campers and three motor homes pulled over for the night. We felt safer there with other people. The next day we proceeded to Burwash/Haines Junction and all the way into Haines.

By the way, I immediately unloaded my shotgun, locked it back in the case, and locked up and separated the ammunition after arriving at the safer spot with the other campers.

I thought about reporting the incident to the mounted police but figured there wouldn't be anything for them to investigate. It sort of worried me about what would or could possibly happen to other travellers who parked at that same area. Again, it was a very remote area. The closest place would have been that lodge, just a few miles down the road. At any rate, the more we thought about it, and the more we watched the series of *Finding Bigfoot* on TV, we thought we would share this story with you as I guess it has been known for Sasquatch to throw rocks at people. I wished I had searched more in-depth on that ridge for possible tracks in the grassy bank, but I was more concerned for the welfare and safety of my wife and myself at the time."

I have left out the name of the witness who reported the incident to Dr. J. Robert Ally, as I do with all reports, according to my own confidentiality policy.

**Investigation:** During my investigation, I drove the road between Beaver Creek and Burwash Landing in 2013 and again in 2015, with the objective of locating where this incident took place. The closest location that I found would be a pull-out on the south side of a the Koidern River, on the left-hand side driving towards Burwash Landing. I have not observed anything out of the ordinary while I was walking about the site.

One last thing: I would recommend that readers read the various books written by my good friend Robert Alley to find out more about Sasquatch activities in Alaska; his latest book is named *Brushes with Bigfoot: Sasquatch Behaviors Reported in Close Encounters, Native and Non-Native Perspectives.*

**Report #50**
**KENO REGION**
**Sighting by Moose Creek in 2011**
**Location: Coord. 63o 29'42 N 137o 01'20 W**
**(Map: McQuesten 115 P: GR 099 044)**

A Tr'ondëk Hwëch'in woman mentioned to me that she had observed a large and tall bipedal entity she identified as a Sasquatch beside the North Klondike Highway, Yukon Highway #2, about 2 km (1.24 mi) from Moose Creek, on the right-hand side of the road. This was while she was driving in the direction of Dawson City. She explained to me the sighting occurred in mid-August of 2011, at about 1800 hours (6 pm).

She reported this encounter to me while I was attending the 2014 Moosehide Gathering at the Tr'ondëk Hwëch'in's village at Moosehide, Yukon, some 6 km (3.73 mi) downriver from Dawson City in July of 2014. The witness was in her mid-20s at the time and was on her way back to Dawson City, where she resided at the time, along with her then-boyfriend, also from Tr'ondëk Hwëch'in. The couple had been visiting family in the community of Pelly Crossing, members of the Fort Selkirk First Nation, and were returning home to Dawson City.

**Encounter:** The sighting occurred on the right-hand side ditch which was about 1 m (3.2 ft) deep at that point. Various plants were in full growth at the time of the year on both sides of the ditch, mostly clover, along a land clearance of some 100 m (320 ft), which had been cleared of trees earlier that summer and did not provide any tree cover whatsoever between the road and the nearby forest. The forest at this location consisted mostly of black spruce and aspen trees on a gradual elevation to nearby higher ground.

The witness reports that she was riding in the passenger seat of the car, and she first noticed what she thought to be a bear, telling the driver to slow down a bit. At the time, she only noticed the creature bent over, probably busy eating clover, which were growing in large quantities along this stretch of road.

As they got within about 10 m (32.8 ft) or so, the creature stood up and that is when she clearly identified the creature as being a Sasquatch. The witness stated the Sasquatch to be about 213 cm tall (7 ft).

She reports that all of sudden, the Sasquatch that she was clearly observing somehow became gradually transparent at that moment. After probably a minute, as she recalls, it became totally invisible to her.

She also mentioned that at the specific moment when it became invisible, she observed three ravens flying away from the exact spot where she had just observed the Sasquatch, and she stated that she had not noticed any ravens or any other type of animal when she first observed the bipedal creature she identified as a Sasquatch.

She would not venture to explain to me what she thought was happening at the time. As far as I am concerned, this disappearance is another puzzle to be solved, being one of four reports in the Yukon of a Sasquatch disappearing directly in front of the witnesses. Some people interested in the Sasquatch phenomenon have advanced that Sasquatch have an ability to change shape at will, shape-shifting as it is known, as well as a display a cloaking ability. Something else to think about.

Her companion, her boyfriend who was driving the car they were riding in, only observed the bottom half of the Sasquatch when it stood up. He did not see the ravens as they were out of his field of vision.

**Investigation:** I last was at Moose Creek during summer of 2020 and again in fall of 2021 but did not notice anything unusual.

Statistical analyses would reveal that a Sasquatch about 2.13 m (7 ft) tall would weigh between about 267 kg (588 lbs) and 334 kg (736 lbs), would have a footprint measuring about 35.56 cm (14 in), and a step of about 136.9 cm (53.9 in). Such a creature would need some 6,100 calories per day to remain healthy and survive.

Similar disappearances are contained in Reports #15, #37, and #47.

## Report #51
## TAKHINI REGION
## Vocal Incident and Animal Reaction by Taye Lake in 2012
## Location: Coord. 60o 63'44 N 136o 17'37 W
## (Map: Champagne 115 A/16: GR 301 527)

A MAN contacted me by phone in late April of 2012, reporting that he heard a series of strange, unusual and unidentified loud vocals by the Mendenhall River, just south of Taye Lake. The witness was in his early 30s at the time—a resident of Whitehorse who is an outdoor enthusiast and participates in many outdoor activities. He was employed by the Kwanlin Dün First Nation (KDFN) in Whitehorse as an architect. He was on a seven-day back-country ski trip with a number of friends when he experienced these unidentified vocals at around 0200 hours (2 am) on Sunday, April 15, 2012, by Taye Lake.

**Local History:** The area around Taye Lake was depleted of firewood during the time of the paddle wheelers; now with second and third growth reaching maturity, the area is still a source of wood harvesting to some degree. A few small farms have been developed in the general area in recent years, although closer to the Alaska Highway, Yukon Highway #1. The nearby small community of Mendenhall is home to a few people, thirty-five or so, who prefer and enjoy living in the countryside.

**Geography:** The area where the vocals occurred is mostly low ground covered by a lodgepole pine forest where the Mendenhall River meanders slowly through, along with the usual stands of poplar trees and willows. There is a previous report from the area: Footprints Report # 7 by Mendenhall in 2011, which was discovered about 15 km (9 mi) south-southeast of this location and closer to the community of Mendenhall.

The group of seven skiers and two dogs were on a seven-day cross-country ski trip. They had started at a point called Takhini Crossing, some 80 km (50 m) west of Whitehorse. From that location, they had mostly travelled in a north-northwest direction when they experienced the vocals. They were travelling mostly in a southern direction to their planned exit point on a trail reaching the Alaska Hwy 5 km (3 mi) east of the community of Champagne, where they had made arrangements for friends to pick them up late on Sunday afternoon.

**Occurrence:** This event occurred during the night of the 6th to the 7th day of their excursion, the last night. Our witness was woken up at about 0200 hours (2 am) by a very loud and strange type of "wailings" and "whoops." He described these as being guttural and very powerful and seemed to originate from the forest, at a distance of about 40 m (130 ft) or so from his tent, at best as he could judge.

However, the vocals did not appear to be threatening or aggressive to him, but rather protective and somewhat unnerving, according to the reporter. The dogs had been barking for a while before the vocals started, but no one paid any particular attention to them, and they all went to sleep. It should be mentioned that our witness was alone in his tent, which was located some 20 m (65 ft) away from the others.

The vocals lasted for some ten minutes and during that time the dogs were whimpering and, even though they were tied to a nearby tree, they were trying to get into his tent. Because our witness was extremely tired and since it was awfully cold outside, he did not get out of the sleeping bag to investigate the source of these strange vocals.

It was only after he returned to work and mentioned his experience to some of his friends and co-workers, all members of the Kwanlin Dün First Nation, they then suggested the vocals sounded much like vocals that a Sasquatch would make.

**Investigation:** I have interviewed the witness three times, and he has been consistent in all aspects of his report. He heard of me through a local radio program that I had been interviewed on, and this is when he decided that he would contact me.

His tent happened to be the closest to where the vocals came from, while the others were spread out over a fair distance away and below a small rise on the ground, which is probably the reason why he was the only one in the group who heard the vocals. Actually, one of the dogs must have heard them first, as it was the barking of that dog that woke him up.

Surprisingly he had asked the other members of the group if they had heard anything unusual and out of the ordinary; however, no one else had clearly heard these vocals or anything unusual during the night. However, it should be clarified that the members of the group would spread out their tents in mostly low wind-protected ground and distanced them so the snoring from a tent would not disturb the others.

He did not pursue the matter at the time for reasons he would not explain to me. He later stated that he did not know why he did not mention or discuss his experiences with his friends in the morning. A very common human reaction to something unusual that cannot be immediately explained.

## Report #52
## TAKHINI REGION
## Scats Discovered on the Kokanee Lake Road in 2012
## Location: Coord. 60o 44'53 N 135o 29'59 W
## (Map: Whitehorse 105 D/11: GR 738 355)

On Thursday, July 5, 2012, my younger son, Steven, and I came across an extraordinary large pile of excrement while driving on a back road at about 1030 hours (10:30 am). At the time of this sighting, we were out looking for good fishing spots along the Ibex River and exploring the area leading to Kokanee Lake.

**Local History:** The area had been ravaged by a wild forest fire in the mid-1950s, and many trails were pushed through, first to fight the fire and then to salvage the fire-killed trees for firewood. The access to this area is some 40 km (24 mi) northwest of the city of Whitehorse.

This logging road is known locally as the Kokanee Lake Road, located about 16 km (10 mi) south of the Scout Lake Road, which in turn starts midway along the Old Alaska Highway portion northwest of Whitehorse. The location of the excrement was about 1 km (0.6 mi) up the Kokanee Lake Road, from the intersection with the Scout Lake Road and was directly in the middle of the road.

**Geography:** The immediate area of the find consists mostly of small rolling rocky hills covered with small new lodgepole pines with the Ibex River running through the area on the south side of the road at a various distance, with Mount Sumanik at an elevation of 1,710 m (5,610 ft) located on the east-southeast side of the road at a distance of about 5 km (3 mi). Closer to another small, unnamed mountain on the north side, one would find a large number of boulders that have detached themselves from the side of the mountain and rolled about as well as a few small caves.

**Investigation:** As I have not observed whatever or whoever defecated on that road, I simply cannot attach a name to the defecator. The size of these scats, however, is quite different from any other pile of ordinary scats from bears, wolves, or any other animals I have ever noticed anywhere else before.

My measurements taken with a ruler indicated the pile of excrement to be about 30 cm long by 30 cm wide (12 in by 12 in), some 17.8 cm (8 in) high and the individual size of the scats were about the size of a beer can, which is 21 cm (8.5 in) in circumference.

The colour was a deep dark black, which usually indicates blood in the food eaten, with traces of berries showing up, and it seemed very solid and firm in composition when pushed with a branch, with an obvious, extremely strong stench. It was fresh and still steaming when found. However, there were not any tracks of any kind visible around it.

The ground in the immediate area consisted of hard-packed gravel with a cover of dust along the roadway, short grass with pine needles in between the tire tracks, and a large amount of pine needles covering the mostly hard, dry gravel ground on both sides of the trail.

Strangely, no footprints or track prints were visible, although one would think that marks left behind by the claws of bears would have been visible, especially a grizzly bear *(Ursus arctos),* as such a size of excrement could well have been from an extraordinarily huge grizzly bear.

The average adult grizzly bear in the Yukon stands at 2.8 m (8.2 ft), the tallest reported to be about 3 m (9.8 ft). The scat from these animals is usually 15.5 cm (6.1 in) long and 3.8 cm (1.5 in) high, as reported by the Government of Yukon.

We were going to bag the pile of excrement on our way back, in order to limit the amount of time we would have to be exposed to the stink while it was in the vehicle .

But as luck would have it, when we came back some three hours later, the pile of excrement was totally scattered about in an obvious attempt at erasing any signs of it. There were no visible signs of any footprints or animal prints in the immediate vicinity of where the pile had been, nor were there any tire marks that a vehicle would have left if it had driven by.

For a matter of clarity, we had not observed any vehicular activities in the area or along the road in question that day.

It looked as if whatever scattered the stuff about had used a tree branch to do the work, which is not the way bears would scatter this stuff, as when bears defecate, they would simply leave the scats where they fell. Very puzzling indeed. That area requires more exploration and observation in the future.

## Report #53
## SQUANGA REGION
## Sightings by Fox Point in 2012
## Location: Coord. 60o 10'47 N 132o 47'39 W
## (Map: Teslin 105 C/2: GR 226 735)

A WOMAN FRIEND OF MINE from the Teslin Tlingit Council mentioned that a young girl had experienced multiple sightings of an ambulating bipedal creature, described as a Sasquatch, over a few months during the summer of 2012.

**Encounter:** One early evening, at about 2000 hours (8 pm), the mother noticed her daughter smiling and waving at someone or something out of the living room window. The mother asked her what she was waving at and the young girl replied, "He is back again." "Who's back?" the mother responded. The young girl said, "You know . . . the boogeyman. He's back again".

The mother then asked her, "What do you mean he's back again?" To which the girl replied, "He is back again. He always comes by and smiles at me in the window." Somewhat shocked, the mother stood still for a few moments, and by the time she went over to the window, the "boogeyman" in question could not be observed by the mother. The residence of the young girl is located at the northwest end of the community of Teslin, a couple of kilometres north and west of the end of the runway at the Teslin Airport, close to a location known as Fox Point, just a few metres off the shores of Teslin Lake.

The witness is a girl who was seven years of age at the time, and her parents are First Nation members of the Teslin Tlingit Council. Our young witness was watching television in the living room of her house when the repeated sightings reportedly occurred.

There have been a few other sightings reports from the community of Teslin, along with a report of an animal reaction and a report of a strange large shadow over a child in the immediate area of this particular sighting which reportedly occurred on multiple occasions.

**Investigation:** The girl stated to my friend that her boogeyman was all covered in dark hair and always came to the same window at about the same time, looking at her, smiling, and waving in a friendly manner.

As explained to me, the lower part of the window's glass is about 152 cm (5 ft) from the ground, and the top of the boogeyman's head went to about 61cm (24 in) above the lower part of the window's glass, making the creature in question some 213 cm (84 in or 7 ft) tall.

A Sasquatch measuring 213 cm (7 ft) tall would weigh between 267 and 334 kg (588 and 736 lbs), would have a footprint of about 35.56 cm (14 in), a step of about 137 cm (54 in), and would need some 6,100 calories per day to remain healthy.

Unfortunately, the young girl did not pay attention to any facial details besides that the Sasquatch was smiling at her whenever she saw the creature at the window. There was no noise mentioned or any footprints found.

## Report #54
## SQUANGA REGION
## Vocals and Rocks Throwing Incident by Morley Bay on Teslin Lake in 2013
## Location: Coord. 60o 50'31 N 132o 34'55 W
## (Map: Teslin 105 C/2: GR 347 638)

In July 2013, two persons from Teslin were subjected to very loud shrieks and experienced a number of large rocks being thrown in their direction when they were attempting to land at a small beach just past the Morley Bay Point on Teslin Lake.

**Occurrence:** The married couple reside in the community of Teslin and are Teslin Tlingit Council (TTC) members. They had been fishing in the area when they decided to pull ashore and have lunch.

However, as they approached a small bay, they were first subjected to loud yells from an area above them and then from across the lake, which is some 2 km (1.2 mi) away at this point. As they got closer to the beach, rocks started flying from an elevated piece of land about 10 m (33 ft) away and some 20 m high (66 ft). Unfortunately, they could not clearly see the rock throwers, and not feeling safe, they backed off and carried on down the lake a bit farther where they had lunch.

This particular beach is located some 12 km (6.4 mi) from the boat ramp located beside the Nisutlin Bay Inlet Bridge on the Alaska Highway, Yukon Highway #1. These incidents occurred in July of 2013 and were reported to me by a good friend, also from the Teslin Tlingit Council, who had talked to the witnesses shortly after they experienced these occurrences.

**Investigation:** I had planned to conduct an on-site investigation in 2014; however, I was too busy with other investigations, and this one had to wait till the weekend of Friday to Sunday, September 11–13, 2015, when I had the occasion to get on Teslin Lake with a friend who had a big enough boat to handle the dangerous water of the lake.

There was no problem finding the location; we landed without any difficulties. After investigating the area and not finding any footprints or any suspicious signs, I decided to install a game camera and a GoPro camera, along with a food gift of an apple and lollipops.

We then ventured to various locations around a 5 km (3 mi) radius to look for any activity signs and do some fishing. The cameras were picked up on Sunday afternoon, the food was intact, and there were not any signs of activities on the camera's recording, except for the usual small animals foraging for food.

## Report #55
## TAKHINI REGION
## Sighting at Fox Lake in 2014
## Location: Coord. 61o 16'32 N 135o 31'37 W
## (Map: Lake Laberge 105 E: GR 082 093)

A Kwanlin Dün First Nation woman friend reported that a woman in her early 50s was returning to the Fox Lake Government Campground at around 2130 hours (9:30 pm) after a day of fishing, on Saturday, August 16, 2014, when she observed what she described as a Sasquatch, on the west shores of Fox Lake about 3 km (2 mi) north of the campground.

**Encounter:** When talking with the witness, who is from Whitehorse and whom I know quite well, she explained to me that she had been out fishing with her husband at the north end of Fox Lake, and they were in the process of returning to the campground when she observed the creature standing on the west shore.

**Local History:** The Fox Lake Campground is a very popular campground for Whitehorse residents, as it is only an hour away from Whitehorse, and it is owned, operated, and maintained by the Yukon Government. The west shores of Fox Lake are forested with mostly black spruce and lodgepole pine with the odd stands of poplar trees.

There is no beach to speak of at that location, as the forest touches the lake itself and the land gradually increases in height to 5,277 m (17,312 ft). There was another sighting that took place in 1998 along the North Klondike Highway, Yukon Highway #2, just past Fox Lake. A report of strange vocals was recently provided to me which occurred during the very same weekend from the west shores of Little Fox Lake, located only 6 km (4 mi) north of Fox Lake.

**Investigation:** What I could gather from the witness is that she noticed what she first thought to be a large bear standing on two feet. As the boat she was riding in, piloted by her husband, came closer to shore at about 10 m (33 ft) or so away, she then identified the creature standing there as being a Sasquatch. She reported it to be tall, large, very big, and very dark. Unfortunately, the witness could not provide more specific dimensions besides tall and large, which could mean different things to different people.

The time of day was about 2130 hours (9:30 pm) during mid-August. The visibility was still good, and the sun was shining, even though it was quite low and was still above the close-by mountain to the west. I have fished on Fox Lake on a few occasions, and indeed, the area would be suitable for the legendary creatures to make their home.

There is another Sasquatch sighting which took place in 1998, Report #25, and a related vocal indident at Little Fox Lake a few hours after this one, Report #56.

## Report #56
## TAKHINI REGION
## Vocals by Little Fox Lake in 2014
## Location: Coord. 61o 20'24 N 135o 38'36 W
## (Map: Lake Laberge 105 E: GR 455 001)

A FELLOW SASQUATCH ENTHUSIAST, who at the time was residing in Alberta, contacted me by phone to report that he had heard strange unidentified vocals while staying at a friend's cabin on the shores of Little Fox Lake at around 0400 hours (4 am) on Sunday, August 17, 2014. The cabin in question is located on one of the pieces of land that is almost an island, located on the southeast shores of Little Fox Lake.

**Occurrence:** The unidentified vocals originated from the western shores across the lake. The witness is a man in his early 40s who currently resides in Edmonton, Alberta. However, he was in Whitehorse for a job interview and was at the company owner's cabin when these unidentified vocals occurred. Being a fellow Sasquatch enthusiast as well, he had contacted me three weeks earlier when he first arrived in Whitehorse.

**Local History:** The previously forested west shores of Little Fox Lake had been mostly destroyed back in 1998 during a wild forest fire and the forest is now in the process of rejuvenating itself with a new growth of trees and plants. The trees are mostly black spruces and poplars, and the terrain is mostly low-lying land with small hills amongst large boulders crisscrossed by a few creeks and a number of trails made by the firefighters while combating the 1998 fire.

**Investigation:** Besides this vocal report, there was a Sasquatch sighting that had occurred a short distance away on Thursday, July 23, 1998, on the North Klondike Highway, Yukon Highway #2, about 6 km (4 mi) southeast of this location, Report #25.

This more recent sighting was reported to me on Monday, August 18, 2014, and had occurred the evening before this vocal occurrence, at around 2130 hours (9:30 pm) on the west shore of Fox Lake on Saturday, August 16, 2014, Report #55). Fox Lake is located only 10 km (6 mi) farther south of Little Fox Lake.

According to the reporter, originally the vocals were thought to be from a barking dog, as the reporter was sleeping when the vocals started, and it had woken him up. The witness stated that the vocals sounded somewhat similar to dogs barking but were much louder, guttural, and seemed to originate from a powerful chest, a sound that no dogs could produce.

These vocals went on for a good ten minutes and according to the witness, appeared to be moving in a northern direction, away from the cabin's location, probably because the vocal maker was walking towards the north. There was no response from any other source.

This report is quite significant considering that a sighting of a Sasquatch was reported to have occurred just a few hours earlier, five and a half hours earlier, from a location only about 10 km (6 mi) away. Ever since I have been interested in the Sasquatch phenomena, I have never heard of two occurrences taking place in close proximity, within a few hours of each other, and from two different persons who did not know of each other.

It would appear to me that the vocal maker in question, most probably the Sasquatch reported to have been seen by a witness on Fox Lake, was walking in a northern direction that evening, west of the North Klondike Highway and probably might have been trying to get in contact with another of his kinfolks.

I have been to both these lakes on many occasions, mostly fishing for lake trout and have explored the entire area east of both lakes, although not as much on the west side, due to the recent forest wildfire and the dangerous condition of the terrain.

I was at both lakes and did not notice anything out of the ordinary during my last visit to the area in 2021.

**Report #57**
**TAKHINI REGION**
**Vocal by Steamboat Slough in 2014**
**Location: Coord. 60o 56'05 N 135o 03'54 W**
**(Map: Upper Laberge 105 D/14: GR 964 555)**

My youngest son and I were out on an exploration expedition in the area of Steamboat Slough, further investigating a tree thrashing occurrence that I had experienced in 2011, in Report #48, when at 1400 hours (2 pm), on Saturday, August 30, 2014, we heard some loud, unidentified strange vocals.

Occurrence: The loud yells originated from a small island located about 1.5 km (1 mi) south-southwest of the Steamboat keeper's cabin, at a location called Steamboat Slough located on the Yukon River. The exact location is 32 km (21 mi) downstream from the Robert Campbell Bridge crossing the Yukon River in downtown Whitehorse.

At the time, my youngest son and I were eating lunch at the Steamboat Slough keeper's cabin when we both heard the loud yells. We first thought that it was from a wolf. However, a short time later, a pack of wolves started to vocalize at a distance of about one kilometre northeast from where we were, an entirely different location and different sounds. These strange loud yells were clearer, much louder, and more guttural than any wolves would make.

Actually, it was identical to loud yells, recorded at an undetermined location on Vancouver Island, in British Columbia, on Monday, August 4, 2014, by a member of the British Columbia Sasquatch Organization (BCSO), as reported by Cliff Barackman on Monday, September 1, 2014.

The reason we were at this location is that we were investigating a tree-thrashing incident that I had experienced on Friday, July 22, 2011, at 1315 hours (1:15 pm) nearby a small unnamed creek crossing the Livingstone Trail close to Steamboat Slough, when this loud unidentified yell was heard. The island where the vocals came from has a good number of tall black and white spruce trees located in the centre of the island, with alders and willows along the outer edge in a shallow part of the Yukon River.The Steamboat Slough makes its way along the right-hand edge of the island and the Yukon River main channel is on the left-hand side of this unnamed island.

**Investigation:** When we originally heard these loud yells and shrieks, I did not quite know what to think. The possibility that a Sasquatch had made these yells and shrieks had crossed my mind, but I did not mention it to my son just then.

About twenty minutes later, we heard a pack of wolves loudly whining and barking, making quite a racket at a distance estimated to be about 700 m (2,275 ft) ft) north-northeast of the Steamboat Slough keeper's cabin, on the mainland.

My thought at this time was that the first yells had been made by a wolf as well, and I did not further think of these yells until checking Facebook during the afternoon of Monday, September 1, 2014, when clear loud yells, much the same as those heard, were presented by Cliff Barackman on his page. As a result, I compared both yells in my mind, and sure enough, the ones that my son and I heard were exactly the same as the ones on Cliff Barackman's Facebook page.

Some thirty minutes prior to stopping at the Steamboat Slough keeper's cabin, I had conducted a short excursion around an area about 2 km (1.6 mi) directly south of the cabin, trying to reach the Livingstone Trail, which should have been fairly close to this part of the slough. However, I had gotten into an area of the swamp that was pretty bad and became somewhat disoriented while trying to find a way around this swamp.

To get my bearings straight, I called my son, who had stayed by the boat, fishing, using the radios that we carry with us when exploring, and I asked him to blow on his whistle to provide me with a direction in order to make my way back to the boat. Thus, we exchanged a number of whistle blows until I came out of the swamp.

I now figure that as a result of us blowing the two whistles a number of times, the "yell maker" became interested in our presence and decided to contact us by yelling. We later found the Livingstone Trail and explored it for a couple of kilometres in the direction of the tree-thrashing event before turning back during a bad rainstorm and returning to our boat.

Nothing unusual was noticed during this short, wet, and muddy hike. We then put our boat back in the water and fished for northern pike for a couple of hours, successfully I might add, and returned to our boat launch site 5 km (3 mi) away, loading up the boat and started back for Whitehorse around 1830 hours (6:30 pm).

My intentions are to set-up camp on the island where the yells came from for a couple of weeks in the near future and investigate the area in question while conducting a habitation expedition. This is another location where three occurrences took place that I know of, within a very short distance of each other in a radius of 3 km (2 mi).

## Report #58
## KLONDIKE REGION
## Sighting by Moosehide Slide in Dawson City in 2014
## Location: Coord. 64o 04'23 N 139o 25'00 W
## (Map: Dawson 116 B/3: GR 772 059)

A First Nations woman friend and colleague, residing in Dawson City, contacted me in the afternoon of Wednesday, November 5, 2014, to inform me of a sighting she had just experienced.

**Encounter:** Along with one of her co-workers, she was on her way to have lunch when they observed a tall dark Sasquatch walking atop the famous Moosehide Slide, located at the north end of town, at about 1205 hours (12:05 pm). The creature walked from the west side to the east side, a distance of about 300 m (985 ft), in about five minutes at the most.

She later received a phone call from another member of the Tr'ondëk Hwëch'in First Nation (THFN), of which she is a member as well. The caller knew of her interest in the Sasquatch phenomenon and was calling her to report that he had also observed a Sasquatch by the Moosehide. Talking with him, she realized that he was talking about the very same sighting she had observed and later reported to me.

**Local History:** There is an interesting story concerning the Moosehide Slide. The name "Moosehide" refers to what the slide looks like: that of a moose hide hung ready to be tanned. In the Hans language, the name is "Edda Dadhecha," meaning "weathered moose hide hanging."

The First Nations story about Moosehide goes like this:

> "A long time ago, people camped by Tr'ondëk and the land across the river. At one time, a group of people raided the camp, so most local people moved to higher ground and set up a trap should the barbaric raiders come back. This trap consisted of big logs and rocks

> held by some rocks and tree roots. When the barbaric raiders came back, one of the brave members pulled off the rocks and roots holding the other rocks and big logs, and these caused the land to move and buried all the barbaric raiders."

Reality is a bit different though. Geologists have theorized that some eight thousand years ago, a landslide occurred at this specific location, which was caused by an increase in the temperature resulting in the topsoil layer gliding onto an ice-rich basal layer, which is a common condition with permafrost ground as is the case for this immediate area.

**Investigation:** My friend and colleague from the THFN conducted an investigation as follows. The Sasquatch sighted was measured to be at a distance of 1.3 km (0.82 mi) from where the three witnesses were standing, as measured using the Google Map Search. Using various items, such as a tall person and a piece of plywood that is 243.84 cm (8 ft) tall and placed at the same distance of 1.3 km (0.82 mi) on a flat piece of land, with the size fresh in their mind, they estimated that the Sasquatch would have been about 243.84 cm (8 ft) tall or maybe even up to 304.8 cm (10 ft).

Considering they had made the calculation on a flat piece of ground, rather than an uphill piece of ground, which would have resulted in looking up at something from of a person's normal vision and since usually, things would appear taller when looking up, I would be of the opinion that the creature they had observed would have been closer to 243.84 cm (8 ft) than the possible 304.8 cm (10 ft) mentioned.

Regardless, a Sasquatch being 243.84 cm (8 ft) tall is well within the average of a Yukon Sasquatch. According to my statistical data, the average Yukon Sasquatch stands at a height of 251.46 cm (8 ft 3 in). Such a creature of 243.84 cm (8 ft) would have a footprint measuring about 41.275 cm (16.25 in), would weigh from about 310 kg to 388 kg (between 682.5 to 855.5 lbs), and would have a step of about 159 cm (62.5 in). A Sasquatch of that size would need about 7,078 calories per day to remain healthy.

If the Sasquatch observed was about 274.32 cm (9 ft) tall the creature would have had a footprint of about 45.1 cm (17.75 in), would weigh from about 38 to 424 kg (745.5 to 934.5 lbs), and would have a step of about 173.577 cm (68.3 in). A Sasquatch of that size would require about 7,735 calories per day to remain healthy. On the other hand, if the Sasquatch observed was indeed 304.8 cm (10 ft) tall, that would mean a footprint of about 50.165 cm (19.75 in) with a weight of between 376 and 471 kg (829.5 to 1.039.5 lbs) and would have a step of 193.135 cm (76 in or 6 ft 3 in). A Sasquatch of such stature would require some 8,600 calories per day to remain in good health.

**NOTE:** The very same person, in September 2021, experienced another sighting at Angelcomb Peak by Tombstone Territorial Park, reported further in Report #69.

## Report #59
## TAKHINI REGION
## Sighting by the Robinson Roadhouse in 2014
## Location: Coord. 60o 26'56 N 134o 50'35 W
## (Map: Robinson 105 D/7: GR 085 013)

A WOMAN FRIEND called me to mention that one of her cousins had contacted her by phone to mention that she, accompanied by her mother (the sister of the woman friend who called me), had observed what she described as a Sasquatch.

**Encounter:** It was explained to my friend that they noticed the Sasquatch standing beside the road in the vicinity of the Robinson Roadhouse, a small roadside community some twenty-five kilometres down the South Klondike Highway (Carcross Road), Yukon Highway #2, around 2045 hours (8:45 pm) on Sunday, November 16, 2014, while they were returning to the community of Carcross after playing bingo in Whitehorse. The witnesses, who are both from the Carcross/Tagish First Nation (CTFN), stated they were driving at a speed of about 80 kph (50 mph) at the time and only observed the creature for a few seconds.

It would appear the bipedal entity was in the process of crossing the road by the Robinson Roadhouse Rest Area when the car approached. As the creature came into full view, now being visible in the car's headlights, it turned back in front of them and walked away into the bush on the right-hand side of the road where it had come from, with the intention of crossing the road.

**Local History:** This area is part of the Kwanlin Dün First Nation (KDFN) traditional territory and had been used by that First Nation for some eight thousand years at least, with many of its residents having homes along the Carcross Road. In 1898, the White Pass and Yukon Route Railroad Company was in the midst of constructing the railway from Skagway, Alaska, to Whitehorse, Yukon.

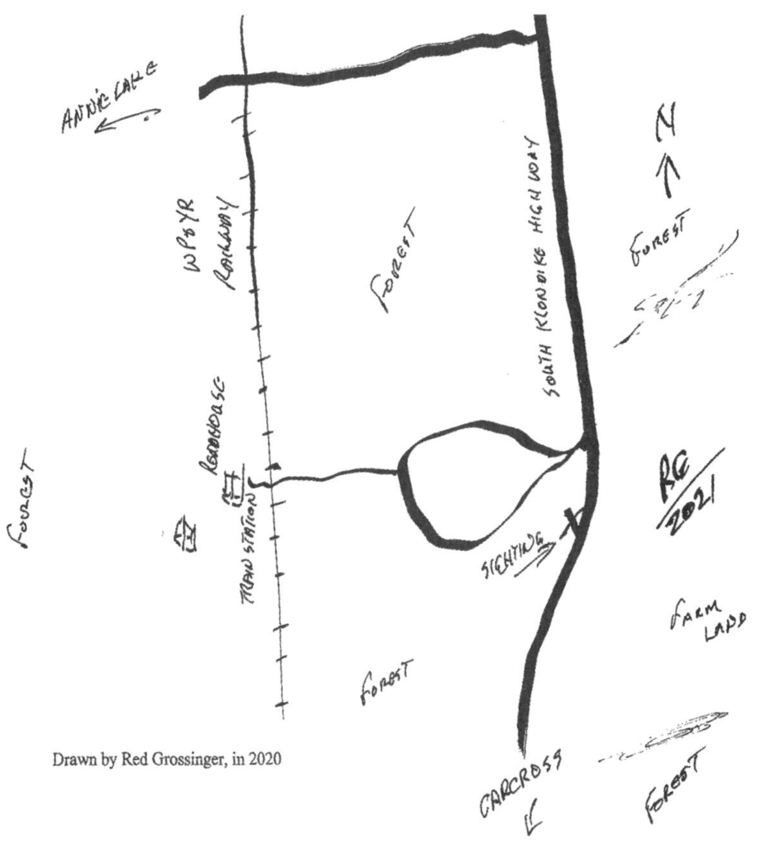


*Takhini Region: Sighting by Robinson Roadhouse,*
*on Sunday Nov. 16, 2014*

A railroad construction camp was built at this site and later, while the YP&YR was operating a roadhouse and train station, the site was called Robinson Roadhouse.

This roadhouse became a step off point from where prospectors would venture into the area of Annie Lake, where gold and other minerals had been discovered in large quantities.

Mining is still taking place in the area, although at a different level than it did over a hundred years ago. Along the Carcross Road, one finds a number of small farms as well as dog kennels and those sorts of activities.

Many Yukoners who enjoy the outdoors have taken up residency along that road as well, as the area is close to high mountain peaks offering their splendour to mountaineering enthusiasts and hikers as well as white water paddlers who would challenge the turbulent waters of the Wheaton and the Watson Rivers.

**Investigation:** The witnesses were not willing to discuss their sighting with me directly. However, my woman friend who is of First Nation descent as well, and the cousin of the witnesses who had originally contacted me, was able to get details concerning the bipedal ambulating entity that was observed that dark evening.

By all indication, the creature, identified as a Sasquatch by the witnesses, appeared to have been about 213 cm (7 ft) tall or so, and according to them had dark black hair, with a bit of reflection from the lights of the car, and no obvious observed breasts.

They only saw the creature for a few seconds, as it stepped back and turned around towards where it first came from.

Therefore, they could not comment on the gait or method of its walking. However, they did notice the hands clenched as if making a fist and the fingers being turned facing its rear, as opposed to the hand position of a human where the fingers face inward and towards the body.

This clenching trait is important, as it is quite similar to another sighting observed in July 2010 by Crestview, a subdivision of Whitehorse.

I should mention that the man who witnessed the Crestview sighting in 2010 is the father of my woman friend in question. Interestingly, the wife of that man is the sister of the Elder First Nation woman from Carcross, who was a witness in this sighting.

Based on the limited description of the Sasquatch observed, the following can be presented: a bipedal ambulating entity said to be 213 cm tall (7 ft) would have a footprint of about 35 cm (13.75 in) or so, would weigh some 262 kg (578 lbs) if of medium size, as this one is reported to have been, or as high as 328 kg (723 lbs) if of a larger frame.

The step of such a creature would be about 134.5 cm (53 in), and in order to remain in good health a Sasquatch of this size would need some 6,000 calories per day.

The paved Carcross Road, as most of us around these parts call it, is officially called the South Klondike Highway. Yukon highway #2, as it is known, was measured to be some 7.4 m (24 ft) wide at this location with a shoulder of 1 m (39 in) on each side of the road. A pullout to the Robinson Roadhouse and Train Station Rest Area, now a historic site, is located at this very site.

There was another sighting that had occurred on Friday, January 6, 2006, only 8 km (5 mi) north on the same road, by what is described as the Cowley Stretch, where a bipedal ambulating creature was observed standing beside a power pole at about 2100 hours (9 pm) by a Kwanlin Dün First Nation woman returning to Whitehorse after visiting family and friends at the Community of Carcross, Report #34. Another Sasquatch occurrence took place on Annie Lake Road in 2010, Report #45.

I was last at these locations in the summer of 2021 and did not observe or hear anything out of the ordinary.

## Report #60
## KLUANE REGION
## Sighting at Marshall Creek in 2015
## Location: Coord. 60o 83'54 N 137o 33'21 W
## (Map: Dezadeash 115A: GR 373 746)

DURING THE EARLY EVENING of Wednesday, July 20, 2015, four ladies from the Champagne Aishihik First Nation (CAFN) were returning home to Haines Junction after spending some time in Whitehorse. As the car approached Marshall Creek, one of them noted that she saw what she thought was a man in dark coveralls picking berries beside the road. She mentioned this to the others, and one of them wondered aloud, "Why is there no vehicle parked by the bridge?" Very odd, they thought.

**Encounter:** As the car slowed down before crossing the Marshall Creek Bridge, one of the ladies said, "That's not a man—that's a Sasquatch." The car driver slowed down and stopped just past the bridge, a couple of metres beside the entity.

All of them had a good look at the creature, who at the time was hunched over picking some berries, only about 2 m (6 ft) from the road where the car had stopped.

A few seconds later, when the creature became aware of the car, it stood up, looked at the car, appearing to be rather curious, intrigued, and not frightened in any way. It did not attempt to move away, according to one of the elderly ladies.

Two other cars went by while their car was stopped. None of those cars' occupants appeared to pay much attention to what was going on.

After two or three minutes, the Sasquatch departed, slowly walking into the bush, and the ladies carried on to their homes in Haines Junction. Upon arrival, one of them contacted a related CAFN man.

This man, whom I have known for a few years, and who is aware of my research work on the matter of Sasquatch, sent me an email the morning of Thursday, July 21, 2015, mentioning the sighting and provided me with all the details he had.

I contacted a friend of mine who is a member of another First Nation, and she contacted one of the witnesses, as she knew that person quite well. She conducted a short interview concerning the sighting on my behalf. This friend passed on the information to me afterward, as it is reported above.

**Local History:** Marshall Creek is located about halfway between the Aishihik River at a point where it crosses the Alaska Highway, Yukon Highway #1, in the small First Nation community of Canyon and the community of Haines Junction, at the junction of the Alaska Highway and the Haines Road, Yukon Highway #8. This area is part of the CAFN traditional territory.

**Investigation:** I visited the location of the sighting on Friday, July 22, 2015, and all I could see were hundreds of foot impressions around trampled plants, tall grass, and a few berry bushes. Apparently, many people from Haines Junction and Champagne had visited the site to pick berries and walked over any possible useful evidence.

The only information from the interview that is useful is that the bipedal ambulating entity, identified as a Sasquatch by the occupants of the car, was about 2.3 m (7 ft) tall with very dark long hair, standing erect on two feet with no apparent breasts. The upper body was muscular but not fat and it did not appear to be afraid of the car or its occupants.

I can gather the following information using the stated height of the observed Sasquatch: the weight would be about 267 kg (588 lbs), his footprint would be about 35 cm (14 in), the step would be some 137 cm (4.5 ft), the stride twice as much. Such an entity would require about 6,000 calories per day to remain healthy.

I make a point of stopping at Marshall Creek when driving in the area to check the countryside. Actually, this is a good fly-fishing spot for Arctic graylings as well.

## Report #61
## SQUANGA REGION
## Footprints and Vocals close to Morley Lake in 2015
## Location: Coord. 59o 57'32 N 132o 04'29 W
## (Map: Atlin 104 N: GR 063 051)

In early October 2015, a man and woman from the community of Langley, in British Columbia, along with two male friends, decided to go moose hunting at a seldom-used location in Northern British Columbia.

This area can only be accessed through a short trail off the present Alaska Highway. That trail is actually part of the Old Alaska Highway in south-central Yukon, only a couple of kilometres from the southwest end of Morley Lake. This lake straddles the 60th parallel of latitude, which is the northern boundary of the province of British Columbia and the southern boundary of the Yukon Territory.

That area, actually being outside of the Yukon, is not usually open for hunting by Yukon hunters unless one gets a special and expensive BC "out-of-province" hunting license.

**Occurrence:** They had arrived in the area during the afternoon of Saturday, October 3, 2015, and had planned to spend a maximum of one week in the area. After setting up camp on the south side and close to the Old Alaska Highway, they settled in for their first night.

Early the next morning, Sunday, October 4, 2015, they set out on foot and within a couple of hours, managed to shoot two moose in an area of about a 200 m (500 ft) radius, fairly close to their campsite. The last one was shot at the edge of a clearing.

After loading up one of the moose, and while loading up the second one in the pickup truck, they had looked around to find a proper location to discard the remains of the animal's guts when a member of the hunting party noticed some extraordinary large human-like footprints (some they had actually destroyed by their own feet while walking over them).

The wife of one hunter, having previously heard of Sasquatch, soon realized that these footprints would have most likely been made by one of those giant bipedal ambulating entities. She studied the footprints for a while, took some photos, that you can see on the next pages, then decided it was worth making a cast of one of the footprints and convinced her husband and his partners that they would need some casting material.

They drove to the community of Teslin, some 60 km (37 mi) away, but could not get what they were looking for at the only grocery store in town. So, they decided to drive to Whitehorse, a distance of 180 km (112 mi) farther northwest, to get the stuff.

Once they had acquired the needed material, they immediately made their way back to the hunting site, arriving at about 1800 hours (6 pm).

Quickly, they poured the casting material and decided to return to Teslin for dinner since they had to wait a good five to six hours for the casting slurry to set properly.

At about midnight, they returned to the location, and as they were digging the cast of the footprint they had made, they started to hear some strange and scary loud noises coming from the nearby forest.

Not knowing what all the noises were at first, they were able to identify the sounds as that of something like a very large bipedal creature was walking around them. By this time, they were simply terrified, and they quickly loaded up the cast in the front passenger seat of the vehicle, and just as quickly, they started piling up in the pickup truck. Then at that moment, a terrifying loud yell could be heard from the forest.

They departed in a hurry, not slowing down until they reached Teslin, where they spent the night at a local motel. The following morning they returned to their campsite to retrieve their tents and camping gear. They noticed some damage to their stuff and a few more of these large human-like footprints but being somewhat afraid and not wanting to stay any longer than needed, they loaded everything up and left the area for good.

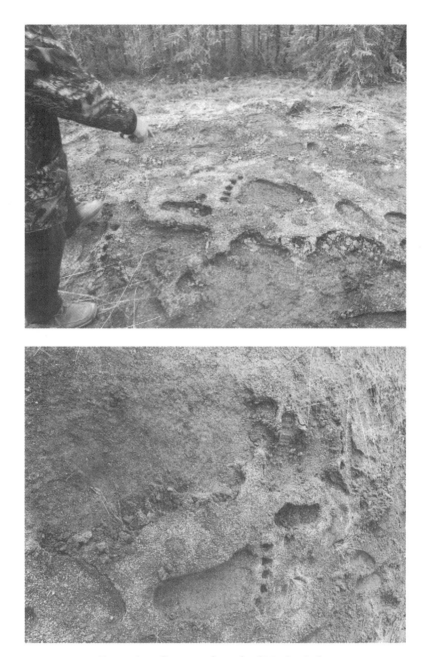

*Footprints discovered south of Morley Lake.*
*Photos courtesy of Vicki Pederson*

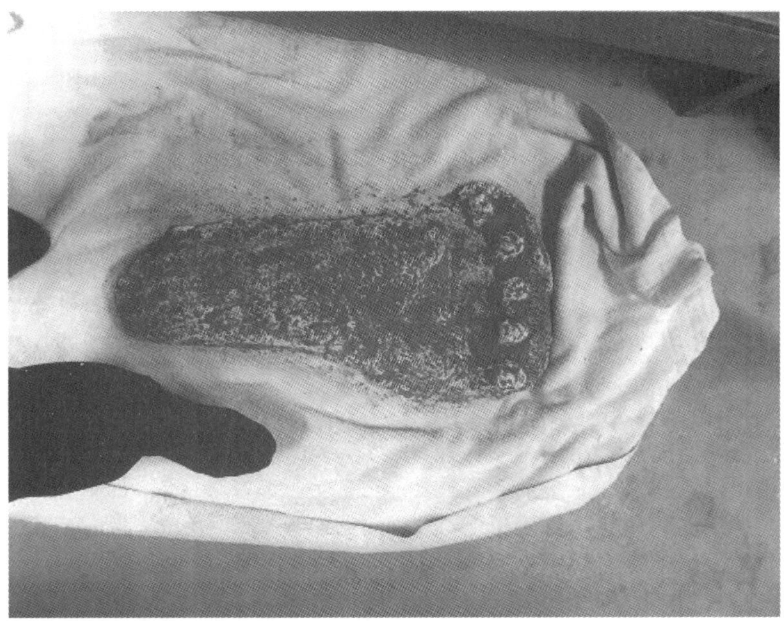

*Footprints discovered south of Morley Lake.*
*Photos courtesy of Vicki Pederson*

They returned home a few days later. The woman had been looking at the cast they had made and was further investigating what the actual source of the print-maker could be. Doing so, she became more and more confident that the footprints they saw could have only been made by a Sasquatch.

**Investigation:** Late in the afternoon of Monday, October 26, 2015, I received an email from one of the news reporters at the *Yukon News,* a Yukon regional newspaper, who had received an email accompanied by a photograph of one footprint from the woman in question, along with her email information.

The first thing I did on Tuesday, October 27, 2015, was to contact the witness, introducing myself as the local Sasquatch enthusiast and investigator in the Yukon. The woman who had sent the email was very responsive to my questions about the footprints, and we exchanged a few emails.

We had a few phone conversations, and she provided me with whatever information I asked for. What had happened is that when they became aware of these human-like footprints they never thought of taking actual ground measurements of the footprints per se, like the length, the width at various locations, the depth, and such. As they simply were not aware of the importance of on-the-ground in situ measurements.

However, the cast they had made was later measured as being 55.88 cm (22 in) long with a width of 27.94 cm (11 in) at the toes, 22.8 cm (9 in) just below the toes (as shown in the attached photo), 16.51 cm (6.5 in) at midfoot, and 13.47 cm (5.5 in) at the heel.

Looking at the photos she had sent me with the various emails, my estimation would indicate a depth of about 2.25 cm (1 in) at the ball of the foot and about 18 mm (0.75 in) at the heel.

That would indicate that the print-maker would have been about 339.191 cm or 3.391 m (11ft) tall with a weight of some 419 kg (924 lbs) if of medium-size, but it was most probably a heavier entity of about 525 kg (1,157 lbs), which would have a step of about 215 cm or 2.15 m (7ft). Such a print-maker would need roughly 9,575 calories per day to remain healthy.

As one can see from the photos on the previous pages, this would indicate a very large print-maker, larger than any previously observed footprints reported in the Yukon. (Or in this case, Northern BC). The photos, as well as the cast, indicate a clear set of five toes, with some earth disturbance around the toes.

There was another set of large human-like footprints very close by which would indicate that the print-maker was actually standing still at that location and these two footprints were not part of a normal walking pattern. Some of the photos also indicated many earth disturbances in the immediate area, some obviously made by the hunting party and others having been made from a two-legged walking entity other than the hunters.

I had intended to drive to the discovery site to investigate in location; however, since I could not get there in October nor in early November, due to my prior commitments in organizing and coordinating the Remembrance Day Ceremony taking place in Whitehorse on Wednesday, November 11, 2015, I just could not find the time to make it out there.

By the time the 12th of November came around, there was some 60 cm (2 ft) of snow on the ground. I was planning an investigative expedition as soon as possible in the spring of 2016; this expedition would be for a period of at least two weeks. I would be setting up my travel trailer fairly close to where the discovery was made, with the intention of attracting and filming a Sasquatch, if lucky. Unfortunately, that expedition had to be postponed, as my wife became quite sick with lung cancer and eventually passed away.

A few other things happened, and it was only in 2017 that I had time to get going. I conducted a three-day expedition to locate the hunting camp and the moose-killing site in July. No interesting signs were found at either location by that time. In 2020, I undertook another short expedition to the same area to look for any interesting activity signs, from Monday, June 25, 2020, to Wednesday, June 27, 2020.

Nothing possibly related to Sasquatch activities was noted during that expedition, although there have been a large number of moose activities in the area.

## Report #62
## SQUANGA REGION
## Vocals and Tree Banging at the South end of Teslin Lake in 2016
## Location: Coord. 59o 73'16 N 132o 06'58 W
## (Map: Atlin 104 N: GR 064 012)

IN THE SUMMER OF 2016, along with four close friends, I participated in an expedition to locate Camp Victoria, which was constructed by the Yukon Field Force in August of 1898, at the point where the Teslin River flows into Teslin Lake in Northern British Columbia.

**Local history:** The Yukon Field Force was formed of members of the Canadian Regular Militia in 1898 to assist the North-West Mounted Police (NWMP) in the Klondike. Departing from Vancouver BC by ship, they had made it as far as the small BC community of Telegraph Creek. From there, they walked 200 km (125 miles) along the Telegraph Trail to Teslin Lake, where they set up Camp Victoria and started constructing boats that would take them to Dawson City in the Klondike.

Our group, which we called "The Legion Five," had organized a few fishing expeditions in the past, usually going to a different location for each voyage. In 2016, we decided to visit Camp Victoria on Teslin Lake from Sunday, July 3, 2016, to Wednesday, July 6, 2016.

**Expedition:** We put the boat in at the Teslin Community's dock and departed around 1100 hours (11 am) on a rainy Sunday, with the objective of finding Camp Victoria. On our way we decided to stop at a point of land that became to be known as "Buday's Point" at the BC/Yukon Border.

Back in March of 1985, the "M" Division of the RCMP from Whitehorse were searching for a hermit-like violent trapper by the name of Michael Oros, better known as "Crazy Mike," who after committing a few crimes, was sought after by the law. Flying in a small plane, the RCMP team located Crazy Mike walking on the frozen lake and decided to land in order to arrest him. While on approach, Crazy Mike fired at the plane, missing it.

But, by now, he was well within BC jurisdiction, and the Yukon RCMP team could not legally make an arrest. The following day, a RCMP team from Prince Rupert, BC arrived in Whitehorse and using the "M" Division's Twin Otter plane, set out to arrest Crazy Mike close to the BC/Yukon Border. After the plane landed, a group of RCMP officers started chasing Crazy Mike, approaching him; he started firing at the officers, killing Constable Michael Buday, near what came to be known as Buday's Point. Later on, a marker was erected at that site. As we approached the point, we decided to stop to pay our respects.

We made a few more stops along the way, and by 1600 hours (4 pm), we started looking for a suitable campsite to spend a few nights. We found an appropriate location in a small, protected bay at GR 064 012. It being still daylight, we decided to explore further south on the lake, hoping to locate Camp Victoria, which we did at around 1930 hours (7:30 pm). We walked around the site to ascertain that indeed it was the right place.

As we were now close to the Teslin River, in a mostly marshy area with millions of mosquitoes, we decided not to stay overnight and returned to the small bay previously located, where we set up our camp for the next few days.

**Occurrence:** One of my companions got up at about 0400 hours (4 am) to answer the call of nature, which was now Monday, July 4, 2016, and while up, he heard a few quiet "whoops" coming from the forest, first from his left, which would have been in the northern direction, then from another direction towards his right.

When I got up around 0600 hours (6 am), he mentioned that what he had heard, whatever or whomever it was, appeared to have been communicating with each other in a subdued manner.

**Investigation:** After breakfast, at around 0900 hours (9 am), even though it was raining hard, my friend and I conducted a walk-about around our piece of land, looking for anything out of the ordinary. Nothing of interest was located, so we joined the rest of the group for lunch, and, as it was still raining, we decided to go fishing rather than return to Camp Victoria.

We caught our limit of fish and went back to our campsite for a dinner of fresh lake trout, after which I installed two trail cameras and a GoPro camera at different locations. The night was uneventful: nothing, no calls or anything of that nature, and no movement detected by the cameras. On Tuesday, the weather finally changed, and that allowed us to visit Camp Victoria and fully explore the area.

We located the remains of four old cabins, as the information about the site had indicated. We cleaned around a cairn erected by the 2nd Battalion of the Royal Canadian Regiment in 1982 and generally made the site more visible. We returned to camp, and after a dinner of ham, I repositioned the cameras again for the night.

**Second Occurrence:** Later that night, at around 2300 hours (11 pm), we heard movement in the forest. It was clear that something bipedal was walking about, at a distance of 200-plus m (210 yd) or so away from our camp, inside the dense forest and away from observation. But that was all. No yells or shouts, just a heavy bipedal walking sound.

In the middle of the night, at about 0330 hours (3:30 am) on the Wednesday, my friend heard a tree banging sound, three distinctive bangs, about five seconds apart, and then some intense shrieking, first from one location to our south, then from the north. This was followed by total silence. I got up early that morning, along with my friend, and we again explored around our campsite. Once more, our search did not reveal anything out of the ordinary and nothing was picked up by the cameras.

After breakfast, we packed up camp and departed, our time being up and some of my other companions needing to return to work.

**Report #63**
**Squanga Region**
**Tree Thrashing with Vocals at south end of Teslin Lake in 2017**
**Location: Coord. 59o 37'16 N 132o 06'58 W**
**(Map: Atlin 104 N: GR 064 012)**

IN 2017, the group of friends and I, called "The Legion Five," returned to Camp Victoria, at the south end of Teslin Lake, where we had been in 2016.

Our yearly expedition took place from Wednesday, July 5, 2017, to Saturday, July 8, 2017, with the objectives of further exploring the site and cleaning the site up a bit more. In addition, two of us were to conduct an investigation concerning Sasquatch-related activities that had taken place in 2016 at the very same location.

We put our boat in the water at the Teslin community's dock again and departed around 1030 hours (10:30 am) in the direction of Camp Victoria. As we approached Buday's Point, we noticed two RCMP boats and a group of RCMP officers as well as BC Conservation officers at the location of Constable Buday's Cairn. We stopped to introduce ourselves and paid our respects.

The group had been cleaning the area around the cairn. We arrived at our destination at around 1700 hours (5 pm) and set-up camp and had dinner, after which I ventured out to set up a couple of cameras.

**Occurrence:** All was quiet during the first night. However, during the second night, July 6–7, we heard some trees being thrashed and banged against each other at around 0430 hours (4:30 am). Then we heard the same thing the following night, July 7–8, at various times, with a few vocals identified as low whoops. These did not seem to be a threat in any way.

**Investigation:** On each occasion, along with a friend, I investigated the area, checked out the cameras, but found no clues as to what made all the racket. There was nothing on the cameras.

Later on, during the third day, I ventured some two kilometres away from camp, investigating in a large circle but could not find any signs indicating any possible activities. We departed as scheduled on Saturday, July 8, 2017, on our way back to Whitehorse as some members of the team had to return to work. Our team now increased to six, we made a trip to Atlin Lake, BC, in 2018 and were subjected to some tree-related activities as well. See related occurrence, Report #66.

**Report #64**
**KLONDIKE REGION**
**Footprints at 40 Mile, in 2017**
**Location: Coord. 64o 25'31 N 140o 32'00 W**
**(Map: Dawson 116 B & 116 C: GR 022 044)**

WHILE ATTENDING a work-related conference in Dawson City, as part of my activities with the Yukon Heritage Resources Board in October 2017, I had the occasion to touch base with my friend and colleague who is a member of the Tr'ondeck Hwech'in First Nation (THFN) in Dawson City.

**Occurrence:** My colleague mentioned that four members of the THFN were on a hunting trip at the 40 Mile (Ch'eda Dek) area in late September of 2017 when they came upon several large human-like footprints, some measuring 38.1 cm (15 in) and some up to 40.64 cm (16 in), along the shores of both the 40 Mile River and the Yukon River.

Knowing of her interest in Sasquatch, they mentioned the discovery to her upon returning to Dawson City.

**Local History:** The name "40 Mile" designates the distance between the Yukon/Alaska border by water, which is 64 km (40 mi) to the former community of Forty Mile. Prior to the large discovery of gold in the Klondike, this small community with a warehouse, a trading post, and the mining registrar office, was located at the confluence of the 40 Mile River to the Yukon River, mostly dealing in fur.

The North-West Mounted Police, now the RCMP, also erected a post at 40 Mile, which they called Fort Reliance.

When gold was discovered in large quantity in Rabbit Creek (now Bonanza Creek) in August 1896, most members of this small community simply moved to what is now Dawson City and claimed most of the land around various creeks and rivers in the area that came to be known as The Klondike.

**Investigation:** As my friend explained, these four hunters had come by boat from Dawson City and arrived at 40 Mile around 1500 hours (3 pm). As soon as they landed, they noticed large human-like footprints, which were probably a couple of days old by then, according to one of the hunters.

They are certain that the footprints were left behind by some Sasquatch, and one of the THFN members noticed two different sizes.

Some of the footprints measured 38 cm (15 in). This would indicate a print-maker being about 231 cm tall (92 in or 7 ft 6 in), weighing around 286 kg (630 lbs) with a step of some 147 cm (58 in), or so. Some 6,535 calories per day would be the intake of such an entity.

Other footprints measured 40.64 cm (16 in) these would indicate the print-maker being some 245 cm tall (97 in or 8 ft). The step taken by this individual would be 156 cm (61 in or 5 ft) tall and would weigh about 305 kg (673 lbs). A Sasquatch of this size would need at least 6,969 calories per day to remain healthy.

I was at Ch'eda Dek (40 Mile River) during the summer of 2020, with my spouse and a couple of friends, and looked for further possible Sasquatch indications but did not find anything.

## Report #65
## KENO REGION
## Vocals and Fleeting Movements north of Mayo in 2017
## Location: Coord. 63o 57'57 N 135o 27'54 W
## (Map: Mount Haldane 105 M/13: GR 624 859)

**A man** called me on Monday, October 30, 2017, reporting strange occurrences he had experienced earlier in October while moose hunting just north of the community of Mayo in central Yukon.

**Occurrence:** He explained his experience to me, and I asked him to write everything down and mail it to me, as emails do not work where he is residing, which he did. The following account describes what he experienced that evening.

At about 1830 hours (6:30 pm) on Saturday, October 28, 2017, the witness was sitting in a hunting hide located by a small forest clearing a few metres away from Haldane Creek and made a couple of moose calls, hoping that a male moose would come by soon, being vigilant and trying not to make his presence known.

All was quiet for about one hour when at about 2000 hours (8 pm), he started hearing slow heavy ambulating footsteps coming from the nearby forest, on his right-hand side. The print-maker then stopped for a few seconds and departed in the direction it came from, running very fast for a short distance and stopping again.

At that moment, a strong unidentified and strange smell, similar to that of a skunk, was noticed by the witness.

The bipedal ambulating entity then started walking again, this time very slowly, still making muffled and squishy noises while walking on a dry ground mostly covered by dry lichen and moss. The reporter could not really see what was moving but could, at times, observe swift undescribed fleeting movements, obviously made by the ambulating entity.

At this time, the witness reports some squirrels started making loud noises further away in the bush. Shortly after, the witness heard a loud "quack," which I take as a tree being hit with another, then about five seconds later, a loud "hoot." This repetition of "quack" and "hoot" went on about eight times, then silence.

About five minutes later, the sound of walking could be heard again, with twigs cracking, from the same location accompanied by a swift indiscernible movement behind the bush, and then all was quiet.

The witness then walked back to his truck, located some 100 m (360 ft) away, and drove about half a kilometre further down the road. He then stopped, got out of his truck, and again made a couple of moose calls, a usual practice when moose hunting.

The response, which appeared to come generally from the location he had just left, was a very clear and loud "hoot," then the witness stated that the noise maker kept making vocals in a group of five calls, then would stop for about five seconds, then other similar calls would come from another direction.

Both calls would be repeated with another five vocals in sequence, switching directions each time. This went on for some ten minutes until both callers decided to walk away.

The witness states that no further strange sounds were heard that evening, and he went back home shortly thereafter when it started getting too dark to hunt, at about 2130 hours (9:30 pm).

**Investigation:** My first impression was that this report was made by a credible witness, which was later confirmed after interviewing the witness at his home, a few kilometres north of Mayo and later at the occurrence site. The ambulating bipedal entity in question was walking and the "hooting" was clearly heard by the witness.

I figured the ambulating entity was responding to the moose calls the reporter was making by positioning itself in a close-by location, possibly waiting for a kill.

I mention this point because a few years ago I was visiting a friend in Prince George, BC, and during our conversation he mentioned that a couple of years before my visit he was out hunting moose and after shooting a young one, a large entity identified as a Sasquatch, took hold of the dead moose and took it away.

To be noted, various moose hunters would have a variety of different calls imitating the calls of a female moose and would make them with the hope that a male moose would answer the calls. This is the object of moose hunting: the human callers try to sound like a female moose calling a male moose, then waiting for the male to come by.

After making arrangements with the reporter, I went to Mayo during the period of Friday, July 13, 2018, to Wednesday, July 18, 2018, to conduct an on-site investigation.

He took me to the exact location of the occurrence and explained once more what had occurred without changing the original account. He showed me where the walking took place, not more than 50 m (160 ft) from his location, the trees that were moved, and the location of the unidentified movement that was briefly observed.

I took the time to walk about the location to determine what would have been happening and to get a clearer idea of these reported movements. We later returned to my campsite at the Five Mile Lake Campground and further discussed his experience.

He did not experience anything unusual during the 2018 or 2019 hunting seasons; I was in the Region in 2020 and did not experience or see anything related to Sasquatch.

**Geography:** The area of the occurrences is mostly low ground with the usual types of trees and a creek carrying the water off Mount Haldane which empties into the McQuesten River.

This mountain is some 1,838.5 m (6,032 ft) tall, with a number of mining operations around it.

**Of interest:** A very large gold mining operation, operated by Victoria Gold Ltd, has started some 20 km (12 mi) away from the vocal occurrence location in 2019. Due to a large increase in traffic and overall activities in the area, the upgrading of the access road along with the construction of an electrical power line, it is quite conceivable that any Sasquatch previously in the area would have moved further away.

There have been a few other reports from the immediate area, Reports #16, #24, #37, and #50.

## Report #66
## SQUANGA REGION
## Tree Thrashing on the shores of Atlin Lake in 2018
## Location: Coord. 59o 12'08 N 133o 54'20 W (Map: Sloko Lake, 104 N/4: GR625 629)

In July of 2018, I was out on Atlin Lake, in Northern British Columbia, with a group of friends now called "The Legion Six" on our annual fishing trip. We had left Whitehorse around 1030 hours (10:30 am) on Tuesday, July 3, 2018, arriving at the BC community of Atlin by Atlin Lake at about 1300 hours (1 pm). We soon put the boat in the water, and we departed for the south end of the lake and arrived at our destination at about 1730 hours (5:30 pm).

**Occurrence:** We had set up camp in a small, protected cove on Sloko Island, cut a few logs, and got a fire going. As we were preparing to get dinner ready, we heard some noise in the nearby forest: trees being banged against each other and one large tree being broken right off and thrown to the ground. The interesting part is that there was no wind whatsoever at the time, so the cause of this tree falling was certainly not the wind.

**Investigation:** I immediately went into the forest towards the noise and found the downed tree, which was about 100 cm (40 in) in circumference and was broken at the root system. There were some scuff marks on the ground, but nothing that would indicate what had pushed it.

I looked for moose tracks or bear tracks specifically, but none were visible in the nearby distance from the tree, no clues as to what had pushed this tree over.

We discussed what would have caused the tree banging and what would have caused the tree to fall but could not come to a reasonable conclusion. Later, after dinner that evening, I set up two game cameras. During our entire stay, I checked the cameras twice a day, but nothing was recorded but bird's movements and our walks about the area.

I ventured into the forest and nearby area every day during our four-day stay but found nothing else of significance, except for a number of hard stone spheres embedded into the lakeside hills, locally called "thunder rocks." By judging the trajectory of these stones and the depth into which they were embedded, they probably were catapulted with high velocity. I know of only two other locations where these are found close by, and I actually kept a few for good luck.

## Report #67
## TAKHINI REGION
## Vocals along the Takhini River Valley in 2018
## Location: Coord. 60o 51'21 N 135o 45'20 W
## (Map: Thirty-Seven Mile Creek 105D/13: GR 599 465)

IN EARLY SEPTEMBER OF 2018, a First Nations woman contacted me by email requesting a meeting to report some vocals she had heard on a few occasions along the Takhini River Valley. It so happened that I had planned a weekend camping trip to Kusawa Lake, just a few kilometres southwest of the location where she had heard all these vocals, and we made arrangements to meet up at the campground on Saturday, September 8, 2018, at around 1400 hours (2:00 pm). She arrived with her husband and her young child and started to explain what she had heard. Strange vocals originating from the Takhini River Valley, close to her present home, had started in the winter of 2016, soon after they had moved into their new home.

**Occurrence:** The first time she had heard these strange and odd vocals was in mid-winter when she and her husband had returned home from a shopping trip in Whitehorse at about 0030 hours (12:30 am).

They had unloaded the groceries and were sitting at the dining room table, with the window directly beside them partially open. It had been a warm winter day, one of our warm-wind chinooks, when they first heard their dogs getting wild and barking excessively.

This is when they heard a number of very deep and powerful howls, louder than the barking from all the dogs, overpowering, each howl followed by a sort of loud screaming moan.

The vocals lasted for about three minutes, and then all was quiet. At first, they were both in shock, and they simply stood there. The following day she mentioned the incident to a neighbour who had also heard it.

This person also mentioned that such vocals happened fairly often around these parts, and some people had said they were from a Sasquatch. Since the first night, they have heard the same vocals once or twice a month, between 2300 and 0100 hours (11 pm and 1 am), on one occasion at 0300 hours (3 am).

On Monday, September 3, 2018, she was sitting at the dining room table while her husband was doing dishes. At about 2300 hours (11 pm), she heard a loud and deep moan, which seemed to be coming from across the Takhini River Valley. Her dog was at the door "crying" to get in, as she said.

She grabbed her cell phone and went out and pressed record. She was then lucky enough to record two loud screaming and moaning type of howls, the same as she had often heard before.

**Local History:** The area where all this occurred is a subdivision called Takhini River Subdivision, located fifty kilometres west of the city of Whitehorse on the Alaska Highway. Members of the Champagne Aishihik First Nation (CAFN) have been living here for hundreds of years, and most present inhabitants are First Nations Peoples from various Yukon First Nations.

**Investigation:** When we met on Saturday, September 8, 2018, she played the recording; the content was clearly the type of loud moaning that I had heard on a few occasions around the Yukon and from the recordings of other people found on the internet. For all intents and purposes, this is still an ongoing investigation; I have asked the woman in question to keep a record of any noise and vocals she may hear by date, time, and type. I plan on setting up camp somewhere close by at some time in late spring with recording equipment to see what I can record or observe.

The woman in question, who is a member of the Champagne Aishihik First Nation (CAFN), also mentioned that she had lived in another nearby house with her grandmother in the mid-1990s, and she'd had other similar experiences while living there.

One particular experience that she remembered was that her grandmother had known about a large Sasquatch creature coming across the Takhini Valley about once a month or so, and while her gramma was still alive, she would bring food to a close by location for her Sasquatch visitor.

## Report #68
## TAKHINI REGION
## Tree Thrashing and Footsteps Experienced by Kusawa Lake in 2019
## Location: Coord. 60o 14'06 N 136o 04'06 W (Map: Ark Mountain 115A/1: GR 427 741)

In July of 2019, I was out fishing with a group of friends, "The Legion Six," during our annual fishing/exploration trip around the Yukon. Each year we visit a different lake to fish in, and this year we decided on Kusawa Lake. We left Whitehorse at 1000 hours (10 am) on Thursday, July 2, 2019, arriving at Kusawa Lake at about 1130 hours (11:30 am). Quickly putting the two boats in the water, we departed for our campsite destination, some 50 km (30 mi) down the lake, arriving around 1400 hours (2 pm). We set-up camp, gathered and cut some firewood, and relaxed till dinner at about 1800 hours (6 pm).

**Occurrence:** After a dinner of ham steak, we were relaxing by the campfire, sharing stories and planning the next day's activities, when we heard some thrashing coming from the forest that appeared to be at a distance of 200 to 300 m (650 to 985 ft), at about 2010 hours (8:10 pm), we clearly heard trees being banged against each other and what sounded like a tree being thrown, followed by more general thrashing and vague vocals, yet there was no wind at all that would have caused such activities.

**Investigation:** Four of us immediately went out in the direction of this noise, with the hope of finding out what was the cause of all this racket. We explored the forest for some 300 m (985 ft) with no specific result. I found what could have been part of a tree that could have been thrown but nothing else.

The ground was covered with pine needles, dry soil and hard soil all around us, so no trace of foot impression could be found either. We discussed what could have caused all that racket and dismissed bears, moose, caribou, or other similar large animals, but none of us could identify what or whom could have made the type of tree-thrashing that we had all clearly heard.

Three of us were of the opinion that it could well have been a Sasquatch informing us of his displeasure of us being in his territory, while the other three did not know what to think of this occurrence. I later installed three game cameras at various locations around our campsite with the hope of catching something, but unfortunately, all the photos were only of the six of us wandering about the area, as well as birds and small animals.

At around 0300 hours (3 am) that night, which was now Friday, July 3, 2019, two of us heard the sound of footsteps made by a large bipedal entity walking close by. I got out of my tent into the night but could not see anything, nor did we hear anything further.

The footstep sound was definitely from a heavy ambulating bipedal entity walking slowly close to my tent, but again no traces or foot impressions were found when I closely examined the terrain the following morning.

A friend and I ventured out in the surrounding forest on a regular basis during our four-day stay at our campsite but did not find anything of interest.

**Geography:** Kusawa Lake is situated in a deep valley with mountains reaching up to some 2,438.5m (8,000 ft), upon which numerous ice fields are present. Some 500 m (1,640 ft) north of our campsite the Takhini River flows into Kusawa Lake.

Our campsite was in a forested area with gradual terrain elevation within 300 m (985 ft) of our campsite leading up to the Boundary Range Coast Mountains and only 25 km (15.5 mi) north of the border with British Columbia.

This type of terrain offers plenty of wild animals, trees, fish, and plants suitable to eat, which certainly would be attractive for a Sasquatch family to call home.

## Report #69
## KLONDIKE REGION
## Sighting by Angelcomb Peak in 2021
## Location: Coord. 64o 36'15 N 138o 17'52W
**Map of Tombstone Territorial Park, with the sighting location pinpointed, is attached, along with two "blurry" photographs taken by the witness.**

On Sunday, August 1, 2021, a Tr'ondëk Hwëch'in First Nation woman friend and colleague was hiking up the Angelcomb Peak Trail with a group of friends, when they noticed a large ambulating creature walking down a slope of the Angelcomb Peak, away from any regular trails, about 1 km (0.6 mi) to their left. The group had left the Tombstone Territorial Park campground at 1100 hours (11 am) that day and started their hike at about noon. It was a clear and hot day. There were no other hikers around, nor any vehicles parked at the parking area located at Km 81 of the Dempster Highway, the start of the hiking trail; therefore, they were certain that there was no one else in the area.

**Encounter:** The group had been hiking up the trail for just about one and a half hours when they decided to have something to eat; they found a place to sit and started their lunch break.

While so doing, a member of the group noticed something moving to their left and a bit farther up the mountain. What was observed moving was a large bipedal entity, which was going downhill at this point, and identified by my colleague as a Sasquatch.

She was able to take a couple of photographs with her cell phone; but they are not quite clear enough to easily make out any specific physical details of the ambulating entity. At about the same time, as the Sasquatch also seemed to have noticed the group of hikers, it sat down or crouched down, partly out of sight, no longer moving, watching the hikers, and sort of hiding.

Now being somewhat concerned, the group decided to hike back down the trail while keeping an eye on the creature, which remained still the whole time, watching the hikers hiking back down to the trailhead.

**Investigation:** My colleague was able to discern the entity as being quite large and tall, bipedal, completely covered in dark brown hair, and certainly not human; thus, identifying it as a Sasquatch. No other specific physical details could be observed at the time due to the distance.

She contacted some other members of the Tr'ondëk Hwëch'in First Nation (THFN) later on, discussing the sighting, and she was told that a Sasquatch had indeed been spotted in the area previously.

My colleague also checked with the Tombstone Territorial Park registration desk to see if any other hiking group had registered a hike on the Angelcomb Peak Trail that day, as it is the rule, and no one had. Therefore, there were no other people in that region of the Tombstone Territorial Park.

**History:** The construction of the Dempster Highway, which connects the North Klondike Highway, just east of Dawson City, originally to Inuvik and now to Tuktoyaktuk, started in 1959 when oil was discovered around Eagle Plain. It stopped in 1961 for a while and re-started in 1968. The official opening occurred in August of 1979. I had the occasion of driving the Dempster Highway to Inuvik back in 1982 while serving in the Yukon as the Deputy Commander of the Canadian Armed Forces Northern Region Headquarters (Detachment Yukon).

The route itself roughly follows the old Tr'ondëk Hwëch'in and Vuntut Gwitch'in trails, first marked by these First Nations centuries ago, and which was intensively used by Constable Jack Dempster (1876–1964) of the RNWMP, as part of his northern patrols route for many years.

The access to the Angelcomb Peak Trail is located 10 km (6 mi) north of the Tombstone Territorial Park Campground, along the Dempster Highway, Yukon Hwy #5. This Park is located 71 km (44 mi) north of its junction with the North Klondike Highway, Yukon Hwy #2, some 40 km (25 mi) east of Dawson City.

## SPECIAL REPORT

**Report #70**
**ANVIL REGION**
**Sighting of Two Sasquatch along the Ketza Mine Road and Undefined Movements along the same road in 1995**
**Location of Movements: Coord. 61o 47'47 N 132o 02'42 W**
**(Map Ross River 105/16 GR 559 549)**
**Location of Sighting: Coord. 61o 47'22 N 132o 02'19 W**
**(Map; Ross River 105F/16 GR 559 541)**

I WAS CONTACTED by Grant Pauls, of the Tahltan Nation who shared two Sasquatch experiences with me. These activities had taken place in early August of 1995, along a road leading to the Ketza Mine, some 40 km (26 mi) east of Ross River, which is located on the Robert Campbell Highway, Yukon Highway #4, some 232 km (144 mi) east of Carmacks and 361 km (224 mi) west of Watson Lake. These took place while the man was moose hunting. I have left the content of these Sasquatch-related activities as written by the witness, with his permission, except for a few spelling corrections and edits for clarity, with limited additions, along with the usual calculations to and from metric.

This Report #70 describes an occurrence and an encounter which took place on the 1st and 3rd of August 1995. It should be presented as Report #21; however, since it was forwarded to me in late March 2022, as we were getting ready to go to press, and since I would have had to re-number every report since August 1995, I decided to number this special report as #70.

**Note:** The original report was previously sent to Dr. Melba Ketchum, a veterinarian from Texas, who is the head of DNA Diagnostics Inc. and who was involved in a Sasquatch DNA Project named "The Sasquatch Genome Project," which started in 2012, with final results presented by Dr. Ketchum in 2017.

> Hello, my name is Grant Pauls, and I am a descendent from the Tahltan Tribe from northern British Columbia. I have decided to write about the encounter I had in 1995. I grew up in a small town called Ross River in the Yukon Territory. The community

is made up of approximately 20 per cent non-native people and 80 per cent native (First Nations Peoples), who are mostly of the Kaska Nation, and members of the Ross River First Nation. (Note: As of February 2022, the population of Ross River stands at 410 people.)

As a kid growing up in Ross River, I had heard of many stories from Kaska Elders of their encounters with 'Negaunee' or 'bushman' in which they were described as giants, 10 ft (3 m) tall hairy beings that stole women and children, and you had to be wary of their potential presence while hunting, fishing, or trapping in the bush.

Hearing the stories from time to time was normal, and I just placed it in the back of my mind, thinking it was a long-time legend of prehistoric beings. I had spent a lot of time hunting, fishing, and even working for YTG (Yukon Territorial Government) highway summer camps, as well as various mining companies, so the bush and remote locations were normal for me.

I had been living in Whitehorse and Watson Lake, Yukon, off and on for close to eight years, and I had recently moved back to Ross River. One day I decided I should go hunting for moose, since it was August 1st, meaning it was now officially hunting season and moose were fattening up.

I decided to travel from my mother and father's house, which was about 10 km (6.2 mi) south-east of Ross River, along the Robert Campbell Highway. The location of interest was 40 km (26 mi) east of my mom and dad's house, along the Ketza River Mine Road, an area I knew very well, as I had worked at the mine in 1986/1987, after graduating high school.

(On Tuesday, August 1, 1995) I drove to the mine road after work, and soon realized it was kind of early to hunt moose, as it was a bit too warm. But I thought maybe I would get lucky, so I decided to stop and check out a small lake located 3.5 km (2.2 mi) south of the Campbell Highway, on the west side of the Ketza River Mine Road. (Coord. 61o 47'47 N 132o 02'42 W)

I parked my truck and grabbed my rifle and walked in about 160 m (525 ft) to the lake, but could not reach the lake, as the shore was heavily grown-in with heavy thick willow stands. I decided not to try and bushwhack my way to the lake, as I could hear ducks flapping and quacking along the shore, and I just wanted to take in the moment, so I decided to lay down on the moss and close my eyes, as it was a warm and peaceful evening.

**Occurrence:** After about 20–30 minutes of lying back on the moss with my eyes closed, I could hear something or some things moving around, approximately 50 m (164 ft) behind me, towards the direction of the road where I was parked. I originally thought it was birds or squirrels, but realized the movement was too heavy and quick to be either.

I thought it might possibly be a bear; I knew I didn't want to be lying down in moss with a curious bear around, so I quickly jumped up to my feet and headed towards my parked truck with my rifle in hand. All the movements stopped, and I felt weirded out but continued my short walk back to the truck. I thought nothing more of the noises and headed back to my parents' house.

Two days later, (Thursday, August 3, 1995) I decided to head back to the same location on the mine road again, but this time I was going to park 0.5 km (1640 ft) further, at kilometre #4 (1.2 mi), where there was a 40 to 50 ft (12 to 15 m) high gravel knoll on the east side of the road, giving me a perfect view of a small chain of lakes east of the road.

I parked the truck at the base of the knoll, climbed to the top of the little knoll, and decided to try a couple of moose calls. After about ten minutes, I realized it was getting dusk sooner than expected, and the area was strangely dead quiet. It was polar opposite to what the area had been just two days earlier. I decided to make a couple of moose calls and started to think about what I should do next, wait around listening for activity or head home.

**Encounter:** Then, I looked down to the bottom of the knoll where the truck was parked, and as I gazed towards the road looking southwest, I noticed two human silhouettes, backlit by the sun, looking in my direction, about 200–220 m (656–721 ft) away. (Coord. 61o 47'22N 132o 02'19W)

The two people were standing just on the right-hand side of the road, next to a small spruce tree, and amongst buckbrush willows. I noticed the buckbrush was waist-high on the person on the left. On the tallest one, there was a shimmer of dark red, brown and black, along his right arm and shoulder. I automatically assumed he was wearing what I thought was a plaid wool bush jacket, without seeing any actual plaid shades.

I noticed the person on the right was moving back and forth

like he or she was antsy. I also noticed the buckbrush was at mid-chest line of the shorter being.

I just stared at them, and they were looking back at me. I could not see their faces, as they were backlit by the sun and it was turning to dusk. I tried hard to see facial details like brow, eyes, nose, and chin, but could not see any of the outline. It was a freaky fleeting moment. I thought to myself 'Bushman,' then my mind raced to rationalize the situation, and I thought, those are locals from Ross River camped at that location, and were likely cutting firewood, as this location was originally an area where a lot of firewood was previously cut.

The being on the right kept looking up at the being on the left, judging by the way it kept cocking its head. It was like the smaller being was motioning to the big being: 'That hunter didn't realize we are here.' And my mind raced to 'Ho no, I was calling a moose and people are watching me.'

I felt immediately embarrassed, as it made sense why it was dead quiet, and there were no signs of game. I decided to face the embarrassment and walk down to the truck, drive towards where I spotted them, say hello, and maybe ask them, "How was my moose call?'

As I walked down the gravel knoll, I gave the people one big wave, as if to say, 'I see you too.'

I climbed into the truck and drove the 0.25 km (820 ft) down the road and noticed they were gone, and I overshot their location a bit.

So, instead of backing up, or trying to turn around on the eroded road, I thought I would drive a 0.5 km (1640 ft) farther, to an area where I knew I could turn around with ease. I got turned around, and I neared the location where I last saw them. I noticed there was no camp or trucks, or anything. It looked like no one had camped in that area in years.

I looked, and there were no recent tire tracks either. I noticed the small spruce tree and the buckbrush where I had seen the two people standing; no one was around. I looked at the buckbrush, and I figured it was as high as the other buckbrush I walked through two days earlier, maybe 5 to 5½ feet tall (1.5 to 1.7 m).

I immediately thought my eyes were playing tricks on me. Did I just see two 'bushmen?' I started to feel the adrenaline building in my system. I thought to myself, 'Go to the top of the gravel knoll and look again, because it could have been shadows. I thought that if I don't, I will never know for sure.'

I drove to the bottom of the knoll, jumped out, grabbed my gun just in case, ran to the top of the knoll, turned back to look towards the small spruce tree and buckbrush, and saw nothing else but the small spruce tree and buckbrush.

I ran back to the truck and hauled ass back to my parents' house, travelling between 140–160 km/h (87–100 mph). I swear to God, my adrenaline was so high and lasted the entire 40 km (26 mi) drive with my body shaking and my mind racing with what I just saw.

I arrived back at my parents' place and came through the doorway pumped up and strangely enough, noticed they were watching a story on television about Bigfoot. I announced to them 'that's what I saw,' and pointed at the TV. I went on and told them of my experience and what I saw. They just listened and didn't say a lot.

The following day, a family friend of ours came to visit us. His name is Frank, and he is a traditional Kaska native man who spent years in that particular area hunting, fishing, and trapping. Before I knew it, I just blurted out to him of what I saw. I expected to be laughed at or to be berated by him.

What he said to me blew me away. He said, 'I know where they live!' I was like ,'What?' 'I know where they live, I saw them, and I followed them to where they live.'

I felt both vindicated for my sighting in an area he knew like the back of his hand, and I was also astounded by what he said.

I shared my story, and he shared his story. My dad was standing there, just shaking his head in amazement and disbelief.

To this day, when I share this story twenty-five years later, the hair stands up on my arms, and I get the heebbie jebbies. I have not been able to shake those feelings of being freaked out.

After this experience, it took me three years to go hunting again. Now when I hunt, my six senses are on high alert. I have become a super-hunter where I can see movement, shape, and sound way before anyone else sees anything. It is truly freaky.

What I saw were two large reddish-brown, dark brown/black, hair-covered beings, with conical-shaped heads, no neck, with the larger one standing between 8–9 ft tall, with a set of shoulders that easily was 4–5 ft across, and weighing 600–750 lbs. The smaller one was 7–8 ft tall and was 500–600 lbs. The only thing to which I could compare the width and height of the larger being, would be like looking at a large Clydesdale horse and seeing the width of its belly and the top of his head standing and looking straight at you. That would begin to give you an idea of the width of its shoulders and height of the beings. For comparison, I am a 6 ft tall (1.8 m) and 280 lbs man, with a shoulder spread of 24" or 2 ft; these beings made me look like a kid.

I can tell you, it's not a matter of whether I believe they exist. It's a matter of what are they exactly, and why are they not acknowledged by the governments? Recently, I heard something on one of those YouTube Bigfoot channels, which helped put me at ease, a thought I never had till then, 'These beings have always been here.'

My name is Grant Pauls. This is my story, and there is Bigfoot or 'Negaunee' in the Yukon Territory.

*Maduu,'* meaning "thank you" in my language.

**Investigation:** I received this email from the witness on Thursday, March 24, 2022. I have contacted the witness to clarify some aspects of his long account of his occurrence on Tuesday, August 1, 1995, and then his encounter with two Sasquatch a couple of days later.

There are many points that come to mind: the activities of the Sasquatch on both occasions and the details mentioned by the witness and his personal reactions, feelings, and conclusions. I last was in the area in the summer of 2015. There are six specific reports from around the area: Report #1, a sighting in Faro in 1970; Report #2, a sighting in Ross River later in 70 as well; report #4, another sighting at Dragon Lake in August of 75; report #33, a sighting by Lapie River in 2004; Report #41, an occurrence by Magundy River in 2010; and report #42, another occurrence on Swim Lake Trail later in 2010.

Readers will note the name given to Sasquatch by the Kaska people, *Negaunee*, is much similar to the title of this book, and the name of the Sasquatch in the Dene language: *Nahganne*. The members of the Kaska Nation are closely related to the Dene Nation and share a similar language.

During the occurrence, on Tuesday, August 1, 1995, the witness heard some heavy walking movement, as if an entity was walking close by and behind him.

From my own bush experiences, I am certain it was not a bear, as bear movements are not what one could call "heavy," and on most occasions, they cannot be heard. Their usual actions when a human is around, as they have a keen sense of smell, is to make their presence known to that human person.

During the encounter, on Thursday, August 3, 1995, the witness observed what he thought were two hunters, two human-shaped persons standing on the side of the road, next to a small spruce tree, amongst buckbrush willows.

However, the witness could not see any specific facial or other details due to the sun's location behind the two entities he was observing, which only showed the outline, the silhouette, of two very large and tall entities.

The witness, however, did notice the overall shape of the subjects and judged them as being heavy, tall, with a sort of conical rounded head shape, without any visible neck and large muscular shoulders.

He mentioned the approximate height and weight of each subject, even to the point of comparing them with a known type of animal, so as to provide an idea of their physiques.

The witness mentions the entities as being reddish-brown, dark-brown black, and covered in hair. This is quite common when describing Sasquatch entities, and I have no qualm accepting his description.

Now for measurements, it is common knowledge that guessing the height and weight of a person at a distance of about 200 m (675 ft or so), could be a problem for most people unless one is used to doing so.

In this instance, I would think that because the witness is an experienced hunter, as one of the required skills of a hunter is judging distance and the height of a prey, I accept the witness's judgment of the height as being pretty close to reality.

Weight is another matter; however, in this case, the witness used his own weight in comparison, and again, as he is an experienced hunter, he used those elements to state the approximative weight of the two Sasquatch, which in my view would be acceptably close to reality.

The witness stated that after waving at what he thought were fellow hunters, he started walking down the small knoll he was on, reached his truck and started driving towards the location of the presumed hunters. However, upon reaching what he thought was their location, a mere 250 m (820 ft) away, they were gone. Which begs the question: where did they go?

Since the witness waved at the two entities, basically sending the message "I see you," the two beings probably felt uneasy or unhappy being located and clearly seen and probably hid in the low ground, out of sight.

He further stated that he searched around, from the safety of his truck, but did not find any traces or signs of them.

Had he searched on foot, he may have seen them again. But neither you nor I were there, so we don't know of his feelings at the time, even though he mentioned in his report that his "adrenaline was high. Was it because of fear? Therefore, in my opinion, his decision to remain inside his truck for safety was probably the right one.

One interesting point he mentioned was a statement made on a television program he had watched: "These beings have always been here." Interesting.

What I found, through my research on the subject of Sasquatch during the last twenty-five years, would indicate that the entity known as Sasquatch, giant bipedal, forest-dwelling, hirsute hominoid entities, would have arrived in North America at about the same time as the first original inhabitants of Beringia, starting some thirty thousand years ago, when the continent of Asia was connected to the continent of America for some fifteen thousand years.

The various Yukon First Nations have known about Sasquatch and have shared their experiences about them ever since.

 260

# PART II

# SASQUATCH STORIES *from the* NORTH

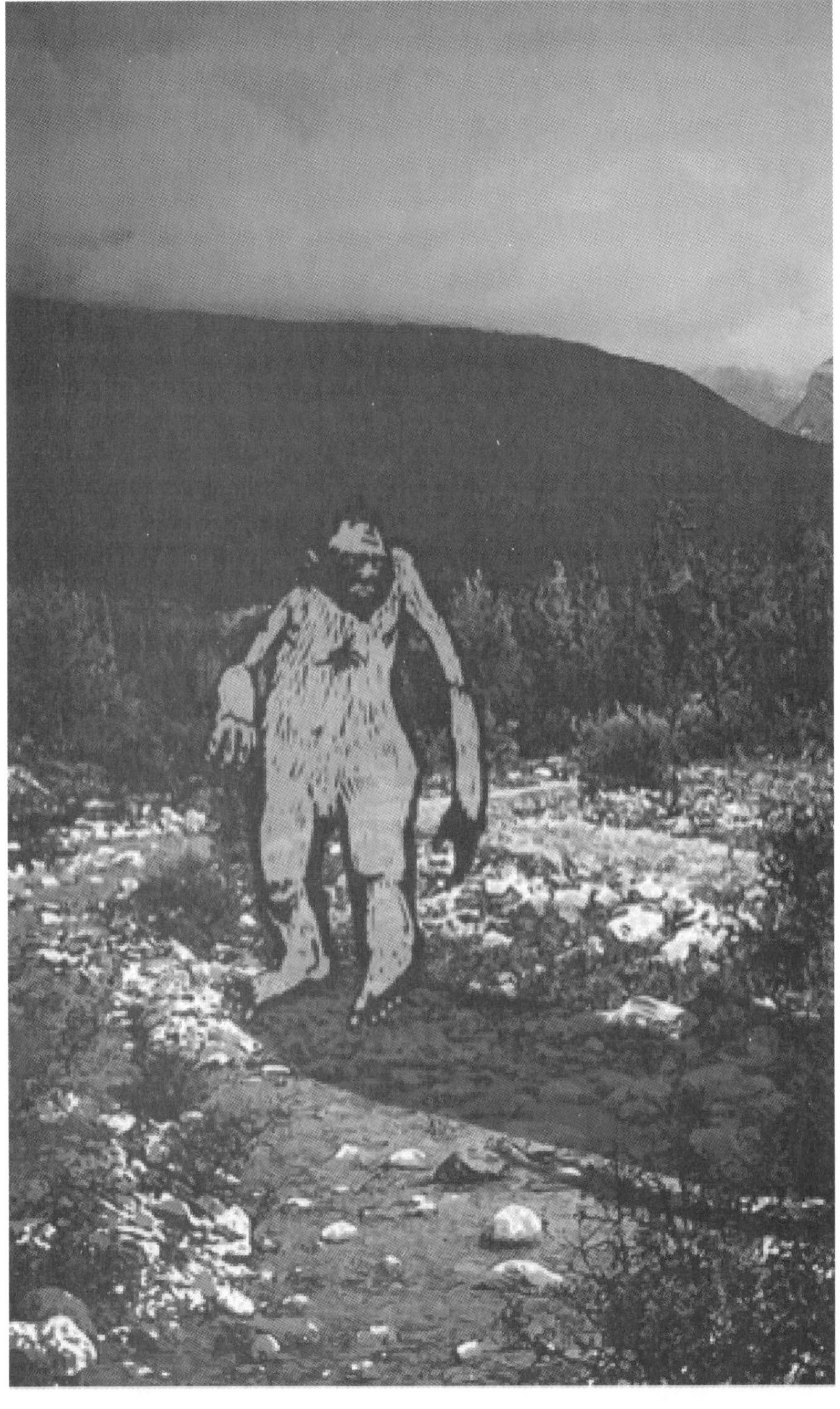

# *Part II*

# *Sasquatch Stories from the Yukon*

THE FOLLOWING SASQUATCH-RELATED STORIES were gathered from many sources while researching, investigating, and writing about Sasquatch during the last few years. Since these Sasquatch-related activities were not investigated, they are labelled as stories and not as Reports.

In 2014, I was lucky enough to have been invited to participate in the 2014 Moosehide Gathering by my friend Kylie of the Tr'ondek Hewch'in Danoja Zho Cultural Centre in Dawson City, with the kind permission of the Tr'ondek Hewch'in First Nation Elder's Council. The gathering took place from Thursday, July 24, 2014, to Sunday, July 27, 2014, at the THFN village of Moosehide, located 6 km (4 mi) down the Yukon River from Dawson City.

Kylie and I hosted the "Sasquatch Talk Program," a program where we discussed the phenomenon of Sasquatch with some of the people attending the gathering, and where we invited people to talk to us about their previous experiences with Sasquatch. Some of the stories are presented here using a different format, because I did not have the opportunity to actually investigate the occurrences presented to us, as I could not access most locations where these activities took place.

### The Swimming Mother

This occurrence took place roughly at the Yukon/Alaska border along the Yukon River, close to the Alaskan community of Eagle, and was relayed to me by an Alaskan First Nation Elder residing in Eagle, Alaska. This story involves four First Nation members of that community who were out hunting moose along the banks of the Yukon River in early 2004.

The members of the hunting party had been boating the Yukon River for a good part of the day and were now looking for a place to set up camp for the night, somewhere close to the Yukon/Alaska border.

They had landed their boat onshore at about 1600 hours (4 pm) by a small, protected cove. A few minutes later, one of the hunters heard what he thought was a baby crying, quite odd for this part of the river, to say the least, as nobody lived around these parts that they knew of.

Being curious, two of the hunters started to walk in the direction of the cries in order to investigate. As they walked around some large boulders, they observed a big and tall bipedal ambulating creature, which they described as being a female Sasquatch, holding a very young Sasquatch by the hand, and the young one was crying.

They immediately stopped walking, and at that moment, the mother Sasquatch noticed them. What happened next really intrigued the hunters, and they witnessed something never seen before. The mother Sasquatch placed her baby on top of her shoulders, with the young holding his or her mother by the long head hairs.

The female Sasquatch then gathered a few broken dead trees lying close by on the shore, and while holding onto those dead trees with both hands, she then threw herself into the water of the Yukon River. Using her feet for paddling and the dead broken trees as a flotation device, she navigated across the river at an angle, taking advantage of the river's current. The hunters stood in amazement, watching this female Sasquatch with her young one swimming away in a manner never observed before.

This is the first time that I know of that mention is made of a Sasquatch making use of dead trees as a flotation device.

**The Wanderer of Moosehide**

This story was relayed to me by an elderly member of the Tr'ondek Hewch'in First Nation who would spend his summer at his cabin in the village of Moosehide.

He mentioned that one evening, in early September 1998 or 1999, just after finishing his supper, he was sitting by a campfire outside of his cabin, smoking a cigarette while relaxing. After a few moments, out of the corner of his eye, he noticed something moving. It could not have been any of the kids, as they had returned to Dawson City in time for the start of school.

Taking a good look, he observed a tall and huge bipedal ambulating creature, which he identified as a Sasquatch, slowly wandering across from the south side of the village by some bushes located close to the church. The creature walked to the other side of the village, into the bush, at a location just north of where the cemetery is presently located. He stated that he did not pay much attention to it, as he knew that some Sasquatch were in the area and they would venture into the village on occasions, probably looking for leftover food or other edible garbage.

This was the first time that he ever mentioned this encounter to anyone, and he figured that the visit took place about fifteen years ago, which would have been around the year 1998 or so.

**The Hunter of Sheep's Mountain**

This was told to me by a friend in his 60s whose son relayed an encounter with a Sasquatch that happened some time ago.

My friend relates that in the spring of 1982 or 1983, his son was part of a group of students from one of the Whitehorse high schools on a day outing to Sheep's Mountain, on the western shores of Kluane Lake. The bus had taken them to the parking area at the foot of the mountain. The group then started climbing the mountain using the footpath.

About thirty minutes into the climb, they had stopped for a break when one student yelled out that a bear had gotten a sheep and was running away with it. However, upon closer examination, the student in question, my friend's son and some of his friends with him that day, identified the wild ambulating bipedal hunter as a Sasquatch rather than a bear.

**The Teslin Visitor**

The following was told to me in the summer of 2010 by a female friend of mine who is a First Nations resident of Teslin in her 60s at the time and a member of the Teslin Tlingit Council.

"For as long as people can remember the community of

Teslin had been visited by a family of Sasquatch on a regular basis, sometimes walking the tree line by the airport, some other times just wandering around the village by the lake. These ambulating creatures appeared to be friendly enough, just looking around, probably searching for food or just being curious."

She mentioned that people came to accept those visits and simply never took the time to report the bipedal creature walking about and around the community. A number of interesting sighting encounters from the area of Teslin are reported in this book.

### The Old Crow Giant

A Vuntut Gwich'in First Nations man in his 70s told me this story in the summer of 2002:

> A long time ago, the village was regularly visited by a giant who would take away the caribou hanging to dry. One day a couple of hunters decided to go after this giant and get rid of him. After they were gone for a few days, the villagers became worried and sent out a search party to find them. Late that day they found the hunters' bodies on top of the small mountains located just outside of Old Crow. They have called that mountain the Giant's Mountain, and villagers have never returned to that location.

### The Never Return Canyon

The following story was told to me by a man in his 40s, a local resident of the town of Mayo, Yukon, during a visit to the area when I went to the region to investigate an occurrence in July of 2018.

In the 1980s, a hydraulic power dam and generating system had been built some nine kilometres north of the community Mayo, on the Mayo River, called the "Mayo Two," at the foot of an unnamed mountain, resulting in a new lake. A small creek running from west to east into that lake and starting in the area of Grid Square (GS) 51 59, on the Mayo Map #105 M/12, is the subject of this story.

For some years, prospectors would venture up this small unnamed creek, in the forever search for the elusive gold—by all reports good quality colours were found along the lower portion of the creek, encouraging prospectors to move on further up this creek's valley, which at one point becomes barely 5 m (15 ft) wide. As the story goes, every time prospectors would enter this restricted canyon, they would be subjected to a volley of rocks being thrown from atop both sides of the high canyon walls, accompanied by loud screams and yells coming from atop these canyon's walls as well.

Needless to say, upon experiencing such unwelcoming behaviour, these prospectors would leave this creek as soon and as fast as they could and, as it was told to me, would never return.

**The Guardians of the Ddhaw Ghro Hot Springs**

These hot springs are located in the Ddhaw Ghro Habitat Protection Area, formerly known as the McArthur Wildlife Sanctuary.

A woman, who was some 50 years of age at the time, had planned to spend a few days by the Ddhaw Ghro Hot Springs. In order to do so, she convinced a helicopter pilot friend in his 50s to take her to these hot springs. The pilot having nothing to do for a few days, decided that he would stay at the hot springs as well. So, one bright morning they took off from the Mayo airport and flew out to the hot springs. They found a place to land fairly close to the springs, unloaded their camping gear, and set out to make camp.

They were in location for about an hour when they started hearing strange yells. Not so loud at first but gradually increasing in volume. At the same time, they started feeling some strange vibes as if they were being watched, and every so often they would hear movements in the bush around them.

They looked around and yet could not see what was walking about, stalking them, nor what or who was making these movements.

The strange feelings increased to the point that both had

hairs standing up on their necks, and they were becoming gradually scared. Although they were both bush-wise, they could not understand what was happening to them.

After another thirty minutes or so, they'd had enough and decided to leave the area and return home to Mayo. Neither of the two ever told their experience to anyone, until this woman shared it with me in 2017 when we were discussing the subject of the Sasquatch.

Of further interest, in May of 2006, I was investigating large human-like footprints that had been noticed in and around the Selkirk First Nation (SFN) community of Pelly Crossing. During my investigation, I was talking with some SFN elders and one of them mentioned that Keecho, their local name for Sasquatch, would usually take refuge in the Ddhaw Ghro Habitat Protection Area during the summer and would move closer to the Pacific Ocean during the winter, crossing close to Pelly Crossing.

**The Stalker of Bennett Lake**

This story was related to me by a woman who currently resides by Marsh Lake, a few kilometres south of Whitehorse.

In the 1980s, her father had a cabin along the west shores of Bennett Lake and would spend time at the cabin whenever he had some free time from his work. This one winter weekend while he was at his cabin, the weather was quite nice and calm, so he decided to take a walk about the area. Donning his snowshoes, he left the cabin and ventured into the nearby forest of pine trees. After walking about one kilometre, he sensed that he was not alone. But yet, looking around, he could not see anything. He then realized that he was being followed by an invisible, or so it seemed, ambulating entity.

He could sense and hear some walking in the snow, in time with his steps. When he stopped, the invisible ambulating entity would stop. When he walked, it would follow him as well, in unison, keeping the same rhythm and speed as he was walking, at a distance he judged to be about 15 to 20 m (45 to 55 ft), becoming more and more unnerving to him.

He could not see what was following him. He could not

discern what the entity was, but it was there for sure. As the woman mentioned to me, her father was an experienced bushman, having spent much time in the forest.

Eventually, her father decided that he'd had enough of this hide-and-seek sort of game and returned to the safety of his cabin. He never mentioned this experienced to anyone, only sharing it with his daughter a few years later.

### The Girl Who Got Away

A few years ago, I was discussing, with friends, various Sasquatch activities that had occurred across the Yukon when one of them, a man in his 50s at the time and resident of Whitehorse, whom I had known for some time, shared this story.

In the fall of 1998, he was on a hunting trip with a friend, who was a member of the Kwanlin Dün First Nation, along the North Canol Road, located north of the community of Ross River.

They were driving north and looking for a site to camp for a few days when they came across a hunter's camp close to Sheldon Lake, set up between the lake and the road. His friend recognized one of the hunters as a person he knew from the Ross River Dene Council, so they stopped and his friend started to talk with the Kaska Dene hunter, who was set-up with his family, inquiring about a possible campsite close by. He pointed out to a site some five hundred metres away, and off they went. They set up camp, looked over the area, and had their dinner. After dinner, they wandered over to the Kaska camp and started talking about hunting with his friend.

At one point, the Kaska Dene fella mentioned they had experienced a visit from a Sasquatch about ten days before. According to the hunter, at around 2015 hours (8:15 pm) that evening, they started hearing sounds like something walking on two feet from a nearby location. They observed some fleeting, fast movements through the bush but could not clearly see what it was. They added more wood to the fire and kept an eye out for any intruder. This lasted most of the evening and until about midnight. The hunter stayed up till about 0300 hours (3 am) or so and went to sleep close to the fire.

The next day, all was quiet, and they went about their business, yet kept watch on what was going on. They had not heard anything till about 1830 hours (6:30 pm) when all of sudden, a large and tall bipedal entity, a Sasquatch, bluntly walked into their camp and swiftly picked up a small girl, the hunter's daughter, and smartly walked away with her under its arm. The hunter quickly picked up his rifle and started shooting over the head of the Sasquatch, who then simply let go of the girl who was about 10 years of age at the time. The Sasquatch disappeared into the bush and was never seen or heard from again until my friend and his partner arrived.

My friend mentioned they were in that location for four days before they bagged their moose and never heard or saw anything out of the ordinary while there. My friend further said that he had been in touch with his Kaska Dene friend and they had harvested two moose, after my friend and his partner had left, and were not bothered again by the Sasquatch while they were at their campsite during that trip.

During my research work and various investigations around the Yukon, I had heard of similar stories about Sasquatch fetching young people, both girls and boys, but this was the first time I had received specific details of such a kidnapping.

*These related actions by Sasquatch shows some sort of familiarity between the Sasquatch and humans. However, I do not feel qualified to speculate as to what the reasons could be for such familiarity, so I will let the readers think about it.*

**The Porcupine River Bushman**

Around 1906, two prospectors were searching for that elusive gold not far from the community of Old Crow, when they reported observing a tall bipedal ambulating entity, which they called a bushman, better known today as Sasquatch, on the banks of the Porcupine River at about mid-point between Caribou Bar Creek and Frog Lake. There is not any mention of what the Sasquatch was actually doing in the old report I found.

## Carmacks Visitor

An old report mentions that in the summer of 1912, a Sasquatch was often observed on the high ground on the left-hand side of the North Klondike Highway, Yukon Highway #2, as one arrives from Whitehorse. This is where a First Nations graveyard is located. Was he visiting a dead friend?

## The Bathing Sasquatch

Three hunters were hiking in the vicinity of Little Creek, just north of the community of Burwash Landing, in the fall of 1981 on their way to an open meadow when they came across a large man-like entity either sitting or lying in the water of a small pound. One of them first observed the Sasquatch when looking through his rifle scope and judged the creature to be about 216 cm (7 ft) tall. The Sasquatch slowly got up and walked over to a large bolder across the pound, and it leaned on it for six to eight minutes, then rolled onto a grassy ground, before walking into the forest, according to the report that I read.

## The North Canol Road Hiker

In late summer of 1949, a group of First Nations persons from the Ross River Dena Council were driving on the North Canol Road one evening, when they came across a bushman, a.k.a. Sasquatch, just past the South MacMillan River Bridge. The Sasquatch was slowly walking on the road while observing the river, or so it seemed, when they approached it. When the entity saw them, it crossed the road and wandered into the forest.

## Walking the Beach

Three fishermen stopped on the shores of the Eastern Arm of Frances Lake, in the summer of 1947, when one of them noticed a number of large human-like footprints in the sand. Each of these footprints measured some 40.6 cm (16 in) in length, as it was mentioned in an old report.

### The Burwash Encounter

In mid-summer of 1927, two prospectors were on the quest to find gold along the creeks north of Burwash Landing when they came across a large creature "covered with black hair," judged to be about 216 cm (7 ft) tall and slowly walking along a small trail. The prospectors were off that trail beside a small creek when they observed the Sasquatch for a good ten minutes or so, which is stated in their report. It would appear the Sasquatch did not see them, and it paid no attention to them at all.

### The Trapping Sasquatch

A trapper was in the process of checking his trap line when he observed a Sasquatch, which appeared to be doing the very same thing, that is, removing dead animals from various traps our trapper had set a couple of weeks before. This took place at a spot where the Road River flows into the upper reaches of the Peel River, in northeastern Yukon, in December of 1935. Our trapper reportedly fired his rifle at the Sasquatch, who ran into the forest emitting a loud high-pitched wail.

### The Sasquatch of the Nanitenee River Valley

I found a number of old reports mentioning numerous Sasquatch sightings, at various time of the years, around this valley in the 1930s and 1940s, made by local trappers and prospectors. This valley is often referred to as "The Deadman Canyon." It is located in the Logan Mountain Range. The small Nanitenee River flows into the Little Hyland River, which in turn empties into the Hyland River in eastern Yukon. The name is often confused with the Nahanni River, which is actually in the Northwest Territories, on the east side of the Logan Mountain Range.

> *"What do you do after Yukon . . . Where do you go after Yukon . . . You are only fooling yourself . . . if you think there's something else . . . 'cause there is nothing left after Yukon!"*
>
> —From the song "Where do you go after Yukon"
> by Hank Karr, Yukon entertainer, songwriter, singer, 2010

# Bibliography

Alley, J.R. *Raincoast Sasquatch.* Blaine, WA: Hancock House Publishers, 2003.

Alley, J.R. *Brushes with Bigfoot: Sasquatch Behaviors Reported in Close Encounters, Native and Non-Native Perspectives.* Ketchikan, AK: Publisher John Robert Alley, 2021.

Bayanov, D. *America's Bigfoot: Fact, Not Fiction.* Moscow, Russia: Crypto-Logos Publishers, 1997.

Bindernagel, J.A. *North America's Great Ape: The Sasquatch.* Courtenay, BC: Beachcomber Books, 1998.

Bindernagel, J.A. *The Discovery of the Sasquatch. Reconciling Culture, History and Science in the Discovery Process.* Courtenay, BC: Beachcomber Books, 2010.

Bord, C. & J. *The Bigfoot Casebook.* Harrisburg, PA: Stackpole Books, 1982.

Burns, J.W. *Introducing B.C.'s Hairy Giants.* Toronto, ON: *Maclean's* magazine, April 1, 1929.

Byrne, P. *The* Search *for Bigfoot: Monster, Myth or Man.* Washington, DC: Acropolis Books, 1975.

Ciochon, R. Olsen J. and James, J. *Other Origins: The Search for the Giant Ape in Human Pre-history.* New York, NY: Bantam Books, 1990.

Coleman, L. *Bigfoot! The True Stories of Apes in America.* New York, NY: Paraview Pocket Books 2003.

Daegling, D. J. *Bigfoot Exposed: An Anthropologist Examines America's Enduring Legend.* Walnut Creek, CA: Alta Mira Press, 2004.

Dahinden, R. & Hunter, D. *Sasquatch.* Toronto, ON: McClelland and Stewart, 1973.

Fahrenbach, W.H. *Cryptozoology. Sasquatch: Size, Scaling, and Statistic.* Beaverton, OR: Self-Published Paper, Vol.13, Pages 47 to 75. 1997-1998.

Ferrell, E. *Strange Stories of Alaska and the Yukon.* Fairbanks, AK: Epicenter Press, 1996.

Green, J. *On the Track of the Sasquatch.* Agassiz, BC: Cheam Publishing, 1968.

Green, J. *Year of the Sasquatch.* Agassiz, BC: Cheam Publishing, 1970.

Green, J. *The Sasquatch File.* Agassiz, BC: Cheam Publishing, 1973.

Green, J. *Sasquatch: The Apes Among Us.* Seattle, WA: Hancock House Publishers, 1978.

Halpin, M & A. *Manlike Monsters on Trial: Early Records and Modern Evidence.* Vancouver, BC: University of British Columbia Press,1980.

Heuvelmans, B. *On the Tracks of Unknown Animals.* Cambridge, MA: MIT Press, 1965.

Krantz, G.S. *Sasquatch Handprints. Northwest Anthropological Research Notes.* New York: North American Research Publishing, 1971.

Krantz, G.S. *Anatomy of the Sasquatch Foot. Northwest Anthropological Research Notes.* New York, NY: North American Research Publishing, 1972.

Krantz, G.S. *Additional Notes on the Sasquatch Foot Anatomy. Northwest Anthropological Research Notes.* New York, NY: North American Research Publishing, 1972.

Krantz, G.S. *Anatomy and Dermatoglyphics of three Sasquatch Footprints. Northwest Anthropological Research Notes.* New York, NY: North American Research Publishing, 1983.

Krantz, G.S. *A Reconstruction of the Skull of Gigantopithecus blackie. Northwest Anthropological Research Notes.* New York, NY: North American research Publishing, 1987.

Krantz, G.S. *Bigfoot Sasquatch Evidence.* Blaine, WA: Hancock House Publishers, 1999.

Markotic, V. *The Sasquatch and Other Unknown Hominoids.* Calgary, AB: Western Publishers, 1984.

McLeod, M. *Anatomy of a Beast: Obsession and Myth on the Trail of Bigfoot.* Berkeley, CA: U of California Press, 2009.

Meldrum, D.J. *SASQUATCH: Legend Meets Science.* New York, NY: Forge Book, 2006.

Murphy, C.L. *Meet the Sasquatch.* Blaine, WA: Hancock Pub, 2004.

Napier, J. *Bigfoot.* New York, NY: Berkely Press, 1972.

Napier, J. *Bigfoot: The Yeti and Sasquatch in Myth and Reality.* New York, NY.: E.P. Dutton & Coy, 1973.

Nolan, A. *Nine Micmac Legends.* Hantsport, NS: Lancelot Press, 1983.

Patterson, R. *Do Abominable Snowmen of America Really Exist?* Yakima, WA: Northwest Research Association, 1966.

Perez, D. *Big Footnotes: A Comprehensive Bibliography Concerning Bigfoot, The Abominable Snowman and Related Beings.* Norwalk, CA: D. Perez Publishing Inc, 1988.

Place, M.T. *On the Track of Bigfoot.* New York, NY: Dodd Mead, 1974.

Sanderson, I.T. *Abominable Snowmen: Legend Come to Life.* Philadelphia, PA: Chilton Books Co., 1961.

Shackley, M. *Still Living? Yeti, Sasquatch and the Neanderthal Enigma.* New York, NY: Thames and Hudson, 1983.

Slate, B.A. & Berry, A. *Bigfoot.* New York, NY: Bantam Books, 1976.

Sprague, R. *The Scientist Looks at the Sasquatch (1).* Moscow, ID: University of Idaho Press, 1977.

Sprague, R. *The Scientist Looks at the Sasquatch (2).* Moscow, ID: University of Idaho Press, 1979.

Steenburg, T. *The Sasquatch in Alberta.* Surrey, BC: Hancock House Publishers,1990.

Steenburg, T. *Sasquatch/Bigfoot: The Continuing Mystery.* Surrey, BC: Hancock House Publishers, 1993.

Steenburg, T. *In Search of Giants.* Surrey, BC: Hancock House Publishers, 1996.

Weidenreich, F. *Apes, Giants and Man.* Chicago, IL: University of Chicago Press, 1946.

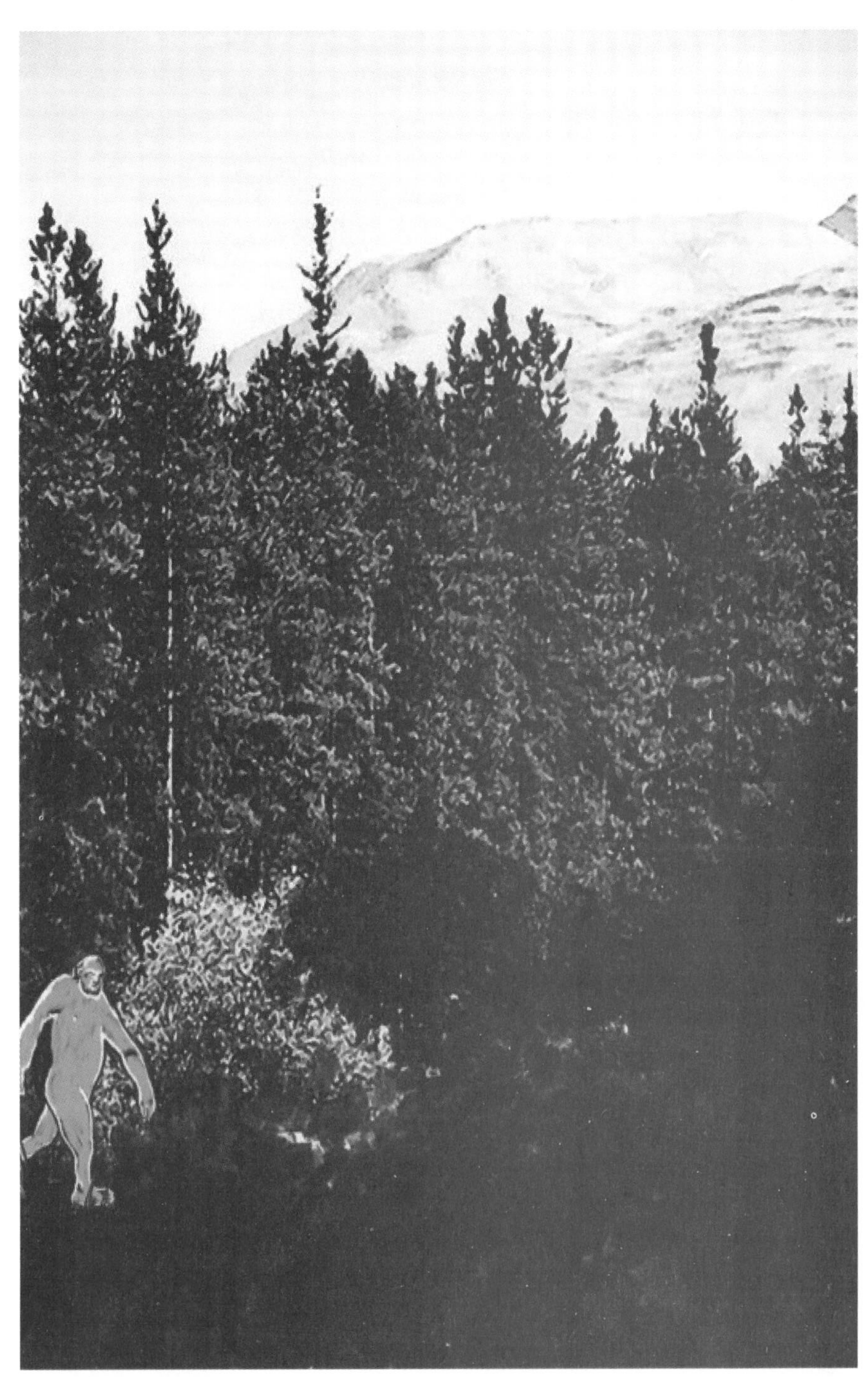

# Acknowledgments

*An open mind is like a fruit-bearing tree . . . it absorbs and feeds on knowledge . . . while the closed mind, on the other hand; is but a bottomless pit . . . from where one never returns. Please open your mind . . . you may well experience something new.* — Red Grossinger, 2022

FIRST AND FOREMOST, Thank you to the people who have had enough internal fortitude and courage to share what they have experienced with me: be it sightings; odd unidentified vocals; strange fleeting movements or activities; unusual animal reactions; the discovery of large human-like footprints; short-term foul smell occurrences; odd unnatural tree occurrences; and strange unusual feelings of not being wanted in a specific area, often accompanied by hirsute reaction, with body hair standing up at the back of your neck and arms, and that sort of thing.

I know there are many more people who have experienced some of these unusual occurrences at some time in their lives, which may well have been caused by one of these unclassified and uncatalogued giant bipedal, forest-dwelling, hirsute hominoids; generally referred to as Sasquatch, at some location around this vast wild land that is the Yukon and other parts of Canada's North.

Maybe they will contact me after discovering this book and report other encounters and occurrences without fear of being ridiculed. I could always write another book to include their experiences.

For many years now, I have been investigating the many stories related to Sasquatch somewhere in the Yukon, away from home, lost in investigations and research work, often in the middle of nowhere, so to speak. While at home, my now deceased wife Marie, learned to do without me being around, much like when I was serving in the Canadian Army somewhere around the world; Thank you, Marie! My sons Darcy and Steve deserve words of appreciation for their constant support, common sense advice and companionship. Steve has been doing some proofreading for this book as well; Thank you, guys!

My good friend Rose Davis, from the Tr'ondëk Hwëch'in First Nation, who often ventured in the Yukon wilds with me, helped me in contacting some of her First Nation relatives and friends around the Yukon. They in turn, would share their knowledge of the land and relate their stories to me. Thank you very much La Rosa; Mahsi Cho! Another woman from the Tr'ondëk Hwëch'in First Nation as well, Kylie Van Every, shared regional stories and sightings of the Sasquatch from the Klondike Region and arranged the "Sasquatch Talks." Thank you so very much, Kylie, much appreciated. Mahsi Cho!

Thank you t o my long-time friends Orval and Anne Turner for their support in relaying Sasquatch-related activities from the Teslin area of the Yukon and helping me in contacting members of their Teslin Tlingit Council; Gunalcheesh! (Unfortunately, Orval passed away in late 2020.)

Special thanks go to Dr. Robert Alley, a a retired professor of Anatomy and Physiology at the University of Alaska at Ketchikan and author of *Raincoast Sasquatch* and *Brushes with Bigfoot*. Robert has kindly given me permission to use an encounter report of a rock-throwing incident that had occurred in the Kluane Region in 2011; Thank you very much, Robert!

I would be amiss not to mention my good friends from Alberta: James Ludwar, Erich Lang, and Brian Baillie, who provided me with many comments and suggestions. Thank you, guys!

I would like to mention a woman from BC who provided me with photographs of very large human-like footprints with two photos of the cast they made of it, when she came across them while moose hunting with her husband and some friends; Thank you to Vicki Pederson.

A huge Merci goes to a very, very special person, who makes my present life worth living again; for being who she is, for her love, her companionships, and for sharing the "great light up above," my wife and companion since 2016, Shanon Cooper.

Thank you to John Nystad for his companionship while investigating some occurrences with me and by providing the sketches of a structure he discovered by Ben-My-Chree in 1995. Dank Je!

I would also like to acknowledge a Dene gentleman who is responsible for the series editing of the book and who has written the Foreword, sharing some interesting stories from the Northwest Territories, Raymond Yakeleya; Mahsi Cho!

To the publisher, Dr. Lorene Shyba of Durvile & UpRoute Books, thank you for trusting me and making my work of twenty years a reality. Thanks also to editors and proofreaders Meghan Whitsitt and Justine Hart.

I know that I have missed some people; sometimes on purpose to keep their identity confidential, some by request, some others totally by accident; if you are one of the latter, please accept my apologies and thank you for your support.

Last but not least, thank you to the readers of this book, who have taken the time to purchase and read about the activities related to the Sasquatch across Yukon and the North.

And remember, as told to me by a Selkirk Yukon First Nation Elder a few years ago:

*"You may not see them, but they are watching over you."*

*— Red*

# SPIRIT OF NATURE SERIES

SERIES EDITORS: RAYMOND YAKELEYA & LORENE SHYBA

## PUBLISHING AUTHORS WHO HAVE THE FORESIGHT TO BRING NEW KNOWLEDGE TO THE WORLD

**THE TREE BY THE WOODPILE**
By Raymond Yakeleya
ISBN: 9781988824031

**LIVING IN THE TALL GRASS**
By Chief R. Stacey Laforme
ISBN: 9781988824055

**LILLIAN & KOKOMIS THE SPIRIT OF DANCE**
By Lynda Partridge
ISBN: 9781988824277

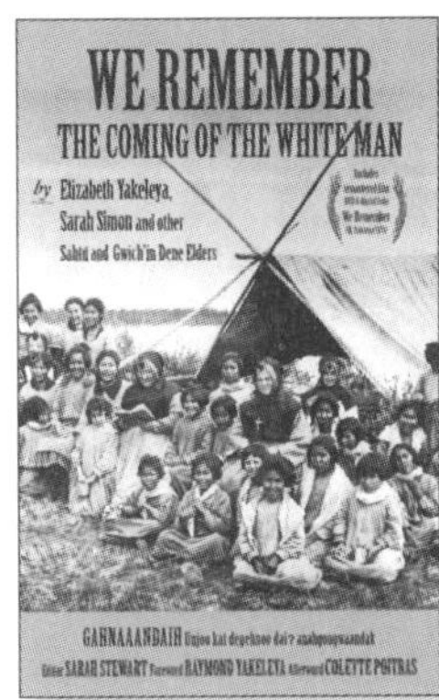


**WE REMEMBER THE COMING OF THE WHITE MAN**
Eds. Stewart & Yakeleya
ISBN: 9781988824246

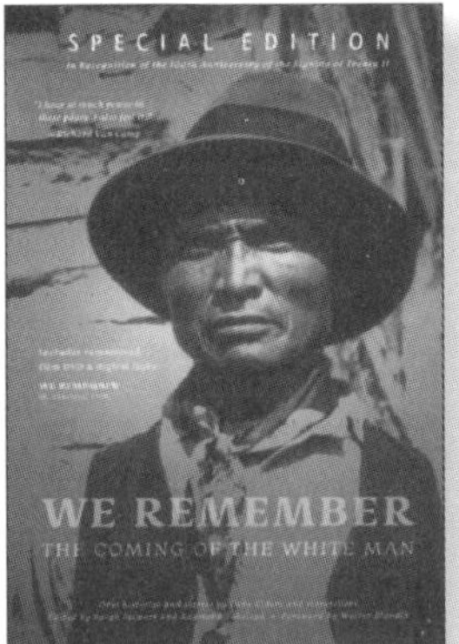


**WE REMEMBER SPECIAL EDITION**
Eds. Stewart & Yakeleya
ISBN: 9781988824635

**STORIES OF METIS WOMEN**
Eds. Oster & Lizee
ISBN: 9781988824215

FOLLOW US ON FACEBOOK
"DURVILEANDUPROUTE"

DURVILE IS A PROUD CANADIAN INDIE PUBLISHER.
DISTRIBUTED BY UNIVERSITY OF TORONTO PRESS (UTP) IN CANADA
AND NATIONAL BOOK NETWOR (NBN) IN THE US.

# SPIRIT OF NATURE SERIES

VISIT DURVILE.COM
OR CLICK THE QR CODE FOR
MORE INFO ON THESE TITLES

**SIKSIKAITSITAPI: STORIES OF THE BLACKFOOT PEOPLE**
By Payne Many Guns *et al*
ISBN: 9781988824833

**WHY ARE YOU STILL HERE?: A LILLIAN MYSTERY**
By Lynda Partridge
ISBN: 9781988824826

**NAHGANNE TALES OF THE NORTHERN SASQUATCH**
By Red Grossinger
ISBN 9781988824598

**CHILD OF MORNING STAR EMBERS OF AN ANCIENT DAWN**
By Antoine Mountain
ISBN: 9781990735103

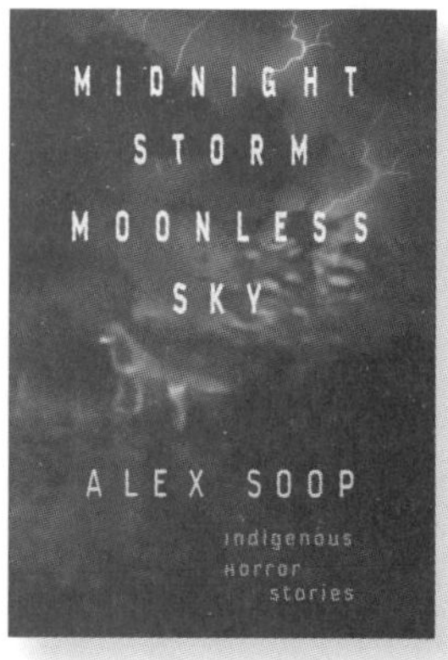


**MIDNIGHT STORM MOONLESS SKY**
By Alex Soop
ISBN: 9781990735127

**THE RAINBOW, THE SONGBIRD & THE MIDWIFE**
By Raymond Yakeleya
ISBN: 9781988824574

A percentage of publisher's proceeds and author royalties have been donated or committed to The Elizabeth Yakeleya Fund; "Home In Our Hearts" for Ukrainian Evacuees; The Canada Ukraine Foundation; Doctors Without Borders; Calgary Communities Against Sexual Abuse; The Canadian Women's Foundation; The Salvation Army; (MMIWG) Missing and Murdered Indigenous Women and Girls; Days for Girls International; Red Door Family Shelter, Toronto; Indigenous Family Shelter, Winnipeg; The Schizophrenia Society of Canada; and The Elizabeth Fry Society.

# About the Author

**RED GROSSINGER**

Red Grossinger is of Algonquin-Huron ancestry and was raised in the Laurentian Region of Quebec. His enthusiasm for Sasquatch can easily be associated with his Indigenous heritage. Red is a decorated military officer now retired from the Canadian Army after thirty years of service with NATO in Canada, Europe, and the United Nations, in the service of peace at many locations around the world. Red is an avid outdoorsman and an open-minded Sasquatch enthusiast who has been roving around the Yukon since 1980. Through these years of travel, Red has acquired an intimate knowledge of the North, which he has used to analyze the many reports presented in this book.

PHOTO: TOM PATRICK,
STAR FLOWER PHOTOGRAPHY